PENGUIN BOOKS

Andrew van Leeuwen has been a motorsport journalist for nearly two decades. He has won multiple Journalist of the Year awards from the Supercars Media Association and Motorsport Australia and is the editorial director at *Speedcafe*. This is his second book, following *Endurance: The Toby Price Story*.

OSCAR PIASTRI
THE ROOKIE

ANDREW VAN LEEUWEN

PENGUIN BOOKS

PENGUIN BOOKS

UK | USA | Canada | Ireland | Australia
India | New Zealand | South Africa | China

Penguin Books is part of the Penguin Random House group of companies whose
addresses can be found at global.penguinrandomhouse.com

Penguin
Random House
Australia

First published by Penguin Books in 2024

Cover photography by Alex Ross Creative
Cover design by Alex Ross Creative © Penguin Random House Australia Pty Ltd
Internal illustrations by Midland Typesetters, Australia
Typeset in 12.5/18 pt Minion Pro by Midland Typesetters, Australia

Printed and bound in Australia by Griffin Press, an accredited
ISO AS/NZS 14001 Environmental Management Systems printer

A catalogue record for this
book is available from the
National Library of Australia

ISBN 978 1 76134 164 9

penguin.com.au

We at Penguin Random House Australia acknowledge that Aboriginal and Torres Strait
Islander peoples are the Traditional Custodians and the first storytellers of the lands
on which we live and work. We honour Aboriginal and Torres Strait Islander peoples'
continuous connection to Country, waters, skies and communities. We celebrate
Aboriginal and Torres Strait Islander stories, traditions and living cultures;
and we pay our respects to Elders past and present.

For John and Glynis van Leeuwen, Chris and Nicole Piastri, and all of the parents who support their kids on their motorsport journey

CONTENTS

INTRODUCTION

'I understand that, without my agreement, Alpine F1 have put out a press release late this afternoon that I am driving for them next year. This is wrong and I have not signed a contract with Alpine for 2023. I will not be driving for Alpine next year.'

—Oscar Piastri, 3 August 2022

It was the Twitter post that rocked Formula 1. Mere hours earlier, the Alpine Formula 1 team had announced that its protégé Oscar Piastri would join its line-up for the 2023 F1 season.

That statement from Alpine made perfect sense. As far as the rest of the world was concerned, the team had been grappling with the decision over who would partner Esteban Ocon the following season. Would it stick with F1 legend Fernando Alonso, a man in age-defying form but still, clearly, closer to the end of his career than the start of it? Or would Alpine look to cash in on its investment in Piastri, to start reaping the benefits of the time and money spent on his meteoric rise through the junior ranks by handing him his F1 debut?

When Alonso made the somewhat unexpected announcement that he was Aston Martin bound at the conclusion of the 2022 campaign, it felt like Alpine's love triangle had sorted itself out. The path was clear. Of course Piastri would step into the seat alongside Ocon for 2023.

Until that tweet.

It was so deliberately worded. If Piastri had indicated that no deal was in place *yet*, then perhaps it could have been chalked up to a quibble over contract details and/or a miscommunication with the team's media department over the timing of the announcement.

But it was the last line that removed any doubt: 'I will not be driving for Alpine next year.' Brutal. Irreversible. Formula 1 was in shock. The media was sent into a frenzy. Alpine had invested so much in Piastri. He was Alpine, through and through. How could it have come to this? How could the relationship have broken down so spectacularly and under such secrecy? And what was going to happen now?

1
STRIKE RATE

The Oscar Piastri story doesn't start with overwhelming success. Not in the standard measurement of trophies and titles, anyway. For Piastri, karting – the traditional first step on the motor-racing ladder – was never about filling the trophy cabinet. It was about getting somewhere. As fast as possible.

A nine-year-old Piastri was just a week into his karting career when James Sera watched him drive at the Oakleigh circuit in Melbourne for the first time. It was 2010 and Sera, a renowned karter-turned-coach, had struck up a relationship with the Piastri family through his karting shop. 'Oscar's dad Chris was sent to me to buy a go-kart. I got to know Chris pretty quickly and we just kind of . . . developed a good friendship straight away,' Sera told me. 'The first time I saw him drive, I thought, "Wow, this kid's really good." I couldn't understand how he was so good because he was so young. But he'd been racing remote-control cars; that's where he started.

3

With go-karting there's obviously a racing line around each track, which is the fastest way around each corner – but a lot of people don't understand that when they first start out. But you could see Oscar knew how that worked; he understood what the racing line was. It looked like he'd been driving for years.

'After watching him for a while, I went home and I said to my wife, "I think we might see this kid in Formula 1 one day."'

If the kid was so good, why didn't he wipe the floor with the opposition at every level of karting? Firstly, it's a discussion that's entirely relative. Piastri did plenty of winning throughout his karting career. He won a state title in 2014. He won the City of Melbourne Titles in the same year. In 2015 he won the opening round of the Australian Kart Championship and the Race of Stars on the Gold Coast. But it's still a pretty thin CV in karting terms, particularly for someone who has since made it all the way to Formula 1.

'Oscar was really fast in a go-kart, but he actually didn't win all that much,' said Sera. 'He didn't necessarily win the big races. He didn't win an Australian championship or anything like that. He didn't dominate anything. He was always much younger and smaller than the kids he was racing . . . always racing a class above where he should have been. He always thought everyone was his mate, and he'd get bullied, bullied off the road. So his results were never what they should have been, because he was batting above his level.

'But he was always, and I mean always, one of the fastest and most consistent drivers.'

You may think that size doesn't matter in a game of horse-power, and once a driver takes the step from karts to cars, that's true. In a full-blown racing car, the suspension does the hard work of vehicle dynamics and, as a driver, you're strapped firmly into a seat moulded to your body. As long as you're strong enough to turn the steering wheel and your neck can deal with the g-force, you're in business. In fact, a driver's career – particularly in open-wheel racing such as Formula 1 – is much more likely to be affected by being tall or heavy than being small or light. If you're too tall, you simply won't fit in the car (or you'll annoy the designers who want to package cars as tightly as possible). If you're too heavy, well, that's more weight that a racing car has to accelerate, then stop, then drag around a corner.

But karting is different. The driver makes up a huge percentage of the total weight of the machine, and there is no suspension to dictate the roadholding. It's not entirely unlike riding a motorbike, in that a driver can use their weight to throw the kart around. And if you're not heavy enough to do that, it can be very hard to make the kart work as intended.

'Oscar was always too small for the class he was in,' said Sera. 'He went to senior karts very early and he needed pedal kits to reach the pedals. He never had the body weight to get the kart to move the way it needed to. But he always found a way . . . we were using my set-ups on his karts and sometimes he'd come in and complain that it wasn't working. And Chris would say, "Hey, it worked for James [Sera], it can work for you." And he'd go back out and make it work. He would just make it happen.'

Even in karting, there were signs of the measured, yet extremely laid-back, approach Piastri takes to his racing – the approach that has become his trademark. Except, in the cut-throat world of top-level karting, with huge fields of ambitious, driven kids separated by nothing in terms of performance, it wasn't always the asset it would eventually become.

'He was extremely relaxed. If anything, when he was driving for me at least, he lacked that mean streak. If he'd had that, he would have won a lot more races. He came second at the nationals in Newcastle in 2015, and he was racing kids who were four, five years older than him. Some of them were twice his height. He could have easily won . . . he just didn't quite have the mentality to get it done. But he was the quickest in the race and that was a real "wow" moment for me. He was in a fast class as well. Kids his age didn't make that step very often, because the karts were too fast. After that he won the Race of Stars in an even faster class, and that's when he was still only 12, and it was like . . . "Oh shit, this kid is getting good."

'He was an extremely good learner, and he was extremely intelligent. He was always much smarter than the people he was racing. One thing I'll say about Oscar is that when he was karting, he was actually lazy. He only did what he had to do to get the job done. He never did any more or any less. He was calculated in that way.'

Piastri could have been more patient, stuck around in each class a bit longer and won a lot more titles and trophies. But trophies didn't matter. Success was measured on how much Piastri was outperforming the standard trajectory and how quickly Sera could get him into the next class.

At the same time, Sera could see things in Piastri that were bigger than karting. There was an unorthodox element to his karting style, something you'd usually try and coach out of a young driver. But in this case, Sera knew that was a bad idea. By allowing Piastri to use his preferred line, which was 'wider' than usual (a later turn-in, perhaps not as tight to the inside kerb at the apex of the corner), he was setting him up to make the eventual switch to cars.

'He had a funny driving line, a really wide driving line that I don't teach anyone,' Sera explained. 'But if he'd adopted what I tried to teach him, it would have made him a worse driver. So, I stopped trying to change his style. He had his own thing going on and it worked for him . . . What works for most drivers doesn't work for all drivers. Oscar is a perfect example of that.

'I always used to say to Chris, "His driving style will suit open-wheel racing. Once he gets into an open wheeler, he's going to smash everyone."

'That's exactly what has happened. In my eyes [Piastri] was always destined for open-wheel racing. From day one.'

The next step on Piastri's journey to stardom was Europe. UK-based karting team Ricky Flynn Motorsport was, at the time, in a rich vein of form. It had taken Lando Norris, a young driver destined for Formula 1, to a European championship in 2013 and a world championship in 2014. The following year it won another world championship with American Logan Sargeant. That made Ricky Flynn Motorsport the key target for the Piastris as they looked to relocate to the other side of the world with their teenage son.

Piastri's father, Chris, emailed Flynn midway through the 2015 season to see if there was a slot in the OK-Junior class for 2016. A contract was signed and the logistics were sorted, with Flynn helping find the Piastris an apartment near the factory. Piastri was enrolled at Haileybury so he could continue his schooling. He couldn't quite match what Norris and Sargeant had achieved on track, and Piastri finished his debut season in Europe sixth in the OK-Junior World Championship standings. But, like during his Australian karting career, there was no point hanging around for the sake of another shot at a trophy. Piastri was clearly good enough that it would be his final season of karting.

At the end of 2016 Piastri made his competitive debut in an actual racing car at the Yas Marina Circuit in Abu Dhabi as part of the Formula 4 UAE Championship. Formula 4 is first step on the wings-and-slicks (a.k.a. single-seat racing cars with slick tyres and aerodynamics) ladder that, if successfully climbed, leads all the way to Formula 1. The cars don't have much power, downforce or tyre grip. F4's purpose is to introduce young drivers to the dimensions and dynamics of a proper car, with suspension, compared to a kart. From the three rounds and eleven races Piastri took part in while in the Middle East, he scored two podium finishes. Once that cameo was over, Piastri returned to the UK to join the TRS Arden Junior Racing Team for the 2017 F4 British Championship. He won six races and finished the season second in the standings, one place ahead of Sargeant.

The next rung on the ladder was the Formula Renault Eurocup, a series that uses single seaters that are slightly more complex than an F4 car and powered by a two-litre Renault motor. Piastri continued as part of the Arden squad and finished the season eighth in the standings, with three podiums. It wasn't necessarily a spectacular debut on the full European car-racing scene, but the signs of a driver able to perform with remarkable consistency were, in hindsight, right there.

It was during that two-season stint with Arden that Piastri had a brush with the famous Red Bull Junior program. Over the years, the energy-drink giant has nurtured the careers of Daniel Ricciardo, Sebastian Vettel, Max Verstappen and many more. With Arden originally founded by Red Bull Formula 1 boss, Christian Horner, Red Bull looked into whether Piastri would be a good fit for the junior program across the 2017 and 2018 seasons. Eventually, it decided to pass. Four years later, Horner would admit it was a decision worth regretting.

Piastri stayed in the Formula Renault Eurocup for the 2019 season but switched to the France-based R-ace GP team, which was coming off titles in both 2017 and 2018. In that sophomore season, both his raw pace and his ability to piece together a title-winning campaign became obvious. Piastri found himself locked in a tense battle with Frenchman Victor Martins. Between them they won 13 of the year's 20 races. Piastri set up his title with a strong start to the season, which included clean sweeps at Silverstone and the Nürburgring. Martins came home strong with four wins from the final six races, but it wasn't enough. Piastri closed out the title expertly with victory in the first race of the final round in Abu Dhabi and placing fourth in the second. For the first time since switching from karts to cars, Oscar Piastri was a champion.

What few would have predicted was that needing two years to conquer a class would become the exception for Piastri, not the rule. Given Red Bull's snub during his Arden days, Piastri wasn't tied to a junior team when he secured that Eurocup title in 2019. But Renault had seen more than enough, and, in late January 2020, it was announced that Piastri was officially part of the Renault Sport Academy, the forerunner to the Alpine Academy. He also had a plumb drive locked away for the coming Formula 3 season.

Formula 3 is the first step on the final climb to the summit of international motor racing. It's an official feeder series to Formula 1, with races taking place on grand prix weekends. That means there is a level of visibility, to both the public and the Formula 1 paddock, that a driver doesn't get until they reach that point. They're now on the biggest stage of world motorsport. There is pressure to perform. They're part of the Formula 1 ecosystem.

For the 2020 F3 season Piastri signed with Prema Racing. The Italian squad is widely regarded as one of the best modern developers of young talent in the world. In recent years, the likes of Kamui Kobayashi, Esteban Ocon, Pierre Gasly, Lance Stroll, Mick Schumacher and Guanyu Zhou have all come through the Prema system en route to Formula 1.

Prema was founded in the early 1980s by Angelo Rosin. These days it's run by Angelo's son René, a passionate, boisterous and immensely popular Italian who lives and breathes motorsport. Like his father, the young Rosin knows a thing or two about young drivers. He's seen all sorts come through the door: fast drivers, slow drivers, complicated drivers, drivers who are easy to work with . . . and when Rosin sat down with Oscar and Chris Piastri ahead of the 2020 FIA Formula 3 season, he immediately liked what he saw and heard.

'He did a very good job in the Formula Renault Eurocup in 2019, and we'd been following him,' he told me. 'We sat down with him before the season and immediately it was a good impression. He was a good kid, level-headed, didn't talk too much . . . it was a very good first impression. We did a test in Valencia, and he was immediately there. Immediately on the pace. He wasn't sitting in first position at the end of the test, but we weren't looking for performance. We were looking to see how the drivers were working with the team. We immediately signed a deal . . .'

Piastri was perfectly placed heading into the 2020 season. He had a contract with the benchmark junior race team in the world. He was just 18 years old and about to debut in the third tier of wings-and-slicks racing, only two steps below Formula 1. And he also found himself under the wing of two highly influential people in the F1 paddock – Australian ex-F1 racer Mark Webber and his partner in business and life, Ann Neal. They had seen that Piastri's star was on the rise and signed him to their JAM Sports Management business. In Webber, Piastri had landed himself a straight-talking, no bullshit kind of manager. The scene was set.

Until, of course, Piastri returned to Australia in March to work the paddock at the 2020 Australian Grand Prix – and got stuck there when the world went into lockdown due to the COVID-19 pandemic. Most of the F1 paddock fled Australia for Europe as soon as the 2020 race was infamously cancelled, but given the uncertainty, Piastri decided to stay put with his family in Melbourne. As the pandemic worsened, Piastri became more and more stuck. In no time at all, Australia had banned people from travelling overseas altogether.

Piastri was meant to be home for a week. His season was meant to be underway not long after that. But it wasn't until eight weeks after arriving in Australia, at the end of May, that he was granted an exemption to leave the country and return to Europe.

Thanks to the complications of the COVID-19 pandemic, the 2020 F3 season didn't kick off until July, instead of in Bahrain in March as planned. From then on, it was a bizarre schedule, often with back-to-back weekends. Piastri won the first race of the season at the Red Bull Ring in Austria, was on the podium in both races in Hungary and another one at Silverstone. He won again in Barcelona and had a podium in the first race at Monza before his weekend unravelled with a penalty for impeding another driver in qualifying for the second race.

The season boiled down to a title fight between Piastri and Sargeant, the former karting star who had also progressed to cars. And the fight for the title came down to the season finale at Mugello. Piastri went into the weekend with a slender lead, which was erased on the first day as he struggled to come to terms with the unfamiliar track layout in the Tuscan country-side. Sargeant started ahead of Piastri for the very last race of the season, too, before his title hopes were dashed by a first-lap collision with Lirim Zendeli. Piastri finished seventh to become champion.

'It was a difficult season because we started racing every week without a break, almost,' said Rosin. 'He won on his first weekend in Spielberg, then he had some issues with the [drag reduction] system. We found the issue just after Silverstone. But he was always there. If the car was good enough for first, he was first. When it was good enough to be on the podium, he was on the podium. He won with his head more than through pure speed. He was not the most spectacular. But he was just always there. Reverse grid. No reverse grid. He was just there. He did so well. The only time I saw Oscar really pissed off was after the penalty at Monza. He was really, really pissed off.'

With a Formula 3 championship in the bag, Prema moved Piastri up to FIA Formula 2 the following season for the first of what was planned to be two years. But again, Piastri was in a hurry. He was a contender from the word go, winning on debut in Bahrain. Later in the season, he banked five pole positions on the bounce as he sealed the title – his third championship in as many years.

'We had this series of pole positions starting at Silverstone,' recalled Rosin. 'At a certain point after the first set of tyres in qualifying at Silverstone, I said to his engineer, "Is that a fair lap? Or did he go over the track limits?" His time through Maggots and Becketts was mega. The lap was something insane. And from then it was pole position and win in the feature over and over. You could see this guy was so consistent and so level-headed. One of his greatest abilities is how he stays calm and relaxed. Even in difficult moments. When you see him in person, you would never say,

"Oh, there's somebody that will destroy everybody." But when he gets in the car, he's a machine. From my point of view, he did an incredible job. That series of pole positions . . . it was just a pleasure to be a part of.

'And apart from one race in Baku, where he was pushed into the wall, I never saw him crash. And that shows he is in full control of the car. The car isn't driving him; he's driving the car. He has everything under control. And then he's this really easygoing guy. When we catch up, it's still great. He's such a great guy.'

That impeccable strike rate in the junior formulae, as impressive as it was, came at a cost. The progression through F3 and F2 really should have taken twice as long. But by the beginning of 2022, at the tender age of 20, Piastri had nowhere to go except Formula 1 – and he didn't have a seat.

At least Alpine had a solution . . .

2

KEEPING UP APPEARANCES

Laurent Rossi, CEO of the wider Alpine group, beamed like a proud father as he addressed a small group of Australian journalists in the Alpine hospitality unit at Albert Park in Melbourne. It was the Friday evening of the Australian Grand Prix weekend in early April 2022, and the well-spoken Frenchman offered a detailed brief of his team's plans for Oscar Piastri. The emotion in his voice was unmistakable. To those in the room, it felt like there was a connection that went far beyond that of a regular employer–employee relationship.

'He's been fast and breaking record after record . . . I had a couple of conversations with him last year, alone, during the race weekends, during some dinners,' said Rossi when quizzed on how he and his team had become so enamoured with Piastri. 'He's extremely smart and mature for his age. Extremely smart. And that's the CEO of Alpine that says that to you, not the manager of a race team. He was asking

...tions about the way we operate the business of Alpine, ...t just the Formula 1 unit. The whole car business . . . And ...e was smart enough to understand that in the Formula 1 team, the team is built around its drivers and the feedback they can give and the way they mesh into the team. The way they build the performance unit around them, on their side of the garage, but also across the garage and across the factories.

'He was asking a lot of questions to understand how to do that and why they are doing it and observing what they are doing. It was very impressive. I saw the other drivers in the [Alpine] Academy, they weren't as curious as he was. There's a difference between being curious and asking a couple of questions, and being curious and asking smart questions, one after the other . . . I could see that, and I was like, "Okay, I want that. This is promising." So, he's fast, that's great. But it's not enough. He's smart.'

Rossi went on to outline a testing and development plan for Piastri. Given there were no race seats in the stable, Piastri was placed in the test and reserve driver role. Every team has a third driver on hand during a race weekend, ready to step into the seat should something happen to one of the race drivers. That's normal. But for Piastri, Alpine had designed a test and reserve driver program like no other.

The plan was to have Piastri do a lot of testing in older Formula 1 cars and, when the rules allowed, the current car. Expensive, but critical to keep him sharp during his 'gap year'. He would also do all of the simulator work, which has become a critical part of modern Formula 1. Drivers spend hours and hours in state-of-the-art simulators where different car set-ups can be assessed with mind-blowing accuracy. And Piastri would participate in Free Practice 1 outings (as allowed by F1's rules to help give young drivers miles) on select race weekends. Plus, he would be on hand for, and properly involved in, every debrief and every bit of data analysis across the season. 'You can rely on [his feedback],' said Rossi. 'It's not like someone is saying something, and you're like, "Yeah right, what do you know?" He's getting a lot of information, a lot of experience and expertise. It's much more intense than a rookie or reserve driver will get. Even compared to last year, my reserve driver was not necessarily involved in all those briefings or debriefs. Clearly not doing all of the tests. Clearly not going on the simulator so much. And that's normal. Oscar is doing it all.

'We'll make sure that . . . it's not a question of if, but when Oscar steps into Formula 1, he will be as ready as possible. That's the only thing that matters to me.'

The subject of the driver logjam inevitably followed. What was Alpine going to do? Was the team really prepared to decline a new deal for an in-form, but out-of-contract, Fernando Alonso? With the Spaniard at 40 years of age, the long-term benefits of re-signing him were limited. But what about the short-term benefits? Alonso had outperformed fellow Alpine driver Esteban Ocon in 2021, and, as a two-time world champion, was still one of the absolute fan favourites. To have a driver that popular on the books, particularly if his form didn't dip, was going to be difficult to give up.

At the same time, keeping Piastri on the sidelines beyond 2022 surely couldn't be an option either. For his talent to flourish he needed to be racing – in Formula 1.

Rossi held his nerve when pressed on the matter by the local journos. He maintained that the priority was for Piastri to develop his skills as the team's test and reserve driver. Should Alpine decide to re-sign Alonso for 2023, Rossi said the team would consider a loan deal for Piastri.

As in football, it's not uncommon for Formula 1 teams to loan out young drivers that have come through a development program to smaller teams for a set time period to help them gain experience in a racing environment. Then, they are drafted back when needed. Max Verstappen cut his teeth at Red Bull's junior team, now known as AlphaTauri. Charles Leclerc raced for Sauber before joining Ferrari. Alpine had already shown willingness to share by letting McLaren do a side deal with Piastri as reserve driver for 2022. But any proper loan, according to Rossi, would require a strict framework that ensured a recall to Alpine would be simple.

'If it's a solution that allows me to get him back at some point, I might think about it,' said Rossi. 'I want to develop Oscar; I don't want to leave him sitting on the bench waiting forever. He needs to be ready when the day comes. And the day will come because he's very talented, he's very worthy of one of the top 20 seats [in Formula 1]. And I do believe he has the potential of being a future world champion.

'I would love to have Oscar as my driver for the future Alpine when we get to the top of the podium. For me the ideal scenario is that he wins races and championships with us. That's what we're going to try and achieve.'

Alpine leant hard into the Piastri hype during the Australian Grand Prix weekend in 2022. He was basically treated like one of the race drivers. There were promotional appearances and nonstop one-on-one and group interviews. There was a cardboard cut-out of Piastri at the front of the Alpine hospitality unit in the paddock. He signed autographs on the Melbourne Walk as he came into the circuit each day. It was a full home-race weekend simulation with everything except actually driving the car. In fact, had it not been the first year of a brand-new set of technical regulations, he may well have driven either Ocon's or Alonso's car in Free Practice 1. At one point, that was the plan, only for the team to get cold feet due to not having a spare chassis and not wanting to deprive the race drivers of miles in the new cars.

Despite Alpine's predicament, it seemed inevitable that when the Formula 1 circus returned to Albert Park the following year, there would be a Melbourne driver on the grid for the first time ever. A real hometown hero, not one from Queanbeyan or Perth. And he'd either be in an Alpine, or in another car with Alpine's blessing. Anything else felt impossible.

Midway through May in 2022, four-time Formula 1 world champion Sebastian Vettel appeared on the BBC's *Question Time* TV show. A German racing driver as a panellist on a political talk show, alongside two MPs and an economist, was on the surface a little strange. But he wasn't there as a Formula 1 driver. He was there as an activist. The 34-year-old had increasingly been using his platform to campaign on social and environmental issues. At the 2021 Hungarian Grand Prix he wore a 'Same Love' T-shirt on the grid in protest of Hungary's discriminatory LGBTQIA+ laws. In the same year he staged a karting event for women only in Saudi Arabia ahead of the kingdom's inaugural grand prix. When Formula 1 visited Miami for the first time in 2022, Vettel walked onto the track wearing a T-shirt that read, 'Miami 2060, 1st Grand Prix Under Water, Act Now or Swim Later'.

Vettel more than held his own on *Question Time*. He spoke eloquently about the Ukraine war. About world resources. About Brexit. At one point, host Fiona Bruce decided to test the strength of Vettel's belief system when it came to sustainability. 'It's interesting that you've talked a lot . . . about energy and the need for renewable energy, and here you are, you are a Formula 1 driver, one of the most gas-guzzling sports in the world. Does that make you a hypocrite?' she asked.

Vettel didn't flinch. 'It does, it does and you,' he said as he pointed at the audience, 'are right when you laugh because there are questions I ask myself every day. I am not a saint. I am very concerned when it comes to the future.

'It is something I ask myself,' Vettel continued, to which Bruce asked if he meant whether he should be racing in Formula 1 at all. 'Yeah,' he replied. 'And travelling the world. It is my passion to drive a car and I love it, and every time I step in a car, I love it, but when I get out of the car, of course I am thinking, "Is this something we should do, travel the world, wasting resources?"' He finished with this: 'There are things I do because I feel I can do them better. Do I need to take a plane every time? No, not when I can take a car. There are certain things in my control and certain things outside of my control.'

It was a frank admission of the disconnect between Vettel's very public beliefs about sustainability and the very public platform he was using to express them. It didn't prompt any mass pressure for him to retire, and talk of a new deal with his current F1 team Aston Martin continued, but pundits began to speculate that retirement could be on the horizon. And when, on Thursday 28 July, the week of the 2022 Hungarian Grand Prix, Vettel announced he would indeed walk away from Formula 1 at the end of the season, it didn't come as a great shock to the industry.

It wasn't only the social and environmental campaigning that had influenced Vettel's decision. The Aston Martin package was clearly a handful to drive and not all that competitive, and at his age, with four world championship titles in his pocket, sitting third on the all-time F1 grand prix winners list, there was little left for Vettel to prove.

The somewhat expected news was followed a few days later by some less expected news. Vettel's replacement wouldn't be the clear favourite, Aston Martin's reserve driver Nico Hülkenberg. And it wouldn't be Vettel's protégé Mick Schumacher – son of the great Michael Schumacher and driving for Haas at the time – whom Vettel had recommended to the team when handing in his resignation.

Nope. On the following Monday the press release dropped. The title: 'Fernando Alonso to join Aston Martin F1 in 2023'.

That announcement sent a few shockwaves through the F1 paddock. Alpine seemed particularly blindsided by it, with team principal Otmar Szafnauer telling media that his own confirmation of the news had come from that press release, having left the Hungaroring circuit in Budapest just hours earlier, confident that Alonso would sign a new deal with his current team. 'Obviously, when we're in the paddock, there's all sorts of rumours, and I had heard rumours that Aston were interested [in Alonso], Szafnauer said. 'Once you hear that they're interested, there's probably discussions that took place and there's some other indications that discussions took place, like walking out of the same motorhome at the same time, all that kind of stuff, which I saw. But I was confident that, even with the discussions, and there's nothing wrong with exploring, that we were very close.

'So yes, the first confirmation I had was the press release. I did ask the question [to Alonso]. And I was told: "No, no, I haven't signed anything." So I was a bit surprised.'

Szafnauer explained that when he and Alonso had spoken on the Sunday evening, Alonso had indicated that he and his lawyer were just ironing out a few wrinkles in the new Alpine offer. According to Szafnauer, Alonso had explicitly said, 'Don't worry, I haven't signed with anybody else.'

The wrinkles, it turned out, were centred on the length of the contract. Alpine was offering Alonso what is known as a one-plus-one deal – a one-year guarantee and a second-year option, in the team's favour, which is activated (or not) based on performance. Alonso, however, wanted more security, and was pushing for at least a two-plus-one, a guaranteed two years at the team before being subject to an option. When Aston Martin offered that security, Alonso walked from Alpine.

It seemed like a blessing in disguise. Alpine's driver situation had solved itself. Alonso had extracted himself from the scenario entirely, and now it was as simple as bringing Piastri into the fold for 2023.

The charade of straightforwardness continued when, a few hours after Szafnauer had spoken to the media, Alpine announced Piastri as one of its race drivers for 2023. There was an official statement and everything. Again, on the very surface, it looked legit. The announcement featured glowing quotes from Szafnauer for the media to use: 'Oscar is a bright and rare talent. We are proud to have nurtured and supported him through the difficult pathways of the junior formulae. Through our collaboration over the past four years, we have seen him develop and mature into a driver who is more than capable of taking the step up to Formula 1'. But there wasn't a single quoted word attributed to Piastri in the press release. Highly unusual. And that wasn't the only giveaway that something was up. The rumour mill had already gone into overdrive that all wasn't well between the Alpine and Piastri camps. In fact, questions about Piastri and his potential unrest had come up in Szafnauer's interview earlier in the day.

So instead of the fingers hammering keyboards to spread the news of Alpine's triumphant promotion of Piastri to a race seat for 2023, the stories took a very, very different tone. Jonathan Noble, one of the top journalists in the F1 paddock, published a piece with Motorsport.com titled 'Alpine announces Piastri for F1 2023, but doubts remain'. Noble wrote, 'While there had been suggestions that he could be loaned out to Williams, it is understood that Piastri and his manager Mark Webber had been trying to secure a deal with McLaren instead as a replacement for Daniel Ricciardo. But, with Alonso out of the picture and Alpine having a contractual call on Piastri's services to put him in an F1 race seat, the situation has now changed – and his current bosses claim they have him on board for 2023.'

From the outside, the smart money was still on Alpine and Piastri ironing out whatever differences there were between them. Of course, it was feasible that the team's inaction on securing a race seat for Piastri, at such a critical time in his career when he couldn't afford another year on the sidelines, could have caused some tension. But with the path now clear, everyone could get on with their respective jobs. There was a seat for Piastri. He was, as far as anyone outside the inner sanctum knew, bound to Alpine by contract. His dream of being a Formula 1 race driver was coming true.

And then came the tweet.

On 3 August 2022, Piastri took to the social media platform then known as Twitter with his own statement: 'I understand that, without my agreement, Alpine F1 have put out a press release late this afternoon that I am driving for them next year. This is wrong and I have not signed a contract with Alpine for 2023. I will not be driving for Alpine next year.'

With each announcement – Vettel retiring, Alonso replacing him, Piastri turning down Alpine – the shockwaves were bigger. It wasn't only about Piastri and Alpine, either. How did McLaren fit into the mess? The team did, after all, have a contract with an embattled Daniel Ricciardo for 2023.

Daniel Ricciardo. Incredibly popular. Always smiling. Australian, just like Piastri. A proven racing talent with eight F1 grand prix victories to his name. But, unfortunately for his legions of fans, at that point he was under extreme pressure after being outpaced by younger teammate Lando Norris since joining McLaren ahead of the 2021 season. Ricciardo did boast the squad's only race win of that time with victory at Monza in 2021. But, in the harshest of terms, it was a statistic that flattered the likeable lad from Perth. In 2021, the head-to-head balance went Norris's way in qualifying (15 to 7), races (15 to 7) and points (160 to 115). By the mid-season break in 2022, when all of these wild driver movements were unfolding, Norris was once again well on top. From 13 races he'd out-qualified Ricciardo 9 times. He'd finished ahead of him 10 times. Norris had 76 points to his name, Ricciardo only 19.

Back in May that year, the door for an early end to the McLaren–Ricciardo deal had creaked open when McLaren boss Zak Brown admitted to media, 'I don't want to get into the contract, but there are mechanisms in which we're committed to each other, and mechanisms in which we're not. I spoke with Daniel about it. We're not getting the results that we both hoped for, but we're both going to continue to push.

'I think he showed in Monza [in 2021] he can win races. We also need to develop our race car; it's not capable of winning races. But we'd like to see him further up the grid. And we'll see how things develop and what he wants to do.'

The most immediate danger to Ricciardo's seat was, at that point, thought to be the race to capitalise on F1's booming popularity in the United States by bringing in a driver known to the North American market. With McLaren and Brown's fingers deep in the IndyCar scene, the likes of US-based talent such as Pato O'Ward, Alex Palou and Colton Herta were all being touted by the industry as potential F1 stars of the very near future.

Midway through July in 2022, Ricciardo took to his own social media channels to make what – again, at least on the surface – seemed to be an emphatic statement. 'There have been a lot of rumours around my future in Formula 1, but I want you to hear it from me,' he wrote. 'I am committed to McLaren until the end of next year and am not walking away from the sport. Appreciate it hasn't always been easy, but who wants it easy! I'm working my ass off with the team to make improvements and get the car right and back to the front where it belongs. I still want this more than ever.'

So as of very early August 2022, the situation was: Alonso joining Aston Martin; Alpine adamant it had a contractual right to Piastri; Piastri publicly rebuffing Alpine amid rumoured links to McLaren; Ricciardo publicly committing himself to McLaren. Messy.

And it didn't get any easier to unravel in the immediate aftermath. As Szafnauer continued to tell journalists that Piastri had no choice but to drive for Alpine in 2023, credible reports began to emerge on 5 August that, yes, the incredible was happening. Ricciardo had been told by McLaren that he wouldn't have a race seat for the 2023 season. And his spot wouldn't be taken by an IndyCar driver. It would be taken by Piastri.

The first part of that equation was made official on 24 August when McLaren announced that it had agreed to part ways with

Ricciardo at the conclusion of the 2022 season. But the team wasn't in a position to formally announce his replacement, even if it was the worst kept secret in Formula 1. Instead, it would need to wait for the matter to be heard by the FIA's Contract Recognition Board.

3

CRB

The Contract Recognition Board's existence can be traced back to a traffic crash between Formula 1 driver Bertrand Gachot and a taxi driver in London in December 1990. There was no damage to either car in the fender bender, but it prompted a heated exchange between the pair. In a moment of what Gachot has consistently argued was self-defence, he produced a can of tear gas and took aim at the taxi driver. He'd bought the tear gas at a service station in France and left it in the car, which belonged to his girlfriend, in case she ever needed to defend herself against an attacker. That was considered normal – and legal – in France. But in England, it was considered the illegal use of a weapon.

Gachot spent half an hour at the police station before he was released. Even after learning that what he had done was technically illegal, he wasn't worried. He knew he'd have to face court but, on the advice of a number of lawyers, he was expecting a fine only. At worst, a suspended sentence.

When the case went to trial in August 1991, a week before the Belgian Grand Prix at Spa-Francorchamps, Gachot was shocked when the judge handed down an 18-month prison sentence and put him behind bars immediately.

With Gachot suddenly, and very unexpectedly, locked up, the Jordan Formula 1 team needed a replacement driver. At incredibly short notice.

This prompted one of the most remarkable rookie stories in the history of Formula 1.

The replacement driver that Eddie Jordan and his team landed on was a young German by the name of Michael Schumacher. At that point, Schumacher was doing great things as part of the Mercedes factory sportscar program as he waited for an opportunity to present itself in Formula 1. He hadn't driven a Formula 1 car yet, but with Mercedes willing to spend US$150,000 for Schumacher to race the Jordan at Spa-Francorchamps to gain experience, and the first-year team in a deep financial hole, the deal went ahead.

On the Monday before the Belgian race, Schumacher travelled to Jordan's factory near the Silverstone circuit in the UK. He underwent a seat fitting before the car was towed, on an ordinary trailer because the transporter had already left for Belgium, to the circuit itself for a familiarisation test. The cash-strapped team was nervous about letting a young driver, with zero F1 experience, loose in the car. And those nerves weren't exactly quelled when Schumacher started going very fast, the team anxious that the German driver was pushing too hard in his eagerness to impress.

'The strongest memory I've got is that within five laps, you would've thought Michael had been driving the car all season,' Jordan team manager Trevor Foster recalled to *Motor Sport* magazine 30 years after that Silverstone test. 'He was just instantly on it, flicking the car around, very much in control. When you see a driver get onto it so quickly, you're always a little bit concerned that they're driving over the edge.

'So we called Michael in, and I remember having a conversation with his manager [Willi Weber]. I said, "Really, Willi, please bear in mind, we need to take our time, this car is going into the trailer to Spa!" At the time Michael wasn't 100 per cent confident in his English, so Willi spoke to him, and then replied: "He doesn't have a problem and doesn't know why you're concerned!"'

Several days later, Schumacher reconvened with the Jordan team at Spa. According to folklore, the Schumacher camp had told Eddie Jordan the young driver knew the circuit well – but the reality was he had never turned a lap of the fast, flowing ribbon of tarmac through the Ardennes in his life. He prepared by riding around the circuit on a fold-up pushbike to learn the layout.

When the Belgian Grand Prix weekend got going, Schumacher's incredible talent was evident. He was instantly competitive in Free Practice, to the point where, once again, the team had to question whether he was trying too hard. When a water leak ruled his car temporarily out of action, he jumped into experienced team leader Andrea de Cesaris's car – and immediately outpaced the Italian driver. When qualifying rolled around, Schumacher put his Jordan seventh on the grid, four spots ahead of de Cesaris. Formula 1 was in shock.

The race itself was a non-event, with Schumacher's inexperience finally catching up with him in an early lap when he blew the clutch to smithereens. But despite the unceremonious end to his debut, the stage was set. A star was born, and Schumacher would go on to win seven world championships. To this day he is considered one of, if not the, best of all time.

Before all that could happen, however, there was one hell of a contract dispute.

Eddie Jordan and his team left Belgium under the impression that retaining this freshly unearthed superstar for the rest of 1991 and beyond would be simple. According to a letter of intent dated the Thursday before the Spa race, Schumacher had declared that, should Jordan enter him in Belgium, he would sign 'the' driver agreement that was on the table before the next race, the Italian Grand Prix.

But by the time all the parties involved – Jordan, Schumacher, Weber, Mercedes and their management firm IMG – came together a week after Spa, things had changed. The key was the letter of intent, which had been amended to say Schumacher would sign 'a' driver agreement, not 'the' driver agreement. Suddenly, Schumacher and his men controlled what any driver agreement would say, if Jordan insisted on the letter being honoured. It might not involve driving at all. A day later, Eddie Jordan received a fax from

Schumacher that simply read, 'Dear Eddie, I'm very sorry but I'm not going to be able to drive for your team.'

Allegedly spooked by the prospect of Jordan doing a deal to run the uncompetitive Yamaha engine in 1992, the Schumacher camp had approached the Benetton F1 team to see if it wanted to sign the young German driver. Not for next season. Right now. Benetton recognised the opportunity to snare a once-in-a-generation talent and made its move. Two days after those talks with Jordan, Schumacher tested for Benetton at Silverstone. And then signed a contract with them that started at the 1991 Italian Grand Prix.

A devastated Eddie Jordan did his best to block the move, but the law was on Schumacher's side. Jordan had no claim thanks to that clever manoeuvring from Schumacher's management with the wording of that letter of intent.

Where some legal power did lie, however, was with Brazilian driver Roberto Moreno – the man Benetton axed from its line-up to make way for Schumacher. Moreno had already been told by Benetton, right after Spa, that he was out at the end of the 1991 season. Suddenly, he was out on the spot.

Given he had a contract with Benetton for 1991, Moreno was able to get an injunction right before the Italian Grand Prix. In a late crisis meeting, literally hours before track action got underway, Moreno was offered half a million US dollars to drop the injunction. He tried to hold out for a million, but eventually gave up and took the $500,000 on the table. According to Benetton's then team manager Flavio Briatore, who retold his side of the story to the official Formula 1 podcast in 2020, the decisive factor was the use of the word 'chassis', not 'car', in Moreno's contract. Benetton's legal obligation was to provide Moreno with a chassis – not to fit that chassis with an engine, wheels or anything else it needed to actually circulate on a race track.

Benetton's actions sparked an uproar in the paddock, particularly among Moreno's fellow Brazilian drivers, and almost led to the team's lead driver Nelson Piquet walking out at Monza. Briatore's response was to tell reserve driver Alex Zanardi to put on a driving suit and head towards the garage. Piquet folded.

Eventually the dust settled. And by the end of the 1995 season, Michael Schumacher and Benetton were two-time, back-to-back world champions.

One part of the fallout from the 1991 Jordan–Benetton–Schumacher saga was the establishment of the Contract Recognition Board (CRB). Informal hotel-room trials weren't going to cut it. Neither was tying up civil courts for extended periods of time. The idea was to create an independent board stacked with sharp legal minds to make swift, informed decisions on contract disputes. The obligation to abide by the CRB's decisions was added to the Concorde Agreement, which effectively outlines the terms of entry to Formula 1.

Details of exactly how the CRB operates are few and far between. But in basic terms, its purpose is to act as an archive of all driver contracts – race, reserve and test – in Formula 1. Teams don't have to provide all details of a contract, as some matters may be sensitive and irrelevant to the legalities. But the key terms must go to the CRB.

Its role only becomes public when a dispute springs to life. On those rare occasions, the CRB brings its lawyers together for a hearing. Those lawyers are then required to make their judgement based on the available evidence within three days.

There aren't many high-profile examples of CRB intervention. Back in late 1994, promising British racer David Coulthard signed with McLaren for the 1995 season. Williams, however, believed it had an option on Coulthard for 1995, a case it successfully argued to the CRB. Coulthard had to wait until 1996 to make his move to McLaren.

A decade later, another Brit in Jenson Button signed with Williams, despite having a valid contract with British American Racing (BAR) for the 2005 season. Again, the CRB sided against the 'poacher' and Button was forced to stay with BAR.

In 2007 there was a win for the other side: BMW Sauber test driver Timo Glock signed a race deal with Toyota for 2008, only for BMW Sauber to turn around and claim it had dibs on the German for the following season. In this case, the CRB ruled that BMW Sauber's option relied on a firm offer of a race seat, which hadn't been forthcoming. Toyota, however, *had* made a concrete offer of a race seat, which was enough to secure Glock's services.

In late August 2022, the CRB roared back into the public eye thanks to the showdown between Alpine, McLaren and Piastri. The hearing was scheduled, somewhat ironically given the incident that had initially inspired the CRB, for the Monday after the 2022 Belgian Grand Prix.

It's important to note that, at that point, the general public sentiment was anti-McLaren, and, to a lesser extent, anti-Piastri. McLaren, led by the intimidating Ron Dennis, was once seen as the evil empire, a team so incredibly dominant that its drivers were unbeatable. You were either a McLaren fan, or you weren't – simple as that. But by 2022, the team had emerged from a period of nothingness to become, remarkably, something of a fan favourite. Now led by the charismatic Zak Brown, and with two popular, likeable drivers in Lando Norris and Daniel Ricciardo, there was a kind of 'everyone's second favourite team' feel buzzing around the place. Even if you weren't a McLaren fan, it was okay to like McLaren. It was a nice vibe, but one that was suddenly under threat by what looked to be a ruthless power play straight from the Dennis era. Dumping the universally loved Ricciardo was bad enough. But then stripping poor Alpine of their protégé to replace him? How could they?

Alpine, for its part, kept up the charade of hurt feelings expertly. Three days before the CRB hearing, Otmar Szafnauer told Sky Sports F1: '[Piastri is] a promising young driver. He hasn't driven in F1 yet. And my wish for Oscar was that he had a bit more integrity. He signed a piece of paper as well back in November and we've done everything on our end of the bargain to prepare him for F1. And his end of the bargain was to either drive for us or take a seat where we would place him for the next three years. And I just wish Oscar would have remembered . . . what he signed up to.'

When quizzed further on the matter that Saturday at Spa, Szafnauer continued to paint a picture of duplicitousness from Piastri's side. 'I told Oscar before the announcement was made,' he said when describing how Piastri had taken the news he was being promoted to a race driver. 'He happened to be in the simulator, so I went and found him, and he smiled and was thankful. We made the release very quickly.'

The impending hearing was the hot topic at Spa, and all of the F1 heavyweights were asked about it during their regular media sessions that weekend. When addressing the press pack, Mercedes F1 boss Toto Wolff questioned Piastri's now infamous tweet but stopped short of directly criticising the young Aussie. 'I think it's important that junior programs are being respected,' said Wolff. 'I think some of the kids should be wary on Twitter what they say about multinational organisations. But I have no insight into the contracts.

'I believe in karma. I believe in integrity. But I'm not here to judge because, as I said, I don't know the legal situation.'

Red Bull F1 team principal Christian Horner, who had overseen plenty of drivers coming through the energy drink's own junior development program, seemed amazed that Alpine had let the situation get to this messy point. 'I don't fully understand it, because contractually, that should just never happen,' Horner told Sky Sports F1. 'I think if Renault and Alpine have invested in his junior career, it's because you invest in youth because you're investing in it for the future, and there has to be an element of loyalty within that. So I don't understand obviously contractually what's going on there. But for him to be even in a position to think that he doesn't have to drive for Alpine next year obviously shows there's something not right.'

The tweet aside, neither Piastri nor McLaren had felt comfortable having their say over the matter. It must have been tough. But the collective biting of tongues would pay dividends once the CRB got involved.

On 29 August 2022 the CRB hearing took place. Alpine, McLaren and the Piastri camp, led by nine-time grand prix winner Mark Webber, all had their say. Three days later, the FIA, motorsport's governing body, released a public statement with the CRB's findings: 'A tribunal appointed by the Contract Recognition Board held a meeting on 29 August 2022 when counsel for Alpine Racing Limited, McLaren Racing Limited and Mr Oscar Piastri were heard. The Tribunal has issued a unanimous decision that the only contract to be recognised by the board is the contract between McLaren Racing Limited and Mr Piastri dated 4 July 2022. Mr Piastri is entitled to drive for McLaren Racing Limited for the 2023 and 2024 seasons.'

As per the Concorde Agreement, Alpine's dream of retaining Piastri was over. The team released a short statement to the media that simply read: 'We consider the matter closed on our side and will announce our full 2023 driver line-up in due course. Our immediate focus is the Dutch Grand Prix and securing points in our fight for fourth in the Constructors' Championship.'

Piastri's initial public reaction was a video posted to social media where he effectively reeled off media-release-style quotes about how excited he was to join such a prestigious team and so on. Two days later, however, Piastri opened up about the saga, including Alpine's original announcement and his subsequent tweet, to the official Formula 1 website. 'My decision [to join McLaren] was made well in advance [of Alonso's departure], which made Alpine's announcement probably even more confusing and upsetting because we had told the team that I wasn't going to continue,' said Piastri.

'It was quite upsetting as the announcement was false and it also denied me the opportunity to properly say goodbye to everyone at [Alpine's factory in] Enstone. I had been with the team for a bit over two and a half years now, and for the rest of the team to find out I was leaving in that manner was very upsetting. I still haven't had the opportunity to say goodbye and it's something I want to do to show my gratitude to all the men and women at Enstone.'

Piastri also shed more light on that conversation with Szafnauer in the simulator room. 'That was a bizarre and frankly upsetting episode,' he said. 'It was done publicly in front of some members of the team who were oblivious to the situation and I didn't want to cause a scene in front of them. Once we were in private, I told Otmar what our position was and what he had been told multiple times before that. It was very surprising to me to make that announcement.'

As for the tweet, Piastri added: 'It was the biggest moment of my career and probably my life up to now. To have that falsely announced was something my management and I felt we had to correct and there were also potential legal implications if we didn't deny the announcement. It was not intended to be pointed or in any way anything more than factual. The last line was quite a strong one, but with the CRB ruling, it shows it was purely a fact.'

Piastri also used the interview to offer some insight into what the CRB hearing had uncovered and how McLaren had won the battle. He explained that the CRB 'has confirmed I didn't have a contract for the 2023 season [with Alpine]. I was free to choose my destiny – and I felt McLaren was a great opportunity. They were very straightforward and very keen and enthusiastic to have me. To be completely honest, there was a lack of clarity around my future at the team at Alpine. They publicly stated they wished to continue with Fernando for at least one or two more years. I respect that. But after spending the year out, my hopes were firmly set on an Alpine seat, and [because of] the lack of clarity and, similarly to Fernando, a bit of a strange feeling in negotiations, it didn't feel like it was the right decision for me [to stay at Alpine].'

As the dust settled, the real story of how Alpine had lost not one, but two drivers – and been forced to cough up the best part of £540,000 in legal fees – emerged courtesy of another Jonathan Noble report for Motorsport.com in September 2022. And it didn't reflect well on the French team and its insistence that Piastri's integrity should be questioned.

According to Noble's sources, Alpine had pinned its hopes on a 'terms sheet', which informally laid out the team's plans for Piastri up to 2023, being recognised as a contract. The terms sheet had, at the very least, been lodged with the CRB. The document had also been lodged with Piastri and his manager, Webber, on 15 November 2021. In the correspondence between driver, manager and team that followed there was a clear plan that Alpine would offer Piastri two separate contracts as a progression from the terms sheet. One contract would be as a reserve driver for 2022. The other would be as a race driver for 2023 and 2024.

'In a letter that Alpine CEO Laurent Rossi sent on that date, he promised that a proper F1 agreement would be sent to [Webber] shortly – "with a view to executing the same no later than 10 business days after receipt of the same", wrote Noble. But the proper contracts never arrived. Not the one as a reserve driver, nor the one as a race driver. Webber grew frustrated, a fact clearly outlined in correspondence with Alpine's legal team in the weeks that followed. The team blamed a lack of resources. Then the impending launch of its new car. But, Alpine promised, things would be settled soon. Webber asked the team to have the contract ready by 1 March 2022 so they could evaluate it before the season-opening Bahrain Grand Prix later that month. On 2 March Webber was told he would have the contract later that day. Two days later Webber was finally sent a 'draft reserve driver agreement', accompanied by a note explaining that the race driver deal for 2023 and 2024 would materialise the following week. But again, that promise wasn't honoured. The second deal never landed, something Alpine explained was because of the complications surrounding a shared reserve driver deal with McLaren.

To be eligible to race a Formula 1 car, a driver needs what is called a super licence. The first step to qualifying for a super licence is earning enough points through success in the junior formulae (criteria easily satisfied by Piastri). Then, the relevant team applies for a super licence by lodging an application with the CRB.

As the 2022 season drew closer, pressure grew to get Piastri's super licence application lodged with the CRB. Alpine suggested pushing through the reserve driver deal for 2022 to ensure the super licence was granted and then worrying about the 2023 and 2024 race driver deal later. On 14 March, with neither driver nor team having signed the reserve driver deal, Alpine instead lodged the signed terms sheet to the CRB with a note stating it was a legally binding 'Heads of Terms'. But at the same time the document itself outlined that it was 'subject to contract'.

It wasn't until 19 March that Piastri and Webber finally received a proposal to sign a four-year race driver contract covering 2023 to 2026. But it wasn't to race for Alpine. The deal suggested Piastri would be loaned out to Williams in 2023. What happened in 2024 would depend on Alonso. If Alpine wanted to retain the Spaniard for another season, Piastri would stay with Williams for a second campaign. The only guarantee of Piastri racing for Alpine in the contract was for 2025 and 2026.

That, wrote Noble, is believed to have been the final straw for the Piastri camp. There was no short-term hope at Alpine. There had already been informal talks with McLaren by this point, and Piastri hadn't signed anything beyond 2022.

He, as the CRB would find, was a free agent.

McLaren allegedly told their current race driver Ricciardo that it was looking at other options for 2023 in early May of 2022. The team then signed a preliminary deal with Piastri on 4 June for an unspecified role, in case the Ricciardo divorce became, for whatever reason, impossible. A month later, to the day, things were significantly clearer. The terms sheet lodged to the CRB by Alpine didn't give it any claim over Piastri's services for 2023. McLaren was making headway with its Ricciardo separation. So, on 4 July 2022, Piastri signed the race deal with McLaren for 2023, as referenced in the publicly announced CRB findings, subject to the seat being available.

That detail changes the meaning of Ricciardo's mid-July social media post regarding his commitment to McLaren for 2023. It's a fair assumption, based on the idea that Ricciardo had known since May that the team had other plans, that the statement was a bargaining chip for his exit rather than a heart-felt commitment by a man who didn't know what was coming.

It appears McLaren's plan had been to wait until the Ricciardo split was announced before the team rolled out Piastri as its new signing. That would have been a cleaner, far less dramatic way to broach the matter with the wider Formula 1 fanbase. But then Fernando Alonso walked out on Alpine. And Alpine responded with its Piastri announce-ment. And Piastri responded with the tweet. And news of the McLaren deal bubbled to the surface.

Given the CRB outcome had been delivered on the Friday of the Dutch Grand Prix, there was no way for Szafnauer to avoid speaking to the press about the matter in the immediate aftermath. He acknowledged that, perhaps, the damage in the Piastri–Alpine relationship had pre-dated his own arrival at the team in March 2022. But he stopped short of using that as an excuse. 'All this happened in November of last year, so I guess it's easy to blame people that aren't here any more, but that's not my style,' Szafnauer said. 'The right thing to do is to have a look at what happened, understand where the short-comings were and fix them for the future.' He also doubled down on Alpine's loyalty to Piastri, despite the legal outcome. 'We delivered everything above and beyond what we said we were going to do, including 3500 kilometres in last year's car [and] making him our reserve driver when McLaren and Mercedes asked if we could share him as a reserve because they didn't have one,' he said. 'We allowed him to do that. We paid him. That's our loyalty to Oscar.'

At the same time, the CRB's findings had highlighted that there was nothing opportunistic or untoward about Piastri's actions. He and Webber's frustrations over the lack of formal direction, and commitment, from Alpine were easily justified. And McLaren? Well, it had hardly dumped poor Ricciardo on a whim and stolen Piastri from under Alpine's nose. An opportunity to sign a surprisingly available new talent had presented itself. Who could blame the team for grabbing that chance with both hands?

At the Italian Grand Prix in early September 2022, Rossi faced the media for the first time since the CRB outcome. The fatherly fondness from Albert Park had been replaced by a sense of genuine hurt from the Alpine CEO at how things had played out – and a frank admission that Alpine had taken Piastri's loyalty for granted. 'It's very disappointing because we've been extremely committed and we've been extremely loyal,' he said. 'We made technical mistakes, legal technical mistakes, which basically left the door ajar. But we never thought – and it was a bit of an oversight for sure – that we had to worry about us.

'When you provide so much to a driver, it's almost tradition that you get back in return the driving of that driver for you. George Russell spent three years at Williams, a good school if any, to learn the ropes and then go back to the mothership. Charles Leclerc did the same, a year [at Sauber] before going back to Ferrari. Verstappen did the same, Seb Vettel did the same. The list is long. It's normal to go back to the team that invested so much in you, especially us.

'I think it's not pushing too far to say that we've been extremely disappointed because we were expecting him to stay true to our investment and our work. While we made mistakes, we feel like we stand for values. That didn't happen for him. Obviously he leveraged the opportunity to shop around and get very likely a better deal.

'But I guess things happen for a reason. We don't necessarily share the same values. So perhaps it's better to part ways now.'

At the same time, McLaren was able to bask in what, with the benefit of hindsight, was a clever decision to keep its Piastri cards close to its chest until the CRB had made its decision. On the same weekend that Rossi was addressing the media at Monza, Zak Brown did likewise at Laguna Seca in California, where he was attending the IndyCar season finale. He admitted the fan backlash had made the build-up to the CRB hearing tough to stomach, particularly given that Alpine had been so vocal on the matter. But the vindication since had been worth it.

'Before the CRB ruling, they didn't know what they didn't know and we kept our mouths shut deliberately,' said Brown. 'Now that ruling has come out and some of the detail, I think it's clear what happened there . . . we knew the truth would come out eventually and we could ride it out, as opposed to giving a running commentary.

'At the time we were not oblivious to the noise and some of the direct message notes I got from fans. But now we're very comfortable that the CRB ruling has come out. It's best to let things play out, and we can give a little colour afterwards. If you look at Otmar's comments, he was giving a play-by-play on the CRB and how confident they were, and now I think he looks a little silly. So I think that's why it's best to keep our mouths shut and comment on it afterwards when there's something concrete to say.'

What Alpine did have in its pocket was that reserve driver contract for the 2022 season. In the short term, Piastri continued his simulator work with Alpine – requests for an early release fell on seemingly deaf ears. But then in early November 2022, news broke that Piastri had driven a McLaren Formula 1 car for the first time. He'd spent two days at Circuit Paul Ricard in France driving a 2021-spec MCL35M. That led to confirmation that his ties with Alpine had been severed early and he was going to be able to drive McLaren's 2022 car, the MCL36, at the now-traditional post-season test on the Tuesday after the season-ending Abu Dhabi Grand Prix.

Alpine's turn of lenience was likely linked to its successful luring of Pierre Gasly from Red Bull's junior team AlphaTauri. The young Frenchman had found himself in an interesting position within the Red Bull system. He'd come through Red Bull's junior program and then through the junior F1 team, known as Toro Rosso at the time, to earn promotion to the main Red Bull Racing squad in 2019. But after struggling to match Max Verstappen, he was promptly demoted back to Toro Rosso ahead of the Belgian Grand Prix midway through that same season. Back at the junior squad, rebranded as AlphaTauri, Gasly rebuilt his career with solid results in 2020, 2021 and 2022. But he was still at a dead end. Would Red Bull really re-promote a driver tarnished by a mid-season dumping from the primary team? It's little surprise that the opportunity to join a factory team – a French factory team, at that – in Alpine was too good to turn down.

During the grand prix weekend in Abu Dhabi, Szafnauer didn't waste the opportunity to describe the Piastri debacle, and subsequent Gasly coup, as a blessing in disguise. 'We had to go to the CRB and then get resolution [over Piastri],' he said. 'You know, that's life, that's why you have bodies that . . . [make a judgement] if two sides think differently. Look, let's see how we do next year. I'm happy that our driving pairing with Esteban [Ocon] and Pierre [Gasly] is better than it would have been if we had won that [CRB] case.

'[Gasly is] more experienced, still young. And time will tell, but I think faster.'

*

Against the dramatic silly-season backdrop, with so much driver movement, there were some curious sights at Yas Marina when the post-season test commenced on that Tuesday in December 2022. There was Alonso, wearing black overalls and a camouflage-look helmet, in a sticker-less Aston Martin car due to his ongoing contract with Alpine. And Piastri in the McLaren. And Gasly in the Alpine.

Lap times from testing are about as unpredictable a form guide as you'll ever find and, usually, people pay them very little notice. Without any knowledge of fuel loads or engine modes, just to name two of the hundreds of performance parameters that can affect car speed, it's simply impossible to know what's real and what isn't. The stop watches may be running, but if the results don't really matter you can never truly say who has and hasn't done a good job. But for the record, Gasly was fourth fastest, Alonso twelfth and Piastri fourteenth (half a second quicker than McLaren driver Lando Norris).

That anybody even remotely cared was a precursor to a fascinating 2023 season.

Before 2022 came to a close, there was one sting left in the rollercoaster of a silly season. Back in August, Audi had formally announced that it would enter Formula 1 as a factory team for the 2026 season. It was an open secret that the Sauber team, currently competing under the Alfa Romeo banner, would land the prized German carmaker's Formula 1 business. At the end of October, that too was made official. McLaren's team principal Andreas Seidl, one of the most highly rated technical minds in the Formula 1 paddock, had long been seen as a logical choice to head up Audi's factory effort at some point. Not only was there the German link, but Seidl had made his name running Porsche's prototype sportscar program before joining McLaren, meaning he and his talents were well known within the Volkswagen Group. However, none of that was seen as a short-term issue for McLaren.

That was at least until the second week of December 2022, when news broke that Sauber Group CEO Fred Vassuer, who also held the team principal title, was heading to Ferrari for the 2023 season. A day later there was a simultaneous announcement from Sauber/Audi and McLaren that Seidl would be taking over the Sauber Group CEO role immediately. His McLaren role would be taken over by Andrea Stella. The Seidl split came as somewhat of a shock, given he had a contract with McLaren that ran until 2025. Zak Brown explained at the time that, yes, the plan was for Seidl to see out his contract and then move to Sauber when the Audi deal formally kicked off. But a friendly approach from Sauber had led to the unexpected exit of a key figure in the McLaren team.

'When it became clear that Fred was going to go to Ferrari, [Sauber owner] Finn Rausing, who is someone that I've known for a decade and get along with very well, gave me a call to see if there was a discussion to be had to potentially release Andreas early,' Brown explained. 'My reaction was, if Andrea would be happy to join as team principal, then I'd be very happy to make that change now, which I think puts everyone in their permanent homes for the foreseeable future.'

Interestingly, McLaren didn't slap a garden-leave clause on Seidl's exit, letting him and his brainpower walk straight into a rival garage. 'I know a lot of teams play the garden-leave card,' said Brown. 'But I think, as we've demonstrated at McLaren, there are ways to dissolve relationships, whether that's with racing drivers, or employees, where you can do things on very workable terms for everyone.'

4

THE ROOKIE HANDBOOK

'The first stage of your career is getting to Formula 1. Then the next stage is your time in Formula 1. And then your next stage is your life after F1, whether that's racing other categories or having another career. And there's a very high chance that you'll skip that middle step.'

Among the eyes closely trained on Oscar Piastri heading into the 2023 season were those of Karun Chandhok, once a racer, now permanently embedded in the Formula 1 paddock as part of the broadcast team.

Chandhok knows a thing or two about the grind of working your way to the pinnacle of world motorsport. And while he managed to avoid the unfortunate fate of 'skipping the middle step' of his racing career, as he so perfectly describes it, he did experience the high of the introduction to grand prix racing, and the low of feeling rejected by the sport, in quicker-than-planned succession.

Chandhok dedicated the first 27 years of his life to becoming one of the first drivers from India to make it all the way to Formula 1. He raced karts and junior formulae at home and in Asia before making the move to the European scene in 2002 when he first contested the extremely competitive British Formula 3 Championship. He then continued on a traditional path through the feeder categories and eventually worked his way into what, at the time, was known as the GP2 series – the step below Formula 1. Winning a race in his rookie season in 2007 helped him catch the eye of the Formula 1 paddock and he struck up a relationship with Red Bull Racing. After completing some straight-line tests with the team (development work on an airport runway, a common practice at a time before sophisticated simulators were used to ease young drivers into Formula 1 hardware), he was invited by Red Bull to Barcelona for a proper test in a Formula 1 car. 'As a kid growing up there are various milestones as a driver,' said Chandhok. 'First you want to go and drive a go-kart. Then you want to drive a race car. Then you want to climb the ladder and one day just experience a Formula 1 car.

'That experience of driving a Formula 1 car for the first time was very special. And in my case . . . at the end of 2007, Michael Schumacher, who had retired, came back to do a bunch of testing for Ferrari because he was getting bored at home. And he tested that day at Barcelona, in the car that Kimi Räikkönen had just won the world championship with. Michael was one of my heroes. And I followed him out of the pit lane on my first run. I remember thinking to myself,

"This is nuts." My first lap in a Formula 1 car and I'm following Michael Schumacher out of the pit lane. It was amazing.'

It took two more years following that test for Chandhok to make the next step and land a race seat in Formula 1. Two years of relentless wheeling and dealing to get a foot in the door. His break came at the start of 2010 thanks to the FIA's decision to let three new teams onto the Formula 1 grid. Those teams were Lotus, Virgin and the Hispania Racing Team, or HRT for short. The new teams came into the sport on the promise of a budget cap that would allow them to compete with the established names. But the budget cap never materialised, and the minnow teams spent several years racing themselves at the very back of the field until they all disappeared from the sport.

They did, however, provide six additional seats on the Formula 1 grid for the 2010 season. And that in turn opened the door for Chandhok to sign a deal with HRT and finally realise his dream of becoming a fully fledged Formula 1 driver.

Summarised like that it seems fairly straightforward. Do the hard yards in the junior series, win some races and take your opportunity when it comes. The reality is that in any given year in the modern era of Formula 1, there are 20 to 24 driver seats in total – and only a handful of those are up for grabs each time around. As an athlete there's a finite element to your career; you don't have forever to find your way in. There's a good chance you need to find the funding to take that first step into a team looking for some backing. You need to play the politics just right. It's hard work. And even if you get everything right, sometimes you still need a bit of luck.

'I got lucky in terms of timing – and this is where timing is so important in your Formula 1 career – that in 2010 there were new teams coming onto the grid,' admitted Chandhok. 'Look at Logan Sargeant and his deal with Williams this year; he's got lucky that he's come along at a time when there's three American races and two American-owned teams, and he's the top Europe-based American driver. The timing couldn't be better for him. Timing is very, very important – and it's something that you can't plan. Because there are too many other pieces of the puzzle.

'Taking that last step to Formula 1 is so, so difficult. It's very tough. Oscar is a great example; he has an impeccable CV. You cannot get a better junior formulae CV than what he's got. And the fact he had to take a year out [in 2022] actually really pissed me off. Because there's just not enough seats in Formula 1. There are half a dozen, maybe eight, drivers in F2 that think they deserve a chance. There's a couple of F3 drivers that think they should go straight to F1. There's some in Super Formula in Japan. Some in America. Then there's F1 test drivers. Drivers in Formula E. All of sudden, oh shit, there's 20 drivers chasing the three or four seats that become available every year.

'It's challenging. It's super stressful. Trying to stay moti-vated is the hardest part. Can you talk yourself into getting your arse in the gym and keep training and keep sharp, just in case the opportunity arises? Because you don't know if the opportunity will arise.'

That was exactly what Chandhok did, which meant when the opportunity with HRT came along, literally a month out from the first race of the 2010 season in Bahrain, Chandhok felt ready. 'The deal itself with HRT was done very last minute; I did the deal at the beginning of February,' he explained. 'We did a seat fitting. We did no testing. And then we went straight to the first race. But throughout that winter I'd spoken to Toyota. And Lotus. And Manor. And USF1. And HRT . . . and I was fairly confident that one of those deals would come through.

'So, I made sure [in] the winter that I got myself prepared in the best way possible. I lost some weight, I made sure that I was physically and mentally prepared for when the opportunity came. Yes, the deal was last minute, but I was confident the deal was coming.'

When the ink dried on that HRT contract, Chandhok's dream came true. To some extent. He was about to become an F1 driver, but it wasn't the start of a dream career. The new teams were hopelessly unprepared for Formula 1. They were hopelessly underfunded. And HRT was the worst-placed of all three heading into the season. As Chandhok points out, there was no pre-season testing, a critical process to understanding the car and assessing its pace and reliability. None. HRT arrived in Bahrain still building its cars. In the first Free Practice session on the Friday of the grand prix weekend, Chandhok's teammate Bruno Senna completed three installation laps. Three times he left the pits and came straight back in. Chandhok watched on from the sidelines. In the second session Senna banked 17 laps, the fastest of which was 11.5 seconds off the pace. His session came to an end when a wheel parted ways with the car. Again, Chandhok watched on from the garage. He was a full day into his Formula 1 career and hadn't turned a single lap.

On the Saturday he finally got to drive the car for the first time, against a field of teams and drivers that had been through an entire pre-season of testing and had completed two full practice sessions the previous day. Chandhok logged a total of four laps for the day. Unsurprisingly, he qualified dead last. He then started his first grand prix from the pit lane, after the team decided to make changes overnight not allowed by the regulations of the time. He quickly crashed out of the race on the second lap. It was anything but a dream debut.

It wasn't until the second race of the season, in Melbourne, that Chandhok got to have 'the moment' of starting a grand prix race from the grid. He occupied the very last spot on the grid, but he was there. 'It was the start of the formation lap. It hit me. And it was the only time it hit me,' he explained.

'The grid is chaos, right. There's no other sport in the world where, as a professional athlete, you're expected to talk to VIPs and media a few minutes before you go and perform. At the highest level. That doesn't happen in the locker room at Wimbledon. Or the Melbourne Cricket Ground. Whereas at a Formula 1 race you've got Martin Brundle sticking a microphone and a TV camera in your face as you're putting your helmet on. That's just the nature of the sport. It's so unique.

'Then there's this moment when you get in the car and there's five or six minutes where you're talking to your engineer and getting all the instructions. And then everyone walks away. They all walk away. The engineers and mechanics all go and stand on the edge of the track while the cars pull away for the formation lap [to join the grid].

'And that's when it hit me. There are 24 of us on the planet that are experiencing this, in this moment. It's amazing. This is it. I am a Formula 1 driver. In a Formula 1 race.

'It hit me for the first 30 seconds of the formation lap. I thought, "Fucking hell, this is cool." But then you have to go into race mode. Your race brain kicks into gear very quickly and you start thinking about tyre and brake temperatures. And it was only that first race [that it hit me]. From that point on you don't really think about it.'

These sorts of moments were the good that Chandhok could take out of his rookie Formula 1 season. But 2010 was a tough year. Chandhok's car was wildly uncompetitive and, thanks to a financial dispute between HRT and chassis manufacturer Dallara, didn't receive a single performance upgrade during his time at the wheel, while the rest of the cars in the field kept getting better. Chandhok's best finish was a 14th in Australia, and he didn't make the chequered flag in Spain, Monaco or Turkey. After the British Grand Prix, the 10th race of the 19-race season, his car was handed over to test driver Sakon Yamamoto. Chandhok's rookie season in Formula 1 was finished and it was only July. But while it was hardly the stuff of dreams, Chandhok was at peace with what he had achieved.

'It's a funny thing,' he said, 'but in 2010 I just took all the positives. I was actually in a really good frame of mind. I was like, "Shit, yeah, a lot of things aren't great, and yeah, we're at the back. But I'm a grand prix driver. I'm on the grid."

'I made it to Formula 1. That was my dream. And once you do it, nobody can take it away from you. From that day forward, you will always be a Formula 1 driver. I built good relationships with the engineers and we made the best of a bad situation. We knew we were racing against two other teams. That's all. And we were last of them as well. But we knew if we got ahead of them at the odd race, we'd done a good job.

'I approached it in a very positive way. What was my alternative? To carry on in GP2? Doing even 10 grands prix in 2010 was better than doing 10 weekends as a GP2 driver.'

Chandhok's dream wasn't over. Not quite yet, anyway. For the 2011 season he signed a deal with Lotus to take part in 10 races – including the inaugural Indian Grand Prix. Then, the rug was pulled from under him. Lotus didn't honour the contract, with Chandhok making just a single grand prix start for the year in Germany. He was left devastated by a sport that he had loved his whole life. 'Honestly, it was the worst year of my career from a mental health and happiness standpoint,' he recalled. 'I had a contract to do a certain number of races and they broke the contract. So I only ended up doing one instead of more, including the Indian GP.

'That was devastating . . . it was the only time in my life – and I am a self-confessed Formula 1 super fan – that I fell out of love with Formula 1. I absolutely hated Formula 1. I felt like it was full of people who lie to you. I was so disillusioned by the end of 2011.'

Chandhok's career as a Formula 1 driver was officially over. The hatred for the sport drove him away from the paddock, Chandhok switching to sportscars on the advice of fellow

F1 outcast Anthony Davidson. That gave him time to heal and at least revive his love of racing. 'I was pissed off with Formula 1 as a sport. Anthony, who is a friend of mine, said, "Close the chapter, go and race sportscars and rediscover your love of racing." And that's what I did. I did five years at Le Mans and in the world championship, and I fell in love with the sport again.'

Eventually, Chandhok found his way back to Formula 1. Not as a driver, but as a broadcaster. Commentating and TV punditry had been a side hustle throughout his driving career, something to help pay the bills. It would later become his post-driving career. 'It's a different mindset,' he explained. 'You aren't in the paddock to wheel and deal and talk your way into a drive. You're there to explain to people at home what's going on. It's a different skillset, but a less cutthroat, less political one. You're there to talk about a sport that, deep down, you still love. Even if it burnt you and you got angry with it.'

There are ways in which Piastri's and Chandhok's introduction to grand prix racing couldn't be more different. Chandhok had to fight tooth and nail for the worst seat on the grid. Piastri had two good, midfield teams fighting over his services. At the same time, there are similarities to their situations. One is the sheer challenge of geography: Chandhok had to leave India for the UK to chase his Formula 1 dream; Piastri did likewise, leaving Australia behind for a new life in England.

It may sound incredibly romantic – but it's not a gap year or a Contiki tour. There isn't the excitement of satisfying the wanderlust of early adulthood. For young drivers born outside of Europe, it's often a frightening, lonely experience. Generally, they will be in their early teens when they leave the comfort and safety of home. They are still kids. Sometimes, as with Piastri, family members relocate with them. More often than not, these kids live on their own. The race teams help by sourcing small, affordable apartments near the factory . . . which usually means living somewhere bleak and barren on the edge of an industrial estate in the middle of England. We're not talking about the party-every-night share house in Fulham sort of experience. In the age of social media, it's easy to imagine how difficult it would be for some of these kids to sit alone, watching their friends carry on life at home. The challenge of relocating has broken more than a few young drivers. And the advantage of avoiding that experience contributes to the sheer number of European drivers that make up the Formula 1 field in any given season.

'The Europeans don't understand how fortunate they are,' said Chandhok. 'They are close to home. If they want to pop home and see family and friends, they always can. Some still live at home through their junior career. For people from Australia and Asia and South America, it's much harder. You come to Europe as a teenager and live thousands of miles away in a country where you don't know the people, you may not speak the language, it's a different culture, different weather, different everything. And the only people you know are the mechanics and engineers at your race team.

'I think that is a real challenge of your mental strength. Imagine it's the middle of January, it's pissing rain and freezing cold in the UK, and you've got to get your arse out of bed and go for a run. And someone like Oscar is there thinking, "Fucking hell, I could be in Melbourne [or] sitting on the beach with my friends right now."

'There's two sides to that coin. It's tough and it breaks a lot of drivers [who] don't have the mental strength. But on the positive side, it can make you so mentally tough. And it can also motivate you. You will charge through walls to make things happen at that age. You're young and chasing a dream. You've given everything up: your life with your mates, the cushy family life by the beach. You're in a soulless apartment in the Midlands in the UK. But you're doing it for a reason. And you keep reminding yourself of that reason.

'It can feed the motivation – if you can get to that mind frame. But it's a huge challenge, one that's definitely under-estimated by Europeans.'

Once that sacrifice has paid off and they've realised the dream of getting to Formula 1, whether it's with the worst team on the grid or one of the best, every driver goes through the same basic experience. The experience of being a rookie in Formula 1.

The physical act of driving the car is, to a large extent, the easy part. The feeder series prepare drivers well – in fact, Formula 2 cars don't even have power steering, whereas Formula 1 cars do. So, while a driver is subjected to higher g-forces in Formula 1, the physicality of manhandling the car is less. As for the technical side of driving a highly advanced

Formula 1 car, drivers now spend so much time in the bespoke simulators built by the teams to learn the processes and how to use them on the fly. The simulators are incredibly realistic in terms of car dynamics too, although they still can't replicate the real thing.

'You don't have the sensation of the g-force, you don't have the wow factor,' explained Chandhok. 'Simulators just don't give you that. But that's what the junior categories prepare you for. With GP2, as it was for me, and Formula 2 now, the cars are powerful, they are big, and they've got a lot of down-force. It's perfect preparation for Formula 1. When I got in a Formula 1 car for the first time, yeah, everything happened a bit quicker. Everything was faster and better. But there wasn't a "holy shit, this scares me" moment.

'I have to say, when I first drove a GP2 car after I raced in Formula 3 and Renault V6 Asia, it scared the shit out of me for the first five laps. The jump from F2 to F1 isn't as big as F3 to F2. You very quickly get used to the speed of a Formula 1 car.'

Those years coming through the junior ranks may help prepare your body and mind for the experience of driving a Formula 1 car. But there's one thing the feeder categories can't teach you. And that's what life as a Formula 1 driver is really like. You go from being relatively anonymous, even as a front-running Formula 2 driver, to being an instant superstar. Everyone wants your time: the team, the fans, the media. For the duration of your active Formula 1 career, you'll barely do a single thing outside of your own home that won't be subject to scrutiny. It's here that, once again, the fantasy and the reality don't necessarily align. The grind of being a Formula 1 driver is real and if you haven't set your life up to deal with it, your on-track performance will suffer. The key to mentally preparing for your rookie season is ensuring that you've put all the right people in all the right places so that the grind happens around you, while you only think about going faster.

'It's about creating the structure around you,' said Chandhok. 'There's a lot of things going on in Formula 1 world. When I say the change from F2 to F1 isn't that big behind the wheel, at the same time it's a huge change outside of the car. You've got all of this attention to deal with. Everyone wants a piece of your time.

'Oscar will see the difference when he gets to Bahrain. As a test or reserve driver he could always wander around the paddock pretty anonymously. Nobody really gave a shit that he was there . . . But he'll walk into Bahrain on the first day and he'll have five TV cameras in front of him at every moment. There will be 20 photographers taking his photo at every moment. There will be this explosion of interest in him.

'When you're a Formula 1 driver, the whole minute of every day is scheduled. From the minute you wake up, to when you get in the hire car, to when you arrive at the track . . . every minute of your day at the track is on a schedule. Including when you take a nap. There will be a 10-minute window for that in the schedule. All of a sudden there's media commitments. Nowadays there's social media scrutiny. There's idiots like myself in the commentary box watching every sector that Oscar will be doing in every practice session. Analysing it. Talking about it. So you have to create the structure around you to cope with all of this stuff that's happening.

'Also, from a commercial standpoint, this is your small window to make hay while the sun shines. Oscar probably hasn't made a lot of money in his career so far. Actually, he's probably made no money at all. All of sudden it's like, right, who is going to do the endorsement deals for me? Who is going to manage my time in terms of what personal endorsements I do, versus the endorsement deals I have with the team, versus the marketing days, to the testing and simulator and travel days? Who is going to travel with me? Who is going to be my travelling team, in terms of physios and [executive assistants]? Who is going to handle booking my travel? Who is going to sort out the logistics of my life?

'Once you've got all of those pieces of the puzzle in place, it declutters your mind. You stop thinking about it all. You just think about what you, as a driver, need to do to extract the maximum performance out of yourself. Whether it's in the cockpit. Whether it's working with the team. How can you clear your mind?

'I would often call my engineer and say, "Hey, I just thought about something. What if we did this with the suspension, or maybe we try this with the aero balance?" I would get these brain waves halfway through dinner . . . You want to be clear in your mind to have the mental space to just think about performance, and not worry about, "Shit, which way am I driving to the track tomorrow? How do I avoid the traffic? What time do I need to be at the autograph session?" You don't need to be thinking about that shit. You need someone else to do all that thinking so you can focus on what's important, which is performance.

'Creating that mental space for performance is something all great sportspeople do, I think. I remember seeing an interview with Rafa Nadal where he talked about packing his own kit bag, because then he knows that every racket is exactly what he wants. I saw a documentary about the Australian cricket team and there's a shot of Steve Smith where he'd laid out all of his batting gloves and all of his bats, and he was putting the grips on each of the bats himself. And softening the gloves in the nets himself. He doesn't trust anyone else to do it, because it's his method. It's part of his mental preparation. When he puts on his gloves, and grabs his bat, to head out to the middle, he's not thinking about whether the grip has been put on properly. He can just go and bat.'

That rigid, minute-by-minute way of life isn't easy. And it's a far cry from the rockstar lifestyle enjoyed by some Formula 1 drivers up until the early 2000s (former Ferrari driver Eddie Irvine, one of the last F1 playboys, was famous for misplacing helicopters and was once quoted as saying, "I love the parties, the boat, the plane, getting into nightclubs for free, getting tables at restaurants without queuing, driving for Ferrari and getting the best looking girls"). But it's a necessity of modern professional sport. It's another one of those sacrifices required to reach an elite level of athleticism.

'It becomes so ingrained in you,' added Chandhok. 'Even today, it drives my wife mad. I'll schedule our day to the point where I'll be saying, "At 7.28 a.m. the kids have to be ready because we need two minutes to do the last toilet stop, and then three minutes to strap them in the car, and then [at]

7.33 a.m. we'll be on the road because it takes twelve minutes to get to school."

'That's how I live my life now, because I spent 20 years living that structured life. That's the only way I know how to function; and I think people in the normal world don't function that way. Nobody says, "Let's leave at 7.33 a.m." They say, "Let's leave at 7.30 a.m." and if they are five minutes late, they don't give a shit.'

Add that rigidity to the long list of challenges Piastri was facing ahead of his rookie season.

Chandhok might have been pissed off that winning consecutive Formula 3 and Formula 2 titles didn't earn Piastri an immediate promotion to Formula 1, but he also knew that the unprecedented test program put in place by Alpine was a huge advantage in the modern times of fierce testing restrictions.

'He's a very well-prepared rookie in modern terms. It's not the same as 15 years ago, when the likes of Lewis Hamilton and Heikki Kovalainen came into the sport with thousands of kilometres of testing under their belts before they raced,' Chandhok explained. 'The modern rookies don't have the opportunity to have a test program at all, usually, so Oscar has been quite lucky to have that. But equally I think he did absolutely the right thing by doing the McLaren deal when he did. I was talking to him and Mark Webber a lot about it last year. I'm very close friends with Mark, so I had an idea of what was unfolding. And I think they did the right thing.

Yes, there's the whole thing about loyalty. That's fine. But the reality is, loyalty goes both ways. Alpine made it pretty clear that Fernando Alonso was their first choice.

'Nobody is going to give you your career. You have to make it happen. By Oscar and Mark going to McLaren and doing the deal, they are making things happen. And I like that.'

Chandhok added, 'But it's a very bold move to go to McLaren as well, because you're walking into a team where Lando Norris is very well established, very well liked, and he's driving exceedingly well. And it's obviously a quirky car, as Daniel [Ricciardo] has proved. It's a bit of a make-or-break move. If [Oscar] can match Lando, his reputation is cemented for life. But if he gets his arse kicked by Lando, then . . . that creates a bit of a problem for him long term.'

But before the balance sheet between Piastri and Norris started to take shape, Chandhok had one every important piece of advice for the rookie – enjoy that moment, the one when you realise you're a Formula 1 driver, on the warm-up lap in Bahrain.

'It's important you have that moment. Oscar won't appreciate it at the time, but when you look back, you have to enjoy those moments. Because it is fucking cool. You've spent so much of your life waiting for that day. It would be a shame not to just pause and soak it in and enjoy the moment. Even just briefly. If you're just caught up in the pressure and the stress of it all, you'll miss it. I hope Oscar does soak up that moment, enjoy it.'

5

TESTING

Once upon a time, there was little in the way of testing restrictions in Formula 1. Teams would pound around the circuit of their choosing over and over again as they developed their cars, not only ahead of a new season, but throughout the season as well. For a team like Ferrari, the lawlessness was particularly advantageous, given it could basically drive cars straight out of the workshop and onto its private Fiorano circuit. The Scuderia's legends of yesteryear cut countless laps around that place.

Of course, these relentless testing schedules came at a cost. Racing cars are expensive to run, and the ability to test freely increased the gulf between the financial haves and have-nots in the world of Formula 1. So, over the years, the restrictions got tighter and tighter. The number of kilometres allowed during a season was constantly cut by the FIA. Eventually, in-season testing (with the current cars) was banned altogether.

That is what made Alpine's 2022 test program for Oscar Piastri, using the 2021 model car, so special. For a team to make that level of financial investment was simply remarkable. And it contributed greatly to the team's heartbreak when he jumped ship.

For 2023 the testing rules were more restrictive than ever. In terms of individual testing, each team was only allowed two 'filming days', during which running was limited to 100 kilometres. In other words, a shakedown. Not useful for meaningful performance work. And instead of a pair of official pre-season tests, as had been the case in 2022, there was a single three-day hit-out at the Bahrain International Circuit on the weekend before the season-opening grand prix at the same venue. The three days had to be shared among the drivers, as teams were only permitted to run one car at a time. The split for McLaren was that Piastri would take the morning on Day 1, the afternoon on Day 2 and the morning on Day 3. His fellow McLaren driver, Lando Norris, would be in the car for the other sessions.

Before the team even got to Bahrain, however, expectations were on the decline. When the 2023 McLaren MCL60 was unveiled to the public in mid-February, the tone was reserved, to say the least. The new car had clearly taken some cues from the 2022 Red Bull Racing's RB18, particularly around the sidepod area. Unsurprising, given that model had been the class of the field the previous season. But McLaren made no effort to hide the fact that the aerodynamic numbers being simulated weren't quite good enough. Andrea Stella, the new team principal, was confident the car was a step forward over the MCL36 from 2022, but not that it was a race winner in its launch specification. The issue could be traced back to the same stage of development as the MCL36, 12 months earlier. Pre-season testing with the 2022 car had been badly hampered by brake problems, and getting on top of those issues sucked up resources that should have gone into developing the aerodynamic package. That left McLaren playing catch-up through the 2022 season, and then into the development of the 2023 car, which was always going to be an evolution of the previous year's model.

'In reality, we have to say that assessing our performance last year and looking at comparing those, we identified multiple areas of opportunities,' explained Stella at the launch of the MCL60. 'The good news is that pretty much all of them have been addressed. I wouldn't want to be too specific, but certainly they have to do predominantly with aerodynamics. Aerodynamics is the name of the game in F1, so no mystery, but there's some more areas, for instance in terms of inter-action with the tyres, there's some work that we needed to do and this was done over the winter.

'There's some other areas of the car that, like I said, will be interesting by developments in the early stage of the season. So we are happy – not entirely happy for what is the launch car, but optimistic that should take a good step soon.'

Another issue for McLaren in the lead-up to the 2023 season was wind-tunnel time. Wind tunnels are a vital part of Formula 1 car design, helping engineers to closely and accurately assess aerodynamic figures. A new in-house wind tunnel at McLaren had been in the works since 2019 but, as critical development took place for the MCL60, it still wasn't online. The team had to continue using Toyota's wind tunnel in Cologne, Germany, at significant cost and inconvenience. A planned mid-year debut of McLaren's in-house facility meant it wouldn't be until 2024 that any real performance benefit would be felt.

'There's more associated with the lack of the wind tunnel than we may think,' Stella admitted. 'For instance, there's quite a significant fee to pay [for] the wind tunnel when we rent it. By having our own, we save quite a significant amount of resources that we want to reinvest in expanding the team.

'So if I consider the lack of wind tunnel and ultimately the size of the workforce, I think McLaren has been doing a competitive job in the past. Allow me to use these two factors to say that we are very happy with what's happening on the technical side. And now it's more up to us to provide the technical side with the right equipment and with the right team power to actually be able to compete at the front.'

Between the lines, the message was clear – McLaren was still in a rebuilding phase as a team, and a return to powerhouse status wasn't imminent. The 2023 car was still compromised, particularly in its launch specification. It wasn't about to light the world on fire in testing, or the first three races of the year.

The great hope, however, was the Azerbaijan Grand Prix at the end of April, earmarked by McLaren as the place to bring the first major upgrade to the MCL60.

The launch also drew questions about the team's new driver line-up. Piastri's working relationship with the team was still in its infancy, with on-track experience limited to those early tests with a 2021-spec car in November 2022. But the team was already making some fascinating observations about Piastri. 'There's a characteristic we like a lot,' Stella explained. '[Oscar] is a man of few words . . . but the right words. That's become very apparent. [He's] certainly focused and also demanding. This characteristic you can see already. The focus goes into being demanding to the team. And this will certainly help elevate standards [at McLaren].'

Demanding isn't always a positive way to describe somebody. But Stella went into more detail, explaining that the observation had come from Piastri's reaction to reviewing team radio files from recent seasons. 'We give [the drivers] some audio files to listen to from previous races. The way he gets to the bottom of matters, and is even questioning like, "Why did you guys do this? You could have done that. You could have done this." Somehow he challenges you, if that makes sense, in a very polite and constructive way. But he doesn't take things superficially or stop challenging [you] just for pleasing the environment. This is not what we want; we want to be challenged.

'I said that he's a demanding guy that should help elevate the standards, just by, in a way, being almost constantly a little unhappy. Which is a good position for a driver to be.'

Piastri, meanwhile, was grilled at the launch about his feelings heading into one of the most highly anticipated rookie seasons ever. Would the pressure of the Alpine/McLaren situation be too much for a young athlete to bear? 'I don't think it adds any pressure from that aspect,' said Piastri. 'I think coming into F1 with the previous results I've had in junior categories, I think there's always going to be an element of expectation from that. And I think whilst the drama created a lot of attention, it has nothing to do with my driving. I think the results are more of an area of expectation, I guess. I don't think [the contract dispute] specifically adds anything.

'I'm just trying to get back up to speed, and obviously, there will be a bit of rust having not raced for a year. There are some things without racing that you just can't keep training . . . that's why I'm looking forward to getting back out on track.'

Piastri was equally bullish when asked if he was nervous about stepping into the seat that had effectively brought fellow Australian Daniel Ricciardo's career to a standstill. 'I'm not concerned about that aspect of things and the lack of experience. I think through my junior career, I've had to change car every single year, I've never driven the same car for more than a year. So adaptation is a big strength that you need in the junior categories. So I think for that aspect, I'm not concerned. I've obviously done a bit of testing in the 2021 car, and the post-season test last year with McLaren. So I know a little bit of what to expect. But I think as a driver you always need to adapt; there's always going to be certain things that are maybe not going to suit you quite as well as you want. As a racing driver you always want more grip and more power. So I think there's always some limitations. It's just how you can drive around those.'

And what if those limitations turn out to be significant, based on the undertones of pessimism coming from Stella about the MCL60? 'I think for me, personally, I've got a lot to focus on myself coming into the sport,' Piastri said. 'In my rookie year there'll be a lot to learn. I think being reserve driver last year I got to experience more of the off-track activities of an F1 driver. So that was, I guess, a bit of a soft introduction. But I think for me, just building the foundations for my career [and] getting back up to speed after not racing for so long are the first ports of call to address. And then ultimately trying to push the team forward alongside Lando to be in a position where, in the future, we could be fighting for podiums and race wins.

'I think what looks good for me is if I can learn as much as I can quickly, and just get these processes correct from the beginning and then start [to form] good habits.'

On Thursday 23 February, the sole pre-season test got underway at the Sakhir desert circuit in Bahrain. As Stella had predicted, there were no heroics from McLaren. In the morning session Piastri completed 52 laps, the best of which was 1m 34.888s – 1.9 seconds slower than Max Verstappen in the pace-setting Red Bull Racing RB19. Norris took over the McLaren car in the afternoon and, despite losing time with a wheel fairing issue, did end up fifth on combined times with 1m 33.462s. Verstappen improved to 1m 32.837s, six-tenths clear of Norris and just over two seconds faster than Piastri's morning time.

Norris continued on Friday morning, cutting another 65 laps in the unruly MCL60 to go ninth fastest from the 10 cars, three seconds slower than Carlos Sainz in the Ferrari, with 1m 35.522s. This time it was Piastri's turn to lead the way for McLaren thanks to a time of 1m 33.175s in the afternoon session. That was good enough for ninth on the combined times, 1.5 seconds slower than Sauber's Zhou Guanyu, who set the fastest time on Day 2.

More worrying than the times were trackside observations from experts that the McLaren car looked hard to drive, particularly over the bumps into turn 1 and through turn 12. At the end of the second day of testing, *Autosport's* F1 editor Matt Kew noted: 'The MCL36 of 2022 was blighted by inconsistent balance from one corner to the next. It doesn't appear that this unwelcome habit has been banished by the arrival of the MCL60. Watching Lando Norris in the morning, admittedly when the track temperature has crept above 40 degrees Centigrade and the tyres are quick to overheat, it appears as though he is an unsettled driver. Several sizeable lock-ups into turn 1 don't help his case. But, even between botched braking zones, of which there are many, the front axle looks lazy and slow to respond. The Brit often washes wide and must bide his time until he can jump back on the power. Some of this might be attributed to him circulating with full tanks. Either way, there's not exactly an abundance of evidence to suggest that, underneath it all, there lies a confidence-inspiring chassis. Oscar Piastri also suffering with understeer and being cautious on the throttle in the afternoon and the car appearing to be easily deflected by bumps and over the kerbs suggest both are uncomfortable.'

On that same day both Brown and Stella faced the media. At least, having been so realistic about the car's shortfalls at the launch, tackling the tricky topic of missed targets wasn't unexpected. 'We know we set some goals for development, which we didn't hit, and we felt it was better to be honest about that,' said Brown. 'Like everyone, we have a lot of development coming. So, we are encouraged by what we see around the corner. I think we will be going into the first race off of our projected targets, but it is hard to really know where that means we will be on the grid.'

Stella then offered better insight on a technical front. The issue, he explained, was that the car was too draggy. In the most basic terms, drag and downforce go hand in hand. Downforce, the downward pressure on the car created by the aerodynamic surfaces, helps cars get around corners faster. The trade-off is that these aerodynamic surfaces also need to break through the air on the straights. There are no benefits to downforce on the straights – only the penalty of drag. The key to a successful Formula 1 car is creating as much downforce as possible with as little drag as possible. Get that balance wrong, and you're in trouble. You'll end up with a tough choice to make: do you take the mid-corner grip and pay for it down the straights? Or drop some downforce and sacrifice grip? The technical term for the balance between downforce and drag is 'aerodynamic efficiency'.

'Last year, we had some clear objectives in terms of development,' Stella reiterated, before explaining in more detail. 'They had to do with aerodynamic efficiency, some development related to the exploitation of the tyres, and also some other objectives to improve the balance. The reality is that most of these objectives have actually been met. But the objective in terms of aerodynamic efficiency of the car, that's the one where we are still shy of what was our target.

'Aerodynamic efficiency is still not where we would like it to be . . . to be a top-four contender. So I would say that's the one in which we are still short.'

Again, the good news was that none of this came as a surprise. 'I think based on what I've seen in these two days, our performance is pretty much where I expected it to be,' added Stella. 'No surprises. The data correlates with what we were expecting from an aerodynamic point of view. Even performance-wise, for whatever is possible to assess based on lap times in tests, where we know that lap times can depend on fuel level engine modes, and [track] conditions.'

Based on that, Stella kept the lid well and truly on the team's expectations for the season-opener the following weekend. 'I think we will see again that the midfield is very compact,' he said. 'And this means that if you don't do a good enough job, even in setting up and maximising what you have, you may struggle to get out of Q1. At the same time, you might be a Q3 contender.

'So I think the fork is relatively open, it is relatively wide. I think when I'm talking about competitiveness, I would say our objective through the season is to be a top-four car. At the moment, I would say we are not necessarily in this range.'

*

Saturday was the final day of the Bahrain test. Piastri continued in the McLaren car for the morning session, which was
interrupted by a spin at turn 10 and a lengthy stay in the
garage as the team strengthened the MCL60's wheel brows.
His best lap was a 1m 33.655s, eighth fastest of the 10 cars and
2.6 seconds slower than Ferrari's Charles Leclerc. In the afternoon the benchmark set by Leclerc was lowered to 1m 30.305s
by Red Bull's Sergio Perez. Norris ended up 11th fastest with
a deficit of 1.8 seconds. Piastri was shuffled back to 16th,
3.3 seconds off the pace. It was a low-key end to a difficult
three days for McLaren.

Amid the pessimism, there was a ray of optimism for the
team. It hadn't made headlines during the test, at least not for
the right reasons, but Stella had spotted something that he
liked. 'Oscar is incredibly talented,' he said. 'I think we have
been able to see already some of these characteristics in the
runs we have done on the TPC [testing of a previous car].
Even during the [Bahrain] test, in the sequence of the soft
tyres, he improved massively from one side to the other. Just
cashing in, capitalising on the learning from one set to the
other set. So, these are very promising signs.'

But, like Piastri himself, Stella stopped short of setting
any real-world, results-based expectations for the rookie
heading into the Bahrain Grand Prix. 'What we expect from
Oscar, really, I don't want to set it in terms of results,' he said.
'For me, what's important is [Oscar's] development rate.
What's important is to stick into a process rather than [be
focused] on the results, because results are a consequence
of a process.

'If you focus too much and too early on some result-related objectives, you can be put off, so we try not to do that. Saying you have to be two-tenths off Lando, or two-tenths better than Lando, we think this is not the right way of approaching this.

'Oscar is very focused on himself. We want the team to support this personal journey, and we will compare to Lando in a functional way. You have an overlay in telemetry [the data lines that indicate things like wheel speed, braking points and pressure and so on], and there's always some good information to pick to improve. Let's look at it, but not because we necessarily want to match it. Otherwise, we don't meet our objectives.'

The McLaren didn't look great. All indications were that the team would have to wait until at least Baku in April, and the planned upgrades, for there to be any hopes of being competitive. And even then, upgrades don't traditionally turn a season around on its head. It was fair to assume that Piastri was facing an uphill battle for his rookie campaign.

6

BAHRAIN

Bahrain Grand Prix
Bahrain International Circuit
3–5 March 2023

In the blink of an eye, the brief pre-season test turned into the first race weekend of the 2023 season – and the first of Oscar Piastri's Formula 1 career.

Overall, the Bahrain test provided a reasonably clear form guide, particularly at the front of the field. Red Bull Racing (RBR) looked to have comfortably preserved the advantage it had enjoyed in 2022. Mercedes appeared to have made some gains, at least compared to Ferrari, but was still a way off RBR. And the cat among the pigeons was Aston Martin and Fernando Alonso – the very combination that had sparked the driver merry-go-round that led Piastri to his rookie season in the first place. When first announced, Alonso's move from Alpine to Aston was broadly seen as a sideways step, at absolute best, if not a step backwards. Few people really took the Aston Martin team seriously. Aside from its prestigious name, it was considered little more than a plaything bought by billionaire Lawrence Stroll to give his son Lance, one of the team's drivers, something to do. It made some kind of sense that Alonso would make the move to tap into Stroll's immense wealth and boost his own earning power in the latter stages of his career.

Unless, of course, he knew something the rest of us didn't.

We'll never know what insight Alonso had into what Stroll was cooking up, or even if the team had a plan to rise from the midfield and tackle the front-runners in 2023. Despite all the technology at the fingertips of designers, there can be an element of dumb luck when it comes to an aerodynamic package. But whatever the case, Alonso's move proved to be genius.

Signs of that being the case emerged during that three-day Bahrain test. The Aston Martin looked fast, particularly in Alonso's hands. Even Brazilian Felipe Drugovich, a Formula 2 regular and Aston's reserve driver, snuck into the top 10 on the final day of the test. He'd been drafted in at the last minute to replace Stroll, who'd fallen off his bike and broken his wrist. That he was able to get within half a second of Alonso, despite the gaping gulf in their relative Formula 1 experience, suggested that the Aston Martin AMR23 had a healthy level of compliance. It wasn't clear exactly where this upstart outfit might slot into the pecking order, but at the very least it was expected to be the class of a packed midfield.

From there it was anyone's guess. Alpine, Alfa Romeo, Haas and McLaren were tough to separate. Even the Williams car looked like an improved package compared to 2022. 'I think there's no midfield any more,' said Haas boss Günther Steiner after testing. 'There's the top teams and the rest. That's my opinion, I'm seeing it now.'

At 2.30 p.m. local time on the first Friday in March, the red light at the end of the pit lane turned green. Free Practice 1, the first hour of non-competitive running for every race weekend, was officially underway. Piastri immediately pulled out of the garage, trundled down the lane and set his career as a Formula 1 race driver in motion. But within less than 10 minutes, there was a reality check as he tried to ease the fickle McLaren into turn 7. He was slightly greedy on the inside kerb at the apex, and bang, the rear let go. Piastri quickly opened the steering and let the car straighten up on the large expanse of bitumen run-off. 'Oscar, is the car okay?' was the message over the radio. 'Yep, all okay,' he replied. 'Just had a snap'. The next time by he set his first representative lap, at 1m 36.274s.

As the session wore on, he worked the time down to 1m 34.997s, 2.2 seconds off the pace and good enough for 12th overall. Lando Norris was fourth fastest, 1.4 seconds behind session leader Sergio Perez. Maybe the McLaren wasn't as slow as feared.

In Free Practice 2, once again, the 10-minute mark provided some excitement for Piastri. This time it was at turn 1, where he arrived alongside Yuki Tsunoda – only to find a slow-moving Lance Stroll at the entry of the corner. It took lightning-quick hands from Piastri to avoid a huge shunt, although a lock-up that destroyed the front-right tyre was unavoidable. Unlike a modern road car, Formula 1 cars don't have anti-lock brakes, or ABS. The cars are stopped with knife-edge threshold braking. Perfectly hitting the threshold of the brakes – the moment before they lock – is an exact science, and tough enough to master in a road car. In a Formula 1 car, with the huge loads required to work the brakes at all, that threshold only gets harder and harder to judge. Getting it right is critical for a number of reasons. Firstly, it's the fastest way to slow the car. The second the wheel locks, the tyre stops creating grip and the braking distance extends, significantly. Secondly, once the tyre loses grip, the car won't turn. If the wheel is locked, you can crank the steering as much as you like, but you're going straight on. Thirdly, even a mild lock-up leaves a tyre with what's called a flat spot, which is exactly what it says on the tin. Once a patch of tyre has been tortured across the top of the asphalt, its threshold becomes less than that of the rest of the tyre. So, when you hit the brakes, most of the tyre might want to keep spinning, but the flat spot won't. And the lock-up cycle continues.

Piastri did try and proceed on the same set of rubber, but, as expected, the next time he got down to turn 1, the front-right tyre immediately locked up again. 'Oscar, is everything okay?' he was asked once again. 'Yeah, the flat spot was too bad,' he said. 'Copy, box this lap.' Time for a new set of boots.

Once the 60-minute timer ticked down to zero, Piastri's best lap was 1m 32.024s, 1.1 seconds behind fast man Fernando Alonso. He was faster, and closer to the ultimate pace, than in Free Practice 1. But he ended up three positions further back. In Formula 1 you can be improving, but not by enough.

Saturday marked the first competitive day of the season. Not immediately, though, with a third and final hour of practice midway through the afternoon. Again, there was steady improvement as Piastri snuck into the top 10 with the ninth fastest time, now well within a second of the pace set by Alonso.

Being among the 10 fastest drivers on the Saturday of a grand prix is extremely important. Not in Free Practice 3, but in the qualifying session that follows it. The starting order for a Formula 1 race is determined by a three-part qualifying system. In the first part, known as Q1, all 20 cars take the track for an 18-minute session. You don't have to be fastest in Q1, but you certainly want to be in the top 15. If you're not, you'll be locked into your starting position between 16th and 20th for the race. If you are one of the 15 fastest drivers, you progress to Q2. The times all reset and you have 15 minutes to set one of the 10 fastest times. If you don't, you'll be locked into a grid spot between 11th and 15th. If you do, you're on your way to Q3, where you'll be given a new set of soft-compound tyres, the fastest of the available compounds, and 12 minutes to have a crack at pole position for Sunday's grand prix.

While the races are long, strategic affairs, where teams and drivers have the luxury of time to adapt to situations, qualifying is a pressure cooker. The windows to nail your lap are minuscule. You don't have a full 18, 15 or 12 minutes to drone around and see if you can go faster and faster. You will basically get one shot to do a lap good enough to progress in Q1 and Q2, and one shot at nailing a top grid spot in Q3. That's because of factors such as new-tyre grip and track evolution, where the circuit itself gains speed as cars lay down more rubber. Of course, that means everyone wants to do their critical lap right at the end of the session when the track should be at its absolute fastest, which brings another factor into play – traffic. The last thing you want to do is encounter a slow-moving car at the wrong point on your fast lap. So, it's up to your engineers and strategists to find you the space you need on the racetrack. If they are feeling particularly brave, and there's a long enough straight for it to be a benefit, they might try and find you a tow. That's when you get just close enough to another car in front that they cut a neat, F1-car-sized hole in the air that gives you extra speed in a straight line. Of course, get that wrong and you'll trip over the car in front and ruin your lap. Finding that space, whether it be clear air or a tow, as late as possible in the session, and then nailing the one lap when your tyres are at their best, is an insane amount of pressure. Getting it right weekend in, weekend out, is often what separates the good from the great.

At 6 p.m. local time on the Saturday of the Bahrain Grand Prix, Oscar Piastri's first qualifying session as a Formula 1 driver burst into life. The entire field bolted on soft-compound tyres for their first runs, effectively a warm-up for both car and driver ahead of what's informally known as the 'happy hour' at the end of each segment, where all the stops are pulled out. That's not to say drivers aren't pushing on their first runs, though, and the signs were immediately troubling for the two McLaren drivers. Norris and Piastri were 17th and 18th fastest respectively, the latter almost half a second away from the safety of 15th. With two minutes to go, the McLarens ventured back out onto the track, hoping for a Q2 miracle.

But for Piastri it wasn't to be. His final run was too scrappy, including a chunk of time lost with a snap at turn 2. He improved on his first run but was still left stranded in 18th place. Even the highly experienced Norris only just snuck through to Q2 with the 15th fastest time. He did manage to qualify 11th overall, but there were clear signs that he had outperformed the car to do so. Those signs of hope from practice were long gone. The McLaren looked as uncompetitive as had been feared. Even the Williams, which Piastri had, effectively, gone to great lengths to avoid racing, looked sharper as Logan Sargeant became the best-placed rookie on the grid in 16th. When Piastri faced the press after qualifying, he was the first to admit that he had left some lap time on the table. 'For me, personally, it wasn't the greatest of qualifying sessions,' he said. 'I just made too many mistakes. Looking on the positives, the corners where there were no mistakes were competitive. I think everyone is so tight now that any little mistake, let alone some of the big ones that I had, cost you a lot. So [there's] a lot more to come from myself.'

Mistakes aside, Andrea Stella was still able to see the positives in Piastri's first qualifying session. '[It was] impressive because the snap he had in corner two was huge and he lost two- or three-tenths there – but otherwise he was not too far off Lando, who is obviously a very strong reference in F1,' he said. 'I am impressed with the speed, but I am also impressed by the approach. He has gone step by step, staying always very calm and very aware of his points of strength and to some extent [the] limitations that are associated with being a rookie. It is just a shame this is not reflected in the classification, but actually I think Oscar has done very well so far . . .'

A little under 24 hours later it was time for Piastri to experience the magic of his first grand prix start. There he was, in the thick of the action. Sitting on the grid as VIPs, TV commentators and hundreds of mechanics swarmed around him. Trying to block out the noise and colour as he climbed into the car and was strapped in tight by the six-point harness. Managing his nerves as he focused on getting his tyres and brakes up to temperature on the warm-up lap. Remembering to have all the right differential and engine settings activated for a race start. Carefully pulling into the right grid spot. Watching those red lights like a hawk as they came on one-by-one across the gantry. Dropping the finger-operated clutch at exactly the right time to take off.

It may have been Piastri's first race start in a year, but he didn't look overly rusty – in fact he seemed quite comfortable with the madness of a first lap, cars to the front, left, right and rear of him, as he made up two spots. He then settled into an impressive rhythm in the opening stint. But his progress began to be slowed by experienced German driver Nico Hülkenberg in the Haas ahead of him. At the end of lap 10, Piastri nailed his exit onto the front straight, hit the DRS button and executed a picture-perfect pass for position into turn 1. He ran long on his first stint, and everything looked to be going to plan . . . until the tiny paddles behind the steering wheel, used to change through the eight-speed gearbox, stopped working. Piastri immediately radioed back to the pit wall: 'I've lost the gearbox.'

'Copy,' was the response. 'Keep trying to downshift; we think it's the steering wheel. Box this lap, and we'll swap [it].' Cue a slow crawl back to the pits as the race moved on without him. All the hard work of the first stint, including that flawless pass on Hülkenberg, was gone.

Changing the steering wheel isn't as big a job as it may sound. Formula 1 cars, like most racing cars, are fitted with a quick-release steering wheel system. Because of the tight confines, the steering wheel is removed each time a driver hops in or out of the car. It's as easy as pulling back on a flange on the hub and freeing the wheel from the steering column. It takes seconds . . . but seconds count for too much during a Formula 1 race. Typically, a car is only stationary during a stop for two to three seconds total. But Piastri had to sit there for what felt like an age as he switched off the engine, waited for a mechanic to replace the wheel, re-fired the engine and then let the on-wheel monitor come back to life. More than 20 seconds later, he still hadn't left his pit box. A shake of his helmet told the story. It wasn't a steering wheel issue; it was something more sinister, a deeper electrical gremlin. The team put the car up on the go jacks and pushed it back into the garage. Piastri's maiden grand prix was over after only 14 laps. A costly DNF.

'The steering wheel change didn't fix the problem because the electronic damage was further down the line around the steering column,' explained Stella after the race. 'It was a problem with the [wiring] harness, probably. We are investigating. Not fixable in a short time.'

It may have been short and nowhere near as sweet as planned, but Piastri wasn't too downbeat with his brief debut. 'Once I got past Hülkenberg, the pace wasn't too bad,' he said in the TV pen as the race continued without him. 'It felt reasonably strong. And my first lap was reasonable, given I hadn't done a first lap for a while. It's just getting used to the dirty air and managing the battery at the start of the race, stuff like that. It's all new to me. It was just nice to be back out on track in a race. I learnt last year how much I miss going racing, so just to be out there, even for a short race, it's a lot better than watching from the sidelines.'

Norris made it to the finish of the race, but only just. He was constantly in and out of the pits with a pneumatic leak that meant a refill every 10 laps or so. Given that there were already question marks over the pace of the car, these reliability issues were troubling. For ultimate success in Formula 1, your car needs to be both fast and reliable. To have even the odd good day, it needs to be at least one of those things. Slow *and* unreliable? That's as bad as it gets. Not that Stella was ready to face that outcome just yet, pointing at some positives such as Piastri's promising tyre degradation – how well the tyres continue to make grip – during his first stint. 'I think the most positive element is that, without issues, Lando would have been a strong contender for points,' he said. 'The pace of the car in the race was almost beyond expectation. I think in the race we saw some reward [for] the work we did over the

Oscar Piastri's meteoric rise through the ranks saw him take out two titles in two years across Formula Renault Eurocup (2019) and Formula 3 (2020). Here he's giving his Prema Formula 2 car a workout at Yas Marina, Abu Dhabi, in 2021 to complete the trifecta for a record-breaking three straight titles.
(Photo: Bryn Lennon/Getty Images)

Oscar celebrates his F2 championship with members of the Prema Racing team in parc fermé after the Abu Dhabi sprint race, 11 December 2021.
(Photo: Mark Thompson/Getty Images)

Oscar raises the Formula 2 Championship trophy (and champagne) with Prema Racing team principal René Rosin. René, along with his father, Angelo, were among the first true believers in the young Aussie. (Photo: Joe Portlock – Formula 1/Formula Motorsport Limited via Getty Images)

Alpine's F1 drivers (*l to r*) Oscar Piastri, Esteban Ocon and Fernando Alonso pose with (*l to r*) technical director Matt Harman, team principal Otmar Szafnauer and Alpine CEO Laurent Rossi in Paris during the unveiling of the team's new A522 racing car for the 2022 Formula 1 season, 21 February 2022. (Photo: Marc Piasecki/Getty Images)

Ready to forge ahead in papaya, Oscar and McLaren Racing CEO Zak Brown have a chat before the Canadian GP, Montreal, 18 June 2023. Zak would go on to tell the media, 'We've got a future world champion on our hands . . .' (Photo: Jakub Porzycki/NurPhoto via Getty Images)

Running with the bulls. Oscar poses with the fastest drivers in the F1 world before the first round at the Bahrain International Circuit in Sakhir, 5 March 2023. (*Front, l to r*): Mercedes drivers George Russell and Lewis Hamilton, Red Bull Racing's Sergio Perez and Max Verstappen. (*Behind, l to r*): Aston Martin's Fernando Alonso and Lance Stroll, McLaren's Oscar Piastri and Lando Norris, and Alfa Romeo's Zhou Guanyu. (Photo: Giuseppe Cacace /AFP via Getty Images)

Talk about pressure from a hopeful fanbase . . . A McLaren devotee holds a sign showing their devout support for Lando and Oscar at the fan stage ahead of the Singapore GP, 15 September 2023. (Photo: Dan Istitene – Formula 1 via Getty Images)

Oscar and his manager – and nine-time Formula 1 GP winner – Mark Webber talk tactics ahead of practice for the Qatar GP, 6 October 2023. Having Webber's no-nonsense approach to life on and off the track would be vital to Oscar's transition to F1. (Photo: Qian Jun/MB Media/Getty Images)

Oscar opens his rookie season at the Bahrain GP, 5 March 2023. (Photo by Alex Galli/LiveMedia/NurPhoto via Getty Images)

Homecoming king. Oscar greets a cluster of fans on the Melbourne Walk ahead of the Australian GP, Albert Park, 1 April 2023. (Photo by Quinn Rooney/Getty Images)

Firing down the back straight at Albert Park, with the familiar Melbourne skyline as a backdrop, Oscar would go on to finish in eighth place and, most importantly, pick up the first championship points of his F1 career. (Photo: Quinn Rooney/Getty Images)

Cool, unflappable and dialled-in as ever, Oscar in the shade at the Azerbaijan GP, Baku, 30 April 2023. (Photo by Vince Mignott/MB Media/Getty Images)

Oscar navigates the Baku City Circuit – a narrow, bumpy, highly demanding street circuit – in his newly upgraded car. Battling a nasty stomach bug only added to the degree of difficulty. (Photo: Bryn Lennon – Formula 1/Formula 1 via Getty Images)

Riding the aqua wave, Oscar navigates one of the more 'colourful' tracks at the Miami GP, 6 May 2023. During his driver introductions, he was greeted by hip-hop artist will.i.am's orchestra, cheerleaders and LL Cool J announcing him as 'Australia's Rookie Boy Wonder'. (Photo: Jared C. Tilton/Getty Images)

Oscar leads AlphaTauri's Nyck de Vries and Williams' Alexander Albon through the Grand Hotel Hairpin at the iconic Monaco GP, 28 May 2023. (Photo: Joe Portlock, Formula 1 via Getty Images)

Oscar and Lando catch up with Aston Martin's Fernando Alonso at the drivers' parade prior to the Austrian GP in Spielberg, 2 July 2023. Alonso's shock departure from Alpine started the dominos falling that would lead to Oscar signing with McLaren. (Photo: Dan Istitene – Formula 1 via Getty Images)

With the 2022 dramas behind them, Oscar has a laugh with Daniel Ricciardo at the drivers' press conference ahead of the Hungarian GP, Budapest, 20 July 2023. Ricciardo had just taken over driving duties at AlphaTauri in the wake of Nyck de Vries' sudden departure. (Photo: Bryn Lennon/Getty Images)

Lando and Oscar give chase to Red Bull's Max Verstappen at the British GP, hoping to check the two-time F1 world champion's pursuit of another crown, Northampton, 9 July 2023. (Photo: Ryan Pierse/Getty Images)

The rookie's first sprint podium. Oscar stands tall in P2 next to Verstappen and Alpine's Pierre Gasly after a challenging sprint race in wet conditions, ahead of the Belgian GP, Spa, 29 July 2023. (Photo: Beata Zawrzel/NurPhoto via Getty Images)

Oscar walks away from a crash during Free Practice 2, ahead of the Dutch GP, Zandvoort, 25 August 2023. A tricky track, a simple loss of the rear, an overcorrection . . . and suddenly McLaren's weekend was in jeopardy. (Photo: Vince Mignott/MB Media/Getty Images)

The McLaren crew tend to Piastri's number 81 car at the iconic Italian GP, Monza, 3 September 2023. (Photo: Jakub Porzycki/NurPhoto via Getty Images)

With a new contract in his back pocket that would see him in McLaren papaya through 2026, Oscar celebrates his P3 podium finish at the Japanese GP, Suzuka, 24 September 2023. The vote of confidence came straight from the top, with team principal Andrea Stella saying, 'We want our future to be with Oscar.' (Photo: Gongora/NurPhoto via Getty Images)

Andrea Stella shares a moment with Lando and Oscar after a 2-3 finish by his dynamic young tandem at the Japanese GP. (Photo by Gongora/NurPhoto via Getty Images)

Oscar climbs into his car, under the watchful eye of his crew, at the Qatar GP, Lusail City, 8 October 2023. The weekend would prove to be his most successful yet in an F1 seat. (Photo: Qian Jun/MB Media/Getty Images)

On the road to victory in the sprint race at the Qatar GP. He couldn't call himself a grand prix winner, yet. But he was now a Formula 1 race winner. (Photo by Qian Jun/MB Media/Getty Images)

Oscar (P2) and Lando (P3) exchange a well-earned fist bump at the conclusion of the Qatar GP. Oscar would sum it up, accurate and succinct as ever: 'That was probably the hardest race I've ever had in my life.' (Photo: Gongora/NurPhoto via Getty Images)

The McLaren team (with Andrea Stella posing between his two young guns) celebrate an impressive weekend haul at the Qatar GP – a sure sign of the turning fortunes of their team. (Photo: Clive Rose/Getty Images)

Viva McLaren! Oscar hugs a turn in his final practice laps ahead of the Mexico City GP, 28 October 2023. He would go on to finish in eighth place, allowing Lando to pass so his teammate could run down Ricciardo and Russell. Stella called the race 'a masterpiece'. (Photo: Rudy Carezzevoli/Getty Images)

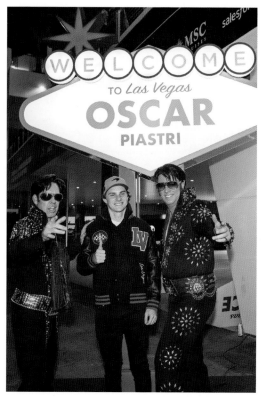

Viva Las Vegas! Oscar poses with a pair of Elvis impersonators in the lead-up to the Las Vegas GP, 15 November 2023. After an embarrassing string of mishaps, the newest jewel in the F1 tour crown delivered in spades. (Photo by Kym Illman/Getty Images)

Oscar leads Lando – for the moment – during the season finale at the Abu Dhabi GP, 26 November 2023. Oscar would finish in sixth place, one spot behind his teammate, to add eight more championship points to his impressive rookie haul of 97, earning him ninth place in the overall standings. (Photo: Mark Thompson/ Getty Images)

The sun might have set on Oscar Piastri's 2023 season in Abu Dhabi, but he left no question that he's a bright star on the rise. (Photo: Clive Rose/Getty Images)

The once and future champion: Oscar Piastri. (Photo: Dan Istitene – Formula 1 via Getty Images)

winter of trying to improve the interaction of the car with the tyres. This was certainly a strong position on Lando's side, but also Oscar, actually, was having good [tyre] degradation in the first stint. He overtook cars. It was a very tight race, so we could have been in the points with two cars. That's the most positive outcome of this event.'

Out front, reigning champion Max Verstappen was unstoppable in the supreme Red Bull. And Fernando Alonso? The wily veteran came home a fine third. The Aston Martin was a genuine surprise package. Pierre Gasly scored his first points as an Alpine driver in ninth, while Esteban Ocon joined Piastri on the list of non-finishers.

Results Summary

Free Practice 1: 12th (1m 34.997s, +2.24s)
Free Practice 2: 15th (1m 32.024s, +1.12s)
Free Practice 3: 9th (1m 33.045s, +0.71s)
Qualifying: 18th (1m 32.101s, +2.39s)
Race: DNF

Bahrain Grand Prix: A brief history

The Bahrain International Circuit: 5.4 kilometres of tarmac that winds through the Sakhir desert, some 30 kilometres from Manama, the capital.

The track is one of many 'Tilkedromes' on the schedule. Tilkedromes are circuits penned by renowned designer Hermann

Tilke. The German rose to prominence when he redesigned the famous Österreichring in Austria in the mid-1990s, turning the old layout into the safer, more modern facility that is now known as the Red Bull Ring. But that wasn't necessarily Tilke's trademark style. The traits of his design became significantly more evident when he created a Formula 1 circuit from scratch for the first time. That was the Sepang International Circuit, ahead of Malaysia's first appearance on the world championship schedule in 1999. Sepang, not currently on the F1 calendar, is a huge, lairy complex with distinctive grandstands and pit buildings. The run-off areas are huge and there are multiple circuit layouts on offer. It is the original Tilkedrome and set the standard for his design – circuits that are incredibly user-friendly, incredibly safe, incredibly hard to crash on, but lacking . . . a bit of character, soul, charm or history.

Bahrain was the second Tilkedrome to join the F1 circus in 2004. More importantly, it was the first time that a world championship grand prix had been held in the Middle East. That inaugural Bahrain Grand Prix was won by Ferrari hero Michael Schumacher, who was joined on the podium by teammate Rubens Barrichello and BAR Honda's Jenson Button. When the trio got on the podium there was no champagne, though. Thanks to the region's strict alcohol laws, they were handed bottles of warrd – a local non-alcoholic drink made of pomegranate and rosewater – to spray about.

Breaking into the lucrative Middle Eastern market was, of course, a boon for Formula 1. The sense of excess and luxury that oozes from the upper classes throughout the Middle East aligns perfectly with one of the richest sports in the world. It's little wonder that Bahrain is now one of four Middle Eastern races on the F1 schedule, along with Saudi Arabia, Qatar and Abu Dhabi. They all have the honour of being night races to highlight their status as marquee events.

Of course, the prominence of F1 in the Middle East hasn't always made for smooth sailing. The early part of 2011 saw the beginning of the Bahraini uprising, a series of anti-government demonstrations and protests that hit its straps when protesters descended on the Pearl Roundabout in Manama on 14 February. What started as a peaceful protest turned bloody during efforts to forcibly clear the roundabout, leaving three people dead. Bahrain had been meant to host the 2011 season-opener on 13 March, but that was swiftly shelved. 'We must focus on immediate issues of national interest and leave the hosting to a later date,' said Crown Prince Sheikh Salman bin Hamad Al Khalifa, the man who had first brought F1 to Bahrain, at the time. 'After the events of the past week, our nation's priority is on overcoming tragedy, healing divisions and rediscovering the fabric that draws this country together – reminding the world of the very best that Bahrain is capable of as a nation once again united.' By June the state of emergency in the kingdom had been lifted and the World Motor Sport Council announced that the race would be rescheduled to 30 October. But Bahrain's reinstatement to the 2011 F1 calendar was short-lived. Tensions were still running high in the region and the decision to name a new date enraged human-rights campaigners, with an online petition against the race going ahead drawing half a million signatures. The teams were uncomfortable too, their objection, at least publicly, on logistical grounds. By mid-July the race had been called off altogether.

Returning to the Bahrain circuit in 2012 wasn't straightforward, either. Protesting hadn't eased in the lead-up to the scheduled race on 22 April, and there was clear apprehension from the teams regarding safety. There was significant speculation that protesters would look to take advantage of such a high-profile, international event. After all, Formula 1 would train the eyes of the world on Bahrain. An unnamed team member told the *Guardian* in the weeks leading up to the race: 'If I'm brutally frank, the only way they can pull this race off without incident is to have a complete military lockdown there. And I think that would be unacceptable, both for F1 and for Bahrain. But I don't see any other way they can do it.'

The race went ahead without the military lockdown. But not without more drama. On the Wednesday before the race, four mechanics from what was then known as the Force India team were caught up in a battle between demonstrators and riot police. Their car was stuck in traffic caused by the incident, with reports of up to eight petrol bombs landing in their vicinity. The shockwaves were felt throughout the sport. Two Force India team members, one of whom had been in the car, immediately flew home due to fears for their safety. The team elected to skip Friday's Free Practice 2 session to ensure it could get its crew members back to the hotel before nightfall and ordered everyone to change into civilian clothes before leaving the track, so they wouldn't be associated with the sport while in public. When the Force India cars were absent from the TV coverage of qualifying on Saturday, there were suspicions it was a blackout, used by Formula 1 management to punish the team for missing practice.

BAHRAIN

Even in 2013, two years into the uprising, there were concerns about racing in Bahrain, particularly when a car bomb was detonated in Manama exactly a week before the grand prix race. But once again it went ahead, as it has every year since and, according to the current contract, will continue to until at least 2036.

7

SAUDI ARABIA

Saudi Arabian Grand Prix
Jeddah Corniche Circuit
17–19 March 2023

Bahrain was a very soft landing for Oscar Piastri. He had raced there in Formula 2. He tested there a week before the 2023 Formula 1 grand prix. In classic Tilkedrome style, there are acres and acres of run-off if you get it a bit wrong (like that snap Piastri had in Free Practice 1).

Saudi Arabia was going to be a significantly tougher assignment. Sure, Piastri had also raced there before. He was a winner on that track in Formula 2. But it's still a street circuit, lined with concrete walls and with very little run-off. And an incredibly fast street circuit where the tiniest of mistakes destroys cars. The place had bit Mick Schumacher twice. In 2021, his rookie season, he tore his Haas to pieces when he lost the rear turning into turn 22 during the race and smacked the wall. The following season he had another big crash, this time in Q2 when he ran slightly wide at the fast turn 12 and ended up on the kerb. That fired him into the wall, the impact a brain-rattling 33g. The German was airlifted to hospital but cleared of any serious injury. Still, he didn't take part in the grand prix itself that year. Anybody would have forgiven Piastri for being a little nervous heading to Jeddah, particularly since there was clearly an issue with the rear-end stability of the McLaren car on corner entry, based on the snaps he'd endured in practice and qualifying in Bahrain.

The pressure was on even before the cars hit the track in Saudi Arabia. Given the controversy that had surrounded Piastri's arrival in Formula 1, there were obviously some curly questions off the back of Bahrain when he sat down with the media on the Thursday of the grand prix in Jeddah. In Bahrain, Pierre Gasly had finished ninth for Alpine, and the team looked significantly better placed than McLaren. Was there any level of regret about how things had played out?

'For me, it was never really a decision of the two teams,' said Piastri. 'It never really came down to that. The rest of the details were all obviously very out there and have been on rinse and repeat a lot. But for me it was clear that I wanted to join McLaren, with the amount of passion that they showed to having me in the team, which was a massive, massive factor in that. So I don't really view it in that same light. I'm very focused on where I am now and trying to help the team move forward and get back to where we want to be. We're obviously not where we want to be at the moment. We've been very open about that. We've got a good development plan in place to try and get ourselves back to where we should be, which is chasing the top three or four teams. To get on the same level as those top three or four teams is difficult. But we can probably take inspiration from what Aston Martin has been able to do over the winter and try and energise ourselves. It is possible to make that jump with a lot of hard work. Obviously we want to try and get back. We'll see what these new developments that we've got in Baku bring for us. But obviously it's going to be [one] step in what's a multi-step plan throughout the year.'

That the challenge of a street circuit, in this fickle McLaren, was more daunting than the wide-open spaces of Bahrain became obvious during Free Practice 1 and 2 on Friday afternoon and evening. There were no heroics from Piastri as he dialled himself into a track that he hadn't driven in two years, and one that looked a whole lot different out the front of a Formula 1 car compared to a Formula 2 car, with those walls approaching a heck of a lot faster.

When practice resumed on Saturday, however, there were signs that Piastri was rapidly getting up to speed. That he was beginning to push became evident right on the halfway mark of the hour-long session, when Piastri ran his car a little too high on the kerb on the way into turn 22 and the back of the car stepped out. Luckily it was one of the few spots on the Jeddah circuit where you could get away with a 'moment' like that, Piastri arresting the slide by taking to the run-off area on his right before continuing with no damage to the car. From there he pressed on, first moving to the back of the top 10 before jumping all the way up to fifth with 14 minutes to go, setting a time of 1m 29.698s on his qualifying sim lap conducted in qualifying-like conditions to assess the one-lap speed of the car. To make it all the more satisfying, the time moved him a spot clear of Gasly in the Alpine. As the rest of FP3 shook out, Piastri was shuffled back to eighth in the order. Still, it was a credible effort, particularly as Lando Norris was only 0.008s faster in seventh. And Gasly also didn't improve, finishing up ninth.

As the sun set over Jeddah, the second qualifying session of the season roared to life. Could the McLaren drivers convert their promising practice pace when it mattered? For Norris, the answer was no. Nine minutes into Q1 he clipped the inside wall at the penultimate corner while on a fast lap. 'I hit the wall . . . it's the front-left steering,' was the sheepish radio call back to the pit wall. He immediately pitted and the crew inspected the car before rolling it back into the garage. The lap he had on the board was never going to be good enough to progress, so the only hope was that the car could be fixed within 10 minutes so he could get back out on the track for another lap. Despite the frantic efforts from the crew, there was no miracle. Norris's day was done. Piastri, meanwhile, was dangling close to the knockout zone as well. Suddenly, McLaren was facing a double Q1 exit. The saviour was a last-gasp effort from Piastri right at the chequered flag that launched him from 17th to 11th, ensuring a career-first Q2 appearance.

The second qualifying segment was a similar story for Piastri as the team walked the tightrope of timing. With just a minute remaining, he was sitting on the Q3 bubble in 10th place while some rapid drivers like Carlos Sainz and Valtteri Bottas lurked behind him, looking to improve. But again, Piastri held his nerve, nailing his final run to finish up ninth and secure passage to the third segment. Pole was never on the cards, based purely on pace, but with Ferrari driver Charles Leclerc nursing a 10-place grid penalty, a spot on the fourth row was up for grabs. Piastri's first run wasn't good enough for it, the 1m 29.710s leaving him slowest of the runners. But his second run did the job as he jumped Gasly right at the flag with a final time of 1m 29.243s. Ninth for the session, and eighth on the starting grid once Leclerc's penalty was applied. It was a remarkable day of ticking career boxes. First Q2 appearance, tick. First Q3 appearance, tick. First time out-qualifying his teammate, tick. Even better, he'd stepped up to the plate on a day when the driver on the other side of the garage made an unforced driving error.

Teammate dynamics are an interesting thing in Formula 1. Unlike the majority of sports, every driver is working with vastly different hardware. Tennis players may use different brands of racquets, but the performance differential is minimal, if existent. But in Formula 1, the only person you can ever be directly compared to is your teammate; he's the only competitor with the exact same hardware at his disposal. The old saying goes that your teammate is the very first person you have to beat. There are countless examples of these relationships turning sour. Across Formula 1 history, at least the professional era, drivers like Alain Prost and Michael Schumacher have demanded lead-driver status in their contracts. The other side of the garage must be occupied by a subservient dedicated to the cause of taking points off the lead driver's rivals. No heroics, thanks.

That wasn't the case at McLaren in 2023. And in the case of Norris versus Piastri, there was never an expectation that the rookie could threaten the experienced driver so entrenched in the team. The driver that had beat eight-time grand prix winner Daniel Ricciardo into submission, despite having never actually won a race himself. So, for Piastri to bank a single-digit grid spot, as Norris was apologising for whacking the fence in what looked every bit like a rookie error, was a neat little win.

Reflecting on the weekend up to that point, Piastri admitted that the fast, concrete-lined circuit had seemed daunting in practice, but that by qualifying he was dialled in, both with the track and the car. 'I think the first few laps in practice on Friday, everything was coming a bit quicker than I remembered from F2!' he explained. 'So that took a bit of getting used to, obviously. But I think more than anything, just getting more comfortable with the car has been beneficial. I feel like if you can get yourself comfortable with the car, then no matter what track you go to, it makes life easier. I feel like I've just been getting more comfortable, even from Bahrain to here. Even throughout this weekend.'

Another critical point was piecing together mistake-free laps, something he hadn't done in qualifying at Bahrain. 'It's just so tight,' he said. 'Even in Q1, I think the difference between being in the top 10 and being out was, like, two-tenths [of a second]. So, you make a small mistake, or a couple of small mistakes, and it looks like a complete disaster. And you put a really good lap together, and you look like a hero.'

*

The better you qualify, the easier your race is likely to be. That may sound like stating the obvious, but it's not only about the position. It's about the drivers you are racing. If you can get on one of the first five rows of the grid, you'll be surrounded by a) fewer cars, and b) better drivers. The start of the race is the most critical. If you're at the back of the grid with the riffraff, avoiding contact early in the race is so much harder.

Of course, there are exceptions to the rule. Such as Oscar Piastri's 2023 Saudi Arabian Grand Prix . . .

The thing with modern Formula 1 cars is that every carbon-fibre flick and edge and angle contributes to the overall downforce of the car – significantly, regardless of how small it may seem. Any bit of contact that sends bodywork flying will cost you dearly in performance. So, when Pierre Gasly ran slightly wide of the tight inside line on the exit of turn 2 during the first lap in Saudi Arabia and brushed Piastri's McLaren that was sitting on the outside line, it was bad news. Piastri ended up ahead of Gasly in that very moment, but it was short-lived. The contact had dislodged the endplate from Piastri's front wing, and the driver knew it immediately. 'I've got damage,' he radioed back to the pits as he felt the front downforce disappear. He plummeted down the order as he battled his way back to the pit entry. Into the lane, new front wing attached, and off he went, now in last position, 38 seconds behind the leader and 25 seconds behind 19th-placed Nyck de Vries.

As the endplate flew from Piastri's car, it was collected by another car further in the pack. Of course, it had to be Lando Norris. He tried to carry on, but at the end of lap 2 he dived into the pits for a new front wing of his own. Nobody's fault, but a disastrous start to the race for the already embattled team. The two McLarens were running 19th (Piastri) and 20th (Norris). With clear air ahead of them, Piastri and Norris clawed their way back to the pack. They had both switched to hard-compound tyres during their unscheduled stops, which meant they could now run long. When the safety car came out on lap 18, Norris opted for a second stop and a move to the medium-compound tyre. The softer, newer rubber meant that, shortly after the restart, Norris was able to breeze by Piastri and grab 17th position.

As the final stint of the race wore on, however, the harder rubber started to come good. Logan Sargeant, running 14th on mediums, created a bottleneck behind his Williams. Eight laps from home, de Vries had had enough and barged past, forcing Sargeant wide in the process. Norris, with Piastri right in his mirrors, tried to get past the American as well, but the draggy nature of the McLaren revealed itself as the Williams pulled clear along the front straight. With seven laps to go, Norris had another crack at Sargeant, but again failed to get through. Two laps later, five to the flag, it was clear that Piastri's hards were better than Norris's mediums. As they kicked off the fifth-last lap, Piastri tried to muscle his way through by getting alongside Norris at turn 1. The McLaren garage held its collective breath as Norris fought back and used what turned into the inside line for turn 2 to retain position after a brief side-by-side. On the fourth-last lap the McLaren pit wall radioed Norris and suggested that he not make life too difficult for Piastri, who fancied his chances of running down Sargeant in 15th. With no points on the line, Norris obliged, letting Piastri through into turn 1 on the third-last lap. Piastri duly found his way past Sargeant on the final lap to secure 15th place, his first classified finish in Formula 1. Norris got next to Sargeant on the run to the finish line, but he couldn't quite get past.

Post-race, Norris tipped his hat to the race craft he'd seen from his rookie teammate as they went wheel to wheel. In keeping with the whole teammate rivalry thing, though, he was quick to point out how easy he'd been on Piastri. 'My first time ever racing with Oscar, so it was good fun,' he said. 'The team told me not to make it too hard for him, so in the end I let him go. I think I would have gotten the Williams myself. But yeah, I let [Oscar] go, I made his life easier. Let him have a chance of getting past the Williams, which he did.'

Piastri himself made no secret of the fact that Norris had waved him through. 'I think we kept sensible,' he said of their on-track stoush. 'Battling for those positions, there's not much to gain. I think there was a call for Lando to, if I had the chance [to pass], not make it too difficult. And in the end, it let me have a shot at Logan, which paid off. [So a nice] bit of teamwork at the end, really. Next time, hopefully, it's for a bit further up.'

What did baffle Piastri was how such minor contact with Gasly during the opening lap had torn the endplate off the front wing of the McLaren. 'I haven't seen [the replay] yet, I'm not 100 per cent sure,' he explained. 'I think it was really just one of those lap 1, turn 1 incidents. The contact felt really small. So I was honestly quite surprised to have damage . . .'

*

Saudi was clearly a step in the right direction for Piastri. He showed he could be a match for Norris on a weekend when the high-speed nature of the circuit suited the McLaren car. Not even a match – between the mistake-free qualifying, and finishing ahead in the race, he'd outperformed his highly rated teammate.

The Formula 1 world took notice. In the days that followed the Saudi race, I interviewed Sky Sports pundit and 1996 Formula 1 world champion Damon Hill, keen to get his thoughts on Piastri's early F1 career form. He agreed that getting into Q3 in Saudi was a critical moment for Piastri, as he exhibited a flash of front-running talent that recent rookies, such as the second-generation Mick Schumacher, had failed to show. 'If you get off to a shaky start, it can take all season to get that [confidence] back again,' Hill told me. 'People are very quick to judge and look for the signs. The great drivers came into Formula 1 with a bang. They arrived. Michael Schumacher, Max Verstappen, Ayrton Senna. They came in and everyone went, "Wow, where did that come from? Who is this guy?" I wouldn't say Oscar has had the opportunity to do quite that, but he has definitely looked very competent and solid. He's not someone who you go, "Oh my god, he looks a bit shaky." Mick Schumacher never really put in one of those "sit up and take notice" performances. And [he] struggled to inspire the confidence people need to have in the driver. Before you know it, it becomes a massive snowball effect where the snowball gets heavier and heavier and you get crushed by it. So far for Oscar, he's not got that problem to think about. He's got very firm footing from which to push off from.'

Being that match for Norris was something Hill felt was incredibly important, more so than dwelling over the fact that Alpine – the team Piastri could have been racing for – had got two cars in the points in Jeddah. 'Alpine are good at the moment; they're not setting the world on fire but looking quite a bit more competitive than McLaren,' conceded Hill. 'But the other side of it is that [Piastri is] up against a driver in Lando that is very highly regarded. It's a curious thing in our sport; you're measured against your teammate as a driver. You can be in a less competitive car, but if you're competitive against a guy who some people think is a world champion in the waiting, then that's all you need.'

Results Summary

Free Practice 1: 14th (1m 31.491s, +1.87s)
Free Practice 2: 19th (1m 30.964s, +1.36s)
Free Practice 3: 8th (1m 29.698s, +1.21s)
Qualifying: 9th (1m 29.243s, +0.98s)
Race: 15th

Saudi Arabian Grand Prix: A brief history

There's been a whiff of controversy attached to the Saudi Arabian Grand Prix since the kingdom's addition to the Formula 1 schedule in 2021.

News of Formula 1's latest foray into the Middle East broke in late 2020, and almost immediately the calls of sportswashing began. The claims were that, once again, Saudi officials were using sport to distract from the country's maligned human rights record – and Formula 1 had taken the bait (well, the money). Human Rights Watch was among the groups to swiftly condemn the event. 'Sporting bodies like Formula 1 and the FIA cannot ignore the fact they and fans are being used for sportswashing,' said Human Rights Watch's Director of Global Initiatives, Minky Worden. 'It is part of a cynical strategy to distract from Saudi Arabia's human rights abuses, detention and torture of human rights defenders and women's rights activists. Formula 1 has made human rights commitments and should explain how the company's operations will improve human rights in Saudi Arabia. Have F1 staff used their negotiations with Saudi leaders to advocate for the release of women's rights activists whose only crime was advocating for the right to drive? Fans, media and race teams should use this moment to say their sport should not be associated with such serious human rights abuses.'

The sportswashing aspect wasn't lost on the driver group, particularly the more socially active like Lewis Hamilton and Sebastian Vettel. But as the first race drew closer, another concern raised its head: the sheer safety of the paddock.

As in Bahrain, fears grew that regional tensions could be amplified by the presence of an international audience. In February 2021, Riyadh hosted the all-electric Formula E World Championship. On the Saturday night of the event, there were reports of bright flashes in the sky over the Saudi capital. Al Jazeera swiftly reported that a Saudi-led coalition had thwarted a missile attack on Riyadh that was blamed on Yemen's Houthi rebels. It all led to an uneasy feeling heading into the inaugural Saudi Arabia F1 race in December 2021, but the money talked and the event went ahead.

Jeddah was bumped up the race order to a late March slot in 2022. And it only took until the first practice session for the drama to begin to unfold. As the cars took to the track, black smoke was seen billowing in the near distance. The Aramco oil refinery, right near the airport and around 16 kilometres from the circuit, was on fire. With TV pictures of the dramatic fire beaming around the world, the Houthi rebels were quick to take responsibility for another missile attack. Right on the doorstep of the grand prix.

Understandably, the attack shook the F1 paddock to its core. Formula 1 CEO Stefano Domenicali called an emergency meeting with the drivers and team principals as the second practice session was delayed. The teams and drivers were told that Formula 1 had been assured that nobody was in any danger, and that the event could proceed as planned. There were more talks after Free Practice 2, talks that went for hours as drivers voiced their concerns. There was talk of a boycott until Domenicali was able to convince the drivers to trust the assurances he had been given by the Saudi authorities. 'We have received total assurances that, for the country, safety is first, no matter the situation – safety has to be guaranteed,' said Domenicali. '[The local officials] are here with their families, actually here at the track, so they have in place all the systems to protect this area, the city and the places we are going.' The boycott was called off, but tensions weren't relieved entirely.

The following day, the Saudi government moved to further quell any concerns. The minister for sport, His Royal Highness Prince Abdulaziz bin Turki Al Faisal, fronted the media and made his position clear. 'The security agencies were all on the highest alert in terms of safety for any of the threats,' he explained. 'Everyone is on 24-hour surveillance, I would say, in terms of where the threat could come from and what to do to action that. We have the security levels very high hosting such an event and we know it's recognised as [being in] the limelight because the media is here, everyone is here. We did realise that from the beginning. And if you see the hit that happened, it's on the outskirts of the city. There were no casualties and it's only a fuel tank what was burning. I was actually landing from the airport during the time. If there is a threat [to the event], rest assured we will cancel the race. But there is no threat and that's what we discussed with everyone.'

The clincher to guarantee safety appeared to be the missile defence system that covered the Jeddah circuit, but not the oil facility. 'You can't cover the whole kingdom,' said Al Faisal. 'So the security agencies cover the areas where there is condensed population, where it had to be covered. That place wasn't covered because it's not a threat to anyone. From the feedback we have got, we were lucky that that's where it happened, but even they were surprised it was that area. So it's not a breach of security.'

The race went ahead and, 12 months later, the Formula 1 circus returned for a third time. The security concerns had all but disappeared, but the human rights issue hadn't. Again, activist groups complained; again, drivers like Hamilton bit their tongues to the best of their abilities. 'The thing is, if I'm not here, Formula 1 will continue without me,' said Hamilton ahead of the 2023 race. 'I still feel that, as a sport going to places with human rights issues such as this one, the sport is duty-bound to raise awareness and try to leave a positive impact. And I feel like it needs to do more. What that is, I don't have all the answers. But I think we always need to do more to raise awareness for things that people are struggling with.'

8

AUSTRALIA

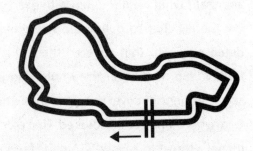

Australian Grand Prix
Albert Park
31 March–2 April 2023

It might just be the greatest moment in Australian Grand Prix history. A moment that marked one of the sport's most sensational debuts – Mark Webber standing on the Albert Park podium in 2002 alongside aviation entrepreneur Paul Stoddart, the pair proudly holding the Australian flag. Webber hadn't actually finished in the top three in what was his first race in Formula 1. But what he had achieved, in the car he had been in, was as remarkable as it gets.

Webber's personal brand is 'Aussie Grit', and it's a perfect way to describe him. Coming through the junior formula series, he was never seen as the most naturally gifted driver. He also never had easy access to the shed-loads of money needed to climb the European open-wheel ladder. But the boy from Queanbeyan knew how to work hard. He knew how to keep the grind going. And he stubbornly climbed that ladder until he made it all the way to the top: Formula 1.

That grit and determination would eventually lead Webber to a top seat at Red Bull Racing. He got painfully close to snatching a world championship title in 2010, only to miss out to teammate Sebastian Vettel. What set his F1 career in motion, however, was his stunning debut in Melbourne in 2002.

Webber's big break came from chain-smoking business-man Stoddart. The man known to many as 'Stoddy' made his money buying and selling planes and plane parts. He eventually set up European Airlines, which gave him the means – and marketing power – to indulge his love of motor racing. He first sponsored Tyrrell Racing before switching his backing to the fun-loving Jordan team in 1999. European Airlines would charter flights to and from the races for the team, and some of the stories from those trips are legend-ary. Tim Edwards, now the CEO at Supercars squad Tickford Racing, was working for Jordan at the time. In 2010 he told *Motorsport News* about some of the on-board antics. 'One of the most popular pursuits was aisle surfing, which involved having one laminated safety card on each foot and one under your backside. You would sit down in the aisle, in a conga line, and wait for take-off. As the plane's nose left the ground, the fun started . . .

'Two occasions of this really were memorable. The first was after we won the Magny Cours GP in 1999 and Murray Walker decided to join the antics. He shot down the aisle as we took off shouting, "Go, go, go." Not a bad effort consider-ing he'd just had his hip replaced.

'The second was when Stoddy had his 747s. On one trip back from Japan, we decided to upgrade the sport from sitting to standing, to make it proper surfing. With four passenger areas on a 747, we also had an aisle three times the length we'd been used to, so you can imagine the speed that they got up to. But the problem was, by the time the conga line made it to the last cabin, there was a bend in the aisle as the rear economy cabin was a slightly different layout. The conga line didn't make it through the chicane and Stoddy took off over the seats and landed somewhere near the dunny at the back of the plane!'

As fun as it was sponsoring F1 teams, what Stoddart really wanted was to own one. His European Racing team fielded Webber in the Formula 3000, the step immediately below F1 at the time, in the year 2000. Twelve months later an opportunity came up for Stoddart to purchase the financially embattled Minardi team – and he grabbed it with both hands. Minardi had been on the F1 grid since the mid-1980s, almost always near the back of it. Back then, world championship points were only paid to sixth place, and points-earning days were few and far between for the Italian minnow team – particularly as car reliability improved and there were fewer DNFs. By the time Stoddart got hold of Minardi, it was in dire financial straits. The prospects of significant improvement were basically zero. The team was in full survival mode.

Stoddart and Webber reunited in 2002 with what was initially a three-race deal for Webber to make his Formula 1 debut. His first race was the Australian Grand Prix, and there was genuine excitement from the local fans to have an Aussie on the Formula 1 grid for the first time since 1994 when David Brabham raced with the woefully uncompetitive Simtek outfit. But expectations were rightly tempered. Webber, lanky by F1 driver standards, barely fit in the underdeveloped car. Even wet weather in qualifying couldn't help him place better than 18th on the grid. The forecast for his finishing position in the race was similar.

And then Ralf Schumacher took flight.

The German made a demon start from the second row of the grid, getting past brother Michael and tucking in behind the Ferrari of Rubens Barrichello on the entry to turn 1. When the Brazilian driver braked slightly earlier than the younger Schumacher was expecting, his Williams climbed over the back of the Ferrari and flew, spectacularly, through the air and into the gravel trap. It triggered a pile-up that took eight cars out of the race. From there it became a rare race of attrition in the modern era as more and more cars dropped out. Through the chaos, Webber suddenly found himself running fifth, a position he held until the finish. He had done the impossible and scored two world championship points, on debut in Formula 1, at his home race, in a Minardi.

To commemorate the extraordinary achievement, Webber and Stoddart were allowed to get up on the podium and celebrate in front of a rabid home crowd. Webber's three races turned into a season-long deal with Minardi, and he was later poached by the better-funded (to an extent, at least) Jaguar team for 2003.

*

Two decades later, Webber was experiencing another first at Albert Park. The first home race for his young star, Oscar Piastri. Home races are a funny thing for a Formula 1 driver. The buzz of being the crowd favourite is nice, and the opportunity to pull off something magical on home soil, as Webber did in 2002, is one to be cherished. But there is also more pressure than at any other race. And the media and sponsor workload is heavier than any other race. Everyone wants a piece of the hometown hero in the week leading up to the event; it can be physically and mentally draining even before a lap has been turned. Daniel Ricciardo often struggled with race week in Melbourne – in fact, he purposely cut down his commitments ahead of the ill-fated 2020 Australian Grand Prix (which was cancelled at the last minute due to the COVID-19 pandemic), having felt burnt out by the end of the 2019 race.

Piastri had at least had a practice run in 2022. Alpine had put him through his hometown-grand-prix paces in terms of media and appearances, so he knew what was coming in 2023. He also had Webber in his corner, something Damon Hill had told me would be invaluable. 'Coming to Melbourne, he'll be getting a lot of attention, and it's about whether that distracts him,' said Hill of Piastri in our post-Saudi chat. 'But he doesn't strike me as the sort of person who is easily distracted or interested in the peripheral stuff that happens in Formula 1. He seems to be a very keen and focused racer. Mark Webber will be giving him all the tips on how to cope with his home grand prix.'

The tips seemed to work. As attention turned away from the pre-race noise, and focus shifted to the on-track action,

McLaren CEO Zak Brown highlighted how well Piastri was weathering the home-race storm. 'He's a very mature 21-year-old, very focused,' Brown said. 'You kind of wouldn't know it's his home grand prix, from his perspective. You can clearly tell around the track that there's an "Oscar-mania", if you like, but he's very focused, head down. You can't really tell the difference between him here or Saudi or Bahrain, and I think that's what's going to make him a really good grand prix driver, his focus and his calmness.'

Despite the promising pace in Saudi Arabia, McLaren's form was still so difficult to predict. It was hard to read too much into the first practice session. At one point, Piastri sat as high as fifth place after a soft-tyre run, but he dropped back to twelfth as the session played out. Ahead of Free Practice 2, all eyes in the pit lane turned to the sky. Melbourne was doing its thing and proving fickle with its weather. 'Oscar, we're expecting rain 20 minutes into the session,' was the radio call. It didn't even take that long for the heavens to open. Rain generally brings practice rounds to a halt. Not the session itself – the clock keeps ticking – but the on-track action stops. Unless there is a solid chance of rain in qualifying or the race, running is meaningless – not to mention risky. Racing cars are supremely difficult to drive in wet conditions. Combine that with slippery painted lines on the track, and the wet grass off it, it only takes the smallest of mistakes to badly damage a car. With 20 minutes to go in FP2, the McLarens ventured out on intermediate wet tyres to assess the conditions. Piastri almost immediately needed the quickest of hands to correct a snap at turn 11 and then again at turn 13. After that, Piastri's pace on the grooved rubber was promising, as he became one of the few drivers lapping in the 1m 31s bracket. Given his relative lack of Formula 1 experience, it was an important bit of wet-weather running. Even better that he brought the car back to the garage with all four wheels attached.

The weather hung around on Saturday, just to the point of being annoying. There was a sprinkle at the end of Free Practice 3, which curtailed any late improvements. For Piastri, the only real action was a rookie mistake right at the end of the session. In some sessions, after taking the chequered flag, drivers are permitted to stay on track and make a practice start on the grid. Piastri, however, went to pull up on the grid before taking the chequered flag, something he later put down to a lack of concentration. The FIA investigated the issue and opted for a slap on the wrist.

The threat of rain lingered until qualifying, but the track stayed dry enough for slick (dry weather) tyres. As in Jeddah, Piastri spent the entirety of Q1 in the drop zone; however, this time there were no late heroics and he ended up on the wrong side of the Q2 bubble. The issue appeared to be that critical window in traffic. He had been forced to a crawl at the very end of his warm-up lap, which would have undoubtedly affected his front-tyre temperature once he started his push lap. That could easily account for the four-hundredths of a second he'd needed to progress.

Sunday was the big day. For the first time since he was in a go-kart, Oscar Piastri was about to take part in a motor race on

Australian soil. Dressed in the proud McLaren papaya orange, he waved to the crowd from an open-top car under beautiful blue autumn skies during the driver parade. A while later, he pulled into his grid spot in front of the packed main grandstands. A proper Melbourne boy on the Melbourne grid. Not an Aussie from Perth, 2700 kilometres away, or even Queanbeyan, 470 kilometres away. The first true hometown hero.

He made a pretty heroic start to the race, too. There was little in the way of rustiness as he made up three places in the frantic opening stages of the race. On lap 7, luck went Piastri's way when Alex Albon hit the wall at turn 6. The collision left the circuit covered in gravel and debris. The first call from race control was a safety car – until it was decided that even a full-course caution wasn't safe enough for the clean-up effort. Out came the red flag.

There's an awkward rule in Formula 1 allowing drivers to change tyres, and satisfy the multi-compound regulations, during a red-flag stoppage. Stopping under safety car conditions is an almost-free pit stop, as the time loss is so heavily reduced. Changing tyres during a red flag? As free as it gets. Some drivers stopped when the safety car was called, looking to take advantage of that and not expecting a red flag. Piastri decided against doing so and filtered up to 11th place as other drivers around him hit the pits. Suddenly, with the race red-flagged, he was able to get fresh boots without losing a single microsecond. He would restart the race in 11th position and on the same tyre strategy as those around him.

In recent years, red flags have been followed by a full, standing restart from the grid. Once the track was clear, the field went out on the Albert Park circuit, lined up on the grid in the staggered two-by-two formation again, and off they went. Early in the second stint, AlphaTauri driver Yuki Tsunoda became a cork in the bottle at the back end of the points-paying positions. Initially, Tsunoda was ninth and Piastri tenth – enough for a single point. That was until a recovering Sergio Perez, in the rapid Red Bull, blasted past the pair of them. Not long after, the two drivers were rounded up by Esteban Ocon in his Alpine. Suddenly they were running 11th and 12th. Getting past Tsunoda was critical to Piastri's hopes of a points finish. Lap after lap, Piastri shadowed Tsunoda's car but couldn't find a way past. The group ahead pulled away as the likes of Zhou Guanyu and Kevin Magnussen closed up the gap behind. Finally, on lap 29, Piastri eased around the outside of Tsunoda at turn 9 to grab 11th place. But all those laps stuck behind the AlphaTauri had been costly. Ocon was already five seconds down the road, the gap between them growing to eight seconds in the laps that followed. With three laps to go, the pursuit of a point seemed hopeless.

At least until Magnussen pulled to the inside of turn 4 and rolled to a stop.

First it was a safety car, a chance for Piastri to close up on Ocon. And then another red flag. It turned out that Magnussen had clipped the wall on the exit of turn 2, and his right-rear wheel hub had disintegrated. Part of the carbon-fibre hub had flown 20 metres in the air, cleared the catch fencing and left a fan with a nasty laceration on his arm. Again, race control called for a safety car – before red-flagging the race for a second time. The entire field returned to the pit lane for new rubber, and, once the debris was cleared, headed back out onto the track for yet another full standing restart for a two-lap dash to the chequered flag. Unprecedented in Formula 1.

Somewhat predictably, the restart was chaos. With rubber marbles from the wearing tyres off the racing line, and with tyres cooling in the evening light, conditions were as difficult as could be imagined for a standing start. As the field raced into turn 1, Carlos Sainz out-braked himself and rammed Fernando Alonso out of the race. The two Alpine drivers then collided on the way out of turn 2 and both ended up in the wall. Out came the red flag for a third time. Confusion reigned as drivers now didn't know whether there would be another standing start, or if the race would be declared. After a lengthy wait, the FIA came to a decision: 'Race resumption behind safety car in the order of the previous start minus cars out,' was the message. 'There will be a rolling start and as there will only be one lap left, the chequered flag will be out as they come back across the line.'

It was a bit of an anti-climax, but good news for Piastri. Through all the madness, he'd ended up ninth on the road. Even better – Sainz was slapped with a five-second penalty for his role in the turn 1 chaos. Given the field would cross the finish line bunched up after the rolling start, the five seconds would dump him way down the order. Piastri's ninth place would, in the final classification, become eighth. Good enough for four world championship points.

On the Sunday evening, as pack-up in the paddock was in full swing, the last round of post-race media roundtables took place. A small group of journalists, myself included, sat down at a table inside the McLaren hospitality unit, waiting to speak to Andrea Stella. Ann Neal, Webber's longtime partner and co-manager of Piastri, was already there, as were a number of McLaren staff. Moments later, in walked a beaming Piastri, still in his race suit, with Webber in tow. It wasn't a wild reception, nothing like when Webber crossed the line in 2002. But the smile on Webber's and Piastri's face clearly showed how good it felt to get some runs on the world championship board – and to do it a few streets from home. Once Stella arrived and the interviews kicked off, I put it to him that while he surely would have liked Piastri's strong grid position in Jeddah to have been converted to points, there was a kind of romance about Piastri scoring his first points in Melbourne. Without a moment of pause, he smiled and said, 'I agree with you. In all this engineering and racing world we want to, for once, have a romantic world, so I am happy that he scored his first points in Melbourne.'

Piastri, meanwhile, saw it less as romance and more as karma after the technical issues in Bahrain and the early contact in Jeddah. 'I feel like the first two races really couldn't have gone that much worse,' he said. 'It was nice to be on the good end of other things going wrong for other people . . .'

Both Piastri and McLaren were now on the world championship board, Norris finishing sixth, a relief to both the team and its drivers. Still, Stella urged caution about the double points finish, in terms of what it meant for McLaren and its spot in the pecking order. '[The result is] important because it was an uncomfortable position to have not scored points, and it's important because, ultimately, [fifth in the constructors' standings], at least, is what we are racing for this season,' he explained. 'At the same time, we can't get carried away. We know that we scored the 12 points in particular circumstances and if we don't improve the car, we are not going to stay P5. This result will have to be converted by the 700 people that work trackside and in Woking into even further energy to develop the car and score regularly, thanks to having a quick car.'

Of course, with a breakthrough points-paying result at Piastri's home grand prix – scored in an uncompetitive car – the Webber comparisons were obvious. But as remarkable as Piastri's day was, it wasn't the same, and that's why there was no repeat of the impromptu podium celebrations. For Minardi, it had been a rare moment of success for F1's longtime battlers. McLaren, however, is a Formula 1 powerhouse. At least, it was in the past, and is determined to regain the status. Podium celebrations, said Stella, would wait until Piastri actually finished on the podium. 'We want to take him on the podium because we gave him a quick car that he will drive to the podium,' he said. 'That's my dream.'

Results Summary

Free Practice 1: 12th (1m 19.777s, +0.99s)
Free Practice 2: 14th (1m 20.380s, +1.49s)
Free Practice 3: 14th (1m 18.713s, +1.15s)
Qualifying: 16th (1m 18.517s, +1.78s)
Race: 8th

Australian Grand Prix: A brief history

The Australian Grand Prix is still a touchy subject in Adelaide.

Back in the 1980s, the sleepy South Australian capital decided to put itself on the world map – by luring the Formula 1 world championship down under. F1 had been investigating staging a race in Australia, and the South Australian government made an aggressive play. The idea was to take F1 directly to the South Aussies with a street track right on the fringe of Adelaide city. A small bit of permanent circuit was laid around Victoria Park and then connected to surrounding roads. In 1985, the Formula 1 circus made its first trip to Australia for the season finale. It immediately fell in love with Adelaide, and Adelaide immediately fell in love with Formula 1. The Australian Grand Prix quickly became Adelaide's thing. 'Adelaide Alive' was the most fitting of marketing slogans. People flocked to the City of Churches from all over the country. Pubs that lined the circuit were packed full for days on end. The most famous was the Stag Hotel, the balcony of which directly looked over turn 9.

Then, after 10 successful years, the race was stolen.

A group of Melbourne powerbrokers, led by Ron Walker, felt the Australian Grand Prix would be a perfect fit for their own city, the self-proclaimed sporting capital of Australia. It was already home to the Australian Open, the famous Melbourne Cricket Ground and the Boxing Day Test, and it was the spiritual home of the Australian Football League, the biggest ball sports code in the country by far. Now it wanted a Formula 1 race as well. The case for a brand-new race around Albert Park Lake, on the outskirts of the Melbourne CBD, was put to then Formula 1 CEO Bernie Ecclestone. And Bernie liked what he heard. It was announced that Melbourne would host the season-opening race in 1996 – which blindsided the South Australian government and infuriated the grand-prix-loving locals.

It technically wasn't the first time Albert Park had hosted the Australian Grand Prix. That was in 1953. Back then it was a non-world-championship event, a status it held until the first Adelaide race in 1985. In the lead-up to the 1996 F1 season, public roads around the parklands were re-profiled and resurfaced to create something that is technically a street track, but not quite a street track. Given it's surrounded by sporting facilities, including a golf course and numerous grassed ovals, there is plenty of run-off and gravel traps, unlike classic street circuits such as the one used for the Saudi Arabian Grand Prix. Instead, Albert Park is typically referred to as a parklands circuit.

The Melbourne version of the Australian Grand Prix has, over time, had its ups and downs. There were record crowds in the first few years, but in other seasons the attendance waned slightly. That was an unfortunate symptom of plonking the event in the middle of a packed sporting landscape. In Adelaide, F1 was pretty much the only show in town. The entire city embraced it. It became part of Adelaide's identity. In Melbourne, it was, in a way, just another major event.

And then it was re-energised by something completely unexpected – COVID-19.

The Australian Grand Prix, in a way, marked the start of the pandemic in Australia. In March 2020, the virus had already arrived, but Australia was kind of just carrying on. Flights had been banned from China, but that was about it. Still, the lead-up to the race was tense and weird. As Italy plunged into coronavirus chaos, there were calls to stop flights from that country as well. Conveniently, that only happened once the two Italian-based F1 teams, Ferrari and AlphaTauri, had arrived in Melbourne. There was a determination from organisers that the event would go ahead, as bizarre as the whole world seemed at the time. On Thursday, the week of the grand prix, media sessions happened as planned, although with drivers physically distanced from journalists and all wearing masks. The supporting formula categories took part in their practice sessions and, as the F1 teams readied themselves for Free Practice on Friday, it felt like there was no turning back.

The Thursday of a grand prix is generally a late day at the track for journalists due to all the media sessions. At some point well into the night, myself and two colleagues, who are permanently embedded in the F1 paddock, made our way into the Melbourne CBD to find somewhere still serving food. We settled on a small Italian restaurant, ordered some dinner and started to debrief about the day. Then, one colleague looked at his phone. Someone had texted him suggesting that a McLaren crew member had contracted the virus. He quickly fired off a text to another person he was sure would know. The second text was immediately read by the recipient, but they didn't respond. Had the tip-off been wrong, it would have been instantly dismissed by the second source. No answer was as good as a yes. Out came the laptops at our dinner table and an already long night got a whole lot longer.

The scenes at Albert Park's gates the next morning were surreal. By that point, McLaren had confirmed that a team member had COVID-19 and they'd withdrawn from the race weekend. Initially, organisers said the event was going ahead and fans flocked to the precinct, only to be told they wouldn't be let in and the event would proceed behind closed doors. The anger and confusion was palpable. Those already inside the precinct were equally confused. The TCR cars were fired up, engines getting warm for the first scheduled on-track session of the day as I walked past their garages. By the time I reached the media centre, multiple Supercars sources had sent texts saying they'd been told to pack up and head home – that the event was off. A short while later, Australian Grand Prix Corporation CEO Andrew Westacott and Liberty Media kingpin Chase Carey, then effectively at the helm of Formula 1, addressed the media in a large outside gathering near the entrance to the paddock to make it official.

Ultimately, they explained, it came down to the F1 teams. If the majority wanted the race weekend to continue, it would. McLaren was already out, and Ferrari said it too would take no further part in this grand prix. Haas and Williams declared they would go with the majority, which left four teams in outright favour of the weekend continuing – Mercedes, Red Bull, AlphaTauri and Racing Point. That made it a tie, leaving Formula 1's managing director Ross Brawn to make the final decision. His preference was to get through Friday's practice sessions and see how things looked. Then, Mercedes F1 boss Toto Wolff's phone rang – it was Daimler CEO Ola Källenius, who didn't necessarily tell Wolff how to vote, but who voiced concerns over the event going ahead amid the deteriorating COVID-19 situation in Europe. Wolff decided to reverse his vote, swinging the majority. In the wee hours of Friday morning, the 2020 Australian Grand Prix's fate was sealed.

It was the first major event that was cancelled in Australia due to the COVID-19 pandemic, and to many it felt like the starting point of almost two years of event cancellations, closed borders – both inside and outside the country – keeping friends and families apart, and people and businesses suffering through successive lockdowns. Melbourne infamously became the most locked-down city in the country as all states pursued an aggressive zero-COVID approach. Of course, that meant the 2021 running of the Australian Grand Prix was cancelled as well.

All of that may sound like bad news – and it was – but the pandemic had a positive effect on both the sport and the event as well. Netflix's *Drive to Survive* docuseries became crucial viewing for bored people stuck in lockdowns around the globe and sent Formula 1's popularity into the stratosphere. The people of Melbourne, meanwhile, emerged from their long lockdowns ready to party. Combine those two factors, and the return of F1 to Albert Park in April 2022 resulted in a wild affair, like nothing I had personally ever seen. These days, an Australian Grand Prix ticket is one of the hottest in town. They sell out, quite literally, in minutes.

9

AZERBAIJAN

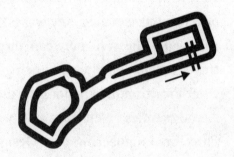

Azerbaijan Grand Prix
Baku City Circuit
28–30 April 2023

Since the launch of the 2023 car, Baku had been seen as the great white hope for McLaren. The return to Europe signalled the introduction of a number of upgrade packages throughout the field. Most notably, an upgrade for McLaren.

In Formula 1 the work never stops. Each team designs a car for the start of the season and then develops the car as the year progresses. Minor changes, mostly to aerodynamics, are made almost race to race, while teams will also work on more significant upgrade packages in the search of a proper performance gain.

McLaren had tempered the relative disappointment of the opening three rounds with the notion that while the launch-spec car was too draggy and too slow, the Baku upgrade would change things. Surely the car would be more competitive.

Surely Lando Norris and Oscar Piastri weren't facing a season of nothingness.

Behind the scenes there had been plenty going on at McLaren. A week before the Australian Grand Prix, when the team was still scoreless in the world championship, it had rolled out a new team structure and vision for the future. The existing structure saw a single technical director, named James Key, who reported to Andrea Stella. It was announced that, effective immediately, Key was out, and the technical director role would be split between three people. Well, eventually three people. For the time being, it would be two. One was Peter Prodromou, who took on the role of Technical Director, Aerodynamics. Neil Houldey was promoted to Technical Director, Engineering and Design. And the team poached David Sanchez from Ferrari to be its Technical Director, Car Concept and Performance – although his garden-leave clause meant he couldn't start working at McLaren until the beginning of January 2024.

'I think there were some limitations somehow associated with the [old] model,' said Stella when he faced the media about the changes. 'In aerodynamics, we wanted to have a technical director that leads aerodynamics. Full empower-ment to this technical director. And we wanted to unleash a very strong resource that we had internally, and that for some reason was under-utilised, like Peter Prodromou, one of the most competent experts in F1 in relation to aerodynamics. And this wasn't happening as efficiently as it should have happened, let's say, so this is something we wanted to fix. And it perfectly fits the model at the same time by giving aerodynamics clear leadership, clear guidance as to the concepts that we wanted to develop and lead to the car.'

A week after McLaren's team restructure went public, a revised upgrades plan was announced. The Baku upgrade would go ahead, but it was no longer expected to be a silver bullet. Instead, it would be the first step of a three-step process for the MCL60. The second update would be the launch of a 'kind of B-spec car' at some point before the European summer break, known in F1 as the 'shutdown', as teams are forced to close their doors to give staff a break. 'We have three main steps: Baku, later on – I don't want to commit to any date, but before shutdown – and then after shutdown,' explained Stella. 'We hope that each of them will be able to provide a few tenths of a second so that we put ourselves in a more realistic position to meet our ambition to become a top-four car towards the end of the season.'

Given drag was an issue with the original spec, it was unsurprisingly a focus for McLaren's Baku upgrade package. There was to be a new floor geometry, aimed at altering suction and improving load, as well as a new lower-drag rear wing, and beam wing elements. 'What we have now is what we should have started the year with,' said Norris of the changes ahead of the grand prix. 'A lot of other teams also have upgrades, so our job is to try and bring slightly bigger things and try to play a little bit of catch-up.

'I think what we have this weekend is just the baseline we should have started the year with. It's about understanding that what we have now is a better baseline and gives more room for improvements. It's certainly going to make us take a small step forward.'

As well as marking the start of the 'European season', where teams tend to start rolling out their major car upgrades, Baku was also the first sprint round of the year. The sprint concept debuted in 2021, the idea being to cut down practice time and add a shorter, additional race to the grand prix weekend. Formula 1 is a very traditional sport with a very traditional structure. Session lengths and qualifying formats had been chopped and changed over the decades, but the concept always remained the same. There was practice, for teams and drivers to tune their cars, followed by qualifying, which would set the grid, fastest to slowest, for a single grand prix. It's a flawed system, in a way. A lack of overtaking is often cited as an issue for F1, but what can you really expect? Each race starts with the fastest cars already at the front . . .

Initially, the sprint format saw a qualifying session to set the grid for the sprint race, and then the grid for the grand prix was set by the outcome of the sprint race. By 2023, however, it had been drastically altered. There would only be a single, 60-minute practice session on the Friday, instead of the usual three. That would be followed by a regular qualifying session on Friday afternoon, which would set the order for Sunday's grand prix. Saturday was therefore a standalone day. There would be a sprint qualifying session that set the grid for a sprint race, significantly shorter than the grand prix, from which the top eight would score world championship points.

*

From the moment Piastri woke up on Friday morning at Baku, he was up against it. Firstly, he and his team were facing just 60 minutes of practice to try and understand the new upgrade package before Piastri would have to qualify and lock in his starting slot for Sunday's race. Secondly, he was battling a nasty stomach bug, thought to be food poisoning, which was going to make tackling the narrow, bumpy and highly demanding street course ridiculously difficult. Despite not being able to eat, Piastri battled through the sole practice session, finishing 12th. Norris was fifth fastest, hinting at progress with the upgraded McLaren.

At 5 p.m. local time on Friday, the field rolled back out for qualifying. Getting out of Q1 was, basically, a game of survival. Eight minutes into the session, Nyck de Vries fired his AlphaTauri into the wall at turn 3. Once the struggling rookie's mangled car was retrieved, the session went green again – for a whole 120 seconds. That was when Pierre Gasly fired his Alpine straight into the barriers that had claimed the AlphaTauri. Eventually, 44 minutes into what was meant to be an 18-minute session, Q1 came to a close with Piastri safely through to the next round in 12th place. Q2 wasn't quite as easy; Piastri was forced to dig deep on his final run to get out of the drop zone. There was a bit of luck with a small tow from Lewis Hamilton, as the rookie jumped the seven-time world champion to scrape through in ninth place.

The Baku City Circuit is a touch over 6 kilometres in length. A lap takes more than 101 seconds. So for Lance Stroll and Oscar Piastri to set identical times in Q3, down to the one-thousandth of a second, was something quite remarkable. Imagine two different people, in two different cars, covering that distance in *exactly* the same amount of time. Unfortunately for Piastri, Stroll had set the time first, which meant he was classified as ninth on the grid, and Piastri tenth. When he faced the TV cameras after the session, Piastri admitted he was feeling a bit 'under the weather'. 'I'll be fine for tomorrow,' he promised. 'I've felt better before, but I'll be fine.'

'Fine' was a little optimistic, but Piastri was indeed there on Saturday. Still struggling to keep food down, and running on next to no sleep, he showed Mark Webber–like resilience as he battled through the sprint shootout and the sprint race itself. He qualified 11th and finished the 17-lap race in 10th place, having benefitted from Norris rolling the dice on tyres. The Briton had elected for the soft-compound Pirellis, which proved to be the wrong choice; he'd plummeted backwards through the field before pitting for mediums and finishing 17th. 'It's been a rough 24 hours,' said Piastri. 'It's been quite the physical journey. I didn't get a whole lot of sleep. I'll try and limber up for tonight.'

Piastri did wake up feeling better on the Sunday morning, but the damage had already been done. He was way undernourished, 3 kilograms lighter than he'd started the weekend and facing a hell of a slog to get through 51 laps. The job was made even harder when an ambitious Alex Albon tagged Piastri's left-rear corner on the way into turn 3. There was no real damage to Piastri's car, but the sideways snap from the contact meant Piastri lost touch with the group of 10 cars in front of him. He battled on and brought the car home in

11th place, one spot outside the points. 'I think the adrenaline's still kicking at the moment,' he said after the race. 'But I felt a bit better this morning, which was good. Today's probably been the best I've felt all weekend, which isn't saying much. But yeah, it's been very difficult, physically. Especially yesterday, I was . . . it was pretty rough. I think I've had about four pieces of toast for the whole weekend. I need to get some food back in me before Miami. It's been tough. Happy to see the end of it.'

It was only once the job was done that Andrea Stella revealed that, at various points across the weekend, McLaren had considered benching Piastri so he could rest and be ready for the grand prix on the Sunday. 'We have had a couple of points during the weekend in which we needed to evaluate, "Is it better to have rest now to make sure that we are okay on Sunday?"' he said. 'I can certainly admit that we have made this evaluation a couple of times; we've been very well supported by our team doctor. And the overall medical support I would like to acknowledge has been excellent in assisting Oscar, like his team. But Oscar has always been very calm, and [said], "Okay, let's try, I'll get in the car. If I can't do it, I will box." And then he has always found the resources to go through the session.'

Stella also noted that the demanding nature of the Baku circuit had made battling through the illness, and performing on limited sleep and calories, so much harder. 'It's one of the hardest [circuits], because of how close you go to the walls,'

Stella explained. 'And it's a moment that you touch the wall like we've seen many drivers have this weekend, in terms of even drivers in top cars, so it's definitely an issue that requires a lot of competent lucidity, and a lot of concentration. And sometimes Oscar after a session said, "I'm really exhausted." It was interesting, he was okay in the session, and then after had kind of a little bit of a drop.'

Despite the physical challenges he was facing, Piastri was the only one of the three rookies in the field not to crash at any point of the Baku weekend.

Results Summary

Free Practice 1: 12th (1m 43.980s, +1.66s)
Qualifying: 10th (1m 41.611s, +1.41s)
Sprint Shootout: 11th (1m 43.427s, +1.73s)
Sprint: 10th
Race: 11th

Azerbaijan Grand Prix: A brief history

In the short history of the Azerbaijan Grand Prix, and the wild Baku street circuit, held for the first time in 2017, there are a number of stories that stand out. But one stands taller than the rest. And it's about a driver who, at the time, hadn't even made it to Formula 1.

In the days leading up to the inaugural 2017 Baku event, which included a round of the FIA Formula 2 Championship, Charles Leclerc was dealt a horrible loss. The loss of his father, Hervé Leclerc.

Leclerc Senior was a competent open-wheel driver in his own right, competing in the junior categories in the 1980s. He passed his passion on to his sons Charles and Arthur, and, by 2017, the former was enjoying a meteoric rise towards Formula 1. At the time, Charles Leclerc was driving for Prema in the second-tier formula series, and he was rumoured to be knocking on the door of F1.

So to lose his father, and greatest supporter, on the eve of an important championship round was significant.

Few would have blamed him for staying at home in Monaco and not travelling to Baku that weekend. But there was Charles, not just in the car but determined to win the race. And win he did. An emotional pole position followed by an emotional feature-race victory. He was 19 years old. His helmet and the rear wing of his car carried stickers reading 'Je T'Aime, Papa' (I love you, Dad). It was about as moving as it got – and close to unfathomable that he was able to do it. To deal with what must have been so much pain and still perform in the car.

'My father, he did many things in my career,' said Leclerc in his podium interview in Baku. 'If I'm here today, it's thanks to him. He made me start [racing] at three years old and since then he has been a huge support for me. And it's a good way to thank him. It won't bring him back, but it's a satisfying thing for me this weekend.'

By that point, Leclerc was already well entrenched in the Ferrari system. He was running in F2 as a Ferrari junior driver, and the Scuderia was weighing up whether to place him at Sauber, somewhat a Ferrari junior team, for the 2018 Formula 1 season. The emotional Baku weekend would later turn out to be pivotal in making that happen. And it wasn't the win; it was the fact he had been there at all. Then Ferrari F1 team principal, Maurizio Arrivabene, later told Sky Italia: 'We were on the same flight to Baku last year and I asked him what he was doing on the flight considering what happened to him. He replied, "I have to win this race, then I'll go back and bury my father." There, I understood that Charles knows how to take his responsibilities. If someone manages to concentrate in such a situation, what is a Formula 1 grand prix compared to this?'

That concentration was undoubtedly helped by Leclerc's regrettable amount of experience when it came to grief. His life had already been turned upside down once before – when Jules Bianchi veered off the Suzuka circuit during the 2014 Japanese Grand Prix and collided with a crane that was removing another car from the gravel.

Like Leclerc, Bianchi was a star on the rise in Formula 1. He was in his second Formula 1 season with the minnow Marussia squad, showing all the right signs in uncompetitive hardware. He had ties to Ferrari and was thought to be in contention to join the team once Fernando Alonso departed at the end of the 2014 season.

He was also a very close friend of the Leclerc family – and Charles Leclerc's godfather.

Everything changed on that afternoon in Japan. The unthinkable happened. It had been so long since somebody had died in a Formula 1 crash. The last had been Ayrton Senna at Imola in 1994. Until the perfect storm of disaster in Japan in 2014. Part of it was a literal storm, Typhoon Phanfone, which was lashing the area with rain. Adrian Sutil had already gone off the track at the corner in his Sauber, which was being recovered by a mobile crane. Bianchi went off at the same corner and hit the crane at speed. In modern motor racing, barriers are designed to be hit by racing cars. And racing cars are designed to hit barriers. But a crane is something else.

Bianchi was transported by road to hospital, the weather having grounded all medical helicopters. He spent a month in hospital in Japan before being relocated to a hospital in France. Then, the months went by. Nine of them, in total. There was no improvement in his condition, and on 17 July 2015, the family announced that he had passed away.

Thanks to Ferrari, Leclerc did end up at Sauber for the 2018 Formula 1 season, and he hit another emotional milestone along the way – taking part in the Monaco Grand Prix, around the streets where he'd grown up. The same streets where he had spent so much time with his late father. The same streets that his father had raced on.

That weekend provided another insight into Leclerc's emotional maturity. In the days leading up to his Monaco GP debut, Leclerc took part in a live video Q and A with renowned Formula 1 presenter Will Buxton. The subject of racing at home was raised, and Leclerc opened up about a white lie he'd told his father shortly before he died. 'Last year, before I actually signed [with Sauber], I told him I had signed in Formula 1 to make him happy,' he said. 'We knew that the end was near. I'm very happy to have managed to do that, and now I'm in Monaco, racing in Formula 1. And he can see that from up there.' The story clearly caught Buxton off guard. He tried to move on to the next question but, for a moment, he couldn't. 'I didn't know that . . . that's choked me up a bit, man,' he said. He tried again to continue the interview: 'Okay, right, questions, questions, questions. Which restaurant to visit in Monaco?' Leclerc started to answer, saw Buxton was still struggling and kindly rested his hand on the presenter's shoulder. There was a moment of composure before Leclerc said: 'There are lots of them. But Stars'N'Bars, if you like cars; there are lots of racing things there. It's pretty nice.'

That maturity stems from Leclerc's trauma, something he makes no secret about. In 2019, he told the *Guardian*: 'There have been moments that I wish never happened, but they have made me grow as a driver and helped me. The loss of my father and Jules. Two incredibly hard moments in my life that made me stronger as a person and a driver. Mentally I am stronger than I used to be. They definitely stay with you forever. Unfortunately I lost my father quite early; it changes you. It changes you forever.'

Leclerc is one of the great modern rookie stories. After that first year in F1 with Sauber, he was promoted straight to Ferrari. As of 2023, he is the lead driver for the most famous team in world motorsport. He's a grand prix winner. He carries Ferrari's hopes of its next world championship.

Monaco may be Leclerc's home. It may be the most famous street race in the world. I'm sure there's no race Leclerc would rather win.

But Baku will always be the place where Charles Leclerc showed the world that, without any doubt, he can deal with whatever life – and sport – throws at him.

10

MIAMI

Miami Grand Prix
Miami International Autodrome
5–7 May 2023

Just days after that punishing Baku outing, Oscar Piastri arrived in Miami for his first taste of being a Formula 1 driver on American soil.

The US was, for decades, a tough nut for Formula 1 to crack. The series did its best to get traction in the massive market, but it faced so much domestic competition. The country literally has its own version of Formula 1 in the IndyCar Series. Perhaps a crude simplification, but basically, that's what it is. Then there's NASCAR, which races 30-something times a year, keeping the average US revhead more than busy. F1 came and went from the US over the years, visiting classic circuits such as Watkins Glen and Indianapolis, until it found a modern home at the new Circuit of the Americas in Austin, Texas, in 2012.

Seven years later, someone at Netflix had the bright idea to make a docuseries about Formula 1. *Drive to Survive* was an immediate hit and sent the popularity of F1 into the stratosphere. Tens of millions of people became F1 fans overnight, and a lot of them were in the US. When the Austin race started rocking from 2019 onwards, Formula 1 responded by adding a race in Miami in 2022 and another in Las Vegas for 2023. Piastri had already faced his home grand prix, and all the pressure and fanfare that came with it; now it was time for a rockstar reception in the US. 'I was here last year, and it was probably by far the craziest weekend of the year that I went to,' said Piastri on the Thursday in Miami. 'There's definitely much more presence here in the US. I think from [a] media and marketing point of view, Melbourne was still the biggest [race] compared to here. But it's so far definitely the next busiest.'

In good news for Piastri, he was feeling significantly better than he had felt in Azerbaijan. 'I need to re-weigh myself first, but I'm pretty much back to how I should be in terms of fitness and just feeling,' he said. 'I don't know how much I weigh yet. But I'll keep an eye on that. I've managed to get food in the last few days, which is good.'

Coming out of Baku, the jury was still out on how successful McLaren's upgrades had been. Lando Norris, who'd finished ninth in the Azerbaijan race, mused that the baseline performance of the car was definitely better, but the unique track layout meant it hadn't translated into a noticeable difference in lap time. '[The changes are not] gonna help that much in the very slow-speed corners that we have [in Baku],' he explained. 'So, if you look at it on a pure lap-time basis, [the upgrades] probably didn't help us too much. A tiny bit, but not too much. Maybe Miami will see some bigger gains with some of the more medium-speed corners. But that's it for now. It's a small step forward; it's more like a different philosophy to have a baseline with. But more of the bigger gains are coming out in the future.'

Practice, however, told a different story. Norris was sixth fastest in Free Practice 2 at Miami, but beyond that, the car didn't look all that fast. Despite the struggles, there were some incredible words of praise from McLaren CEO Zak Brown during a team bosses' media conference. Veteran F1 journalist Adam Cooper asked Brown for his thoughts on Piastri's progress, given he'd been dealt a run of tough street circuits, sometimes completely unfamiliar to him, but was yet to wreck a car. 'Yeah, we're very impressed with him,' said Brown. 'He's very focused and has not really made any big mistakes. Just typical exploring the limits, the odd lock of a wheel here and there. The early indications are we've got a future world champion on our hands. We just need to work to give him a faster car.'

Even if McLaren had made gains, the midfield battle was still do or die. In Free Practice 3, the gap between Max Verstappen and Charles Leclerc in first and second place was four-tenths of a second. You had to go back to sixth on the ladder for the next four-tenths gap. The gap between Nico Hülkenberg in eighth, and Nyck de Vries in last place, was less than a second. Real hero-to-zero stuff if you get your lap right or wrong.

And boy did McLaren get it wrong. Both Norris and Piastri were bundled out in Q1, 16th and 19th respectively. 'It's been a difficult day,' said Piastri after qualifying. 'I think we were struggling for pace throughout the whole session today. It's super, super close. It's been the same story the whole year; we're at risk of going out in Q1 every weekend, but also where we have the chance to be in Q3 every weekend. Today was just at the back end of that bracket, unfortunately.'

Knowing that scoring points on pace wasn't possible, McLaren rolled the dice on tyre strategy for the Sunday's grand prix. Norris and Piastri both fitted soft tyres for the start of the race, which would ultimately make them the only two drivers to use that compound in the race. The plan was to make a fast start on the fastest tyres and then jump ship to the hardest compound for the remainder of the race. Apart from making up a few spots on the first lap, the strategy never looked like working. And to make Piastri's life even harder, his 'BBW' – otherwise known as brake-by-wire – failed a few laps after his pit stop.

Since hybrid technology arrived in Formula 1 in 2014, there has been a lot of complexity added to the braking system. Like most cars, depressing the brake pedal of an F1 car activates two master cylinders. For the front brakes, the master cylinder creates pressure that is transferred to calipers, which contain pistons that then push pads against a disc. The friction slows down the wheels. Quite conventional. But for the rear wheels, there are three pillars to braking – friction, engine braking and energy recovery from the hybrid system. That balance is managed electronically, which means the pressure from the master cylinder activates an electronic sensor that then talks to the engine control unit, which regulates the rear braking. Should that system fail, however, then the braking characteristics change – a huge challenge for a driver.

For Piastri, the BBW failure meant he had what is known in motorsport as a 'long' brake pedal, meaning it takes much more input from the driver before he or she starts to feel the pressure that indicates the car will start slowing down. There is nothing, literally nothing, that erodes driver confidence as comprehensively as a long brake pedal – particularly on a street circuit. How can you possibly drive flat-out towards a concrete wall with even a kernel of doubt that the car will slow down when you ask it to?

Piastri battled on and came home 19th, a fitting end to a difficult weekend. 'I had a brake that was about 10 metres long,' he said after the race. 'It was sudden. I hit the brakes one lap and the pedal went to the floor.' He then detailed why he hadn't fallen in love with the Miami layout. 'I think the first sector is quite cool with all the high-speed sections, but the second half of the lap, with all the slow, clunky bits, in these cars it's really quite slow and awkward. A lot of the corners are blind over crests, so you can't see half the corners. It's very low grip, especially off line.' At the very least, Andrea Stella recognised how well Piastri had dealt with the braking issue. 'Oscar was excellent in being able to cope with it,' he said. 'After having locked the tyres for three or four times, he kind of realised how we needed to adapt the way he was braking to this issue.'

More troubling than the braking issue for Piastri was the outright performance of the updated McLaren car. 'The main takeaway is that, after a decent weekend in Baku from a performance point of view, we had a reality check,' admitted

Stella. Given the lengths to which Piastri had gone to end up at McLaren instead of Alpine, droning around on the track in second-last place seemed particularly disappointing. At the same time, there were signs that all was not well at Alpine, either. While the team had got both its cars in the points in Miami, it followed a heck of a wack from CEO Laurent Rossi on French TV. 'It's disappointing, it's actually bad,' said Rossi about his team's performance up until Miami. 'This year ended up starting with a flawed performance and flawed delivery. It's obvious our position in the standings is not worthy of the resources we spend, and we are quite far – in fact, very far – from this year's end goal. I did not like the first grand prix, because there was a lot of – I'm sorry for saying this – amateur-ishness, which led to a result that wasn't right. It was mediocre, bad. And the last race in Baku was tremendously similar to the one in Bahrain. That is not acceptable.'

Results Summary

Free Practice 1: 12th (1m 31.810s, +1.68s)
Free Practice 2: 16th (1m 29.339s, +1.41s)
Free Practice 3: 18th (1m 29.375s, +1.84s)
Qualifying: 19th (1m 28.484s, +1.64s)
Race: 19th

Miami Grand Prix: A brief history

When Formula 1 started looking at venues for a potential second US race in 2017, Miami was on the shortlist from the start. A proposal for the NFL's Miami Dolphins owner Stephen Ross to promote a Miami street race was put forward to the City Commission, which unanimously voted to begin formal negotiations. Plan A was for the first race to take place in 2019 on a downtown circuit that would wind through Biscayne Boulevard and Bayfront Park, over a bridge and into the Port of Miami. It's no secret that Formula 1 enjoys luxurious yachts as a race backdrop, so it was a good fit. Except for a group of Bayfront Park residents who hated the idea and threatened legal action if the race went ahead in their backyard. The plan eventually got thrown in the 'too hard basket', with Formula 1 conceding that the race wouldn't happen in 2019, while Ross went back to the drawing board. He had already resolved to bring the Miami Open tennis tournament from Key Biscayne to Hard Rock Stadium, home of the Dolphins, in Miami Gardens. So why not take the grand prix there too? With that, the Miami International Autodrome was born.

But it was not clear sailing from there. The Miami Gardens City Commission immediately raised objections, which were overcome with the help of Miami-Dade mayor Carlos Gimenez. Then, a group of Miami Gardens residents gave it a shot, suing Formula 1, Gimenez, Hard Rock Stadium and the Dolphins. But there was no stopping the race this time. A 10-year deal was finally signed, and May 2022 was locked in for the first running of the new Miami Grand Prix.

Formula 1 had got its wish of a Miami race, but not its wish of luxury yachts next to the track. Or so it seemed. As a quirky tip of the hat to the original downtown plan, the organisers – led by Tom Garfinkel, vice chairman and CEO of both the Dolphins and Hard Rock Stadium – decided to build a 2200-square-metre Beach Club Zone . . . which, despite being 16 kilometres from the Atlantic Ocean, would feature a marina with real yachts. 'Initially, when we were looking at downtown [for the race], F1 had some ideas about wanting the shots of the yachts,' Garfinkel later explained to Autosport.com. 'When we moved [to the Hard Rock Stadium] for a number of reasons, most importantly because we didn't think we could have a good racing circuit downtown, I told F1 that you're gonna get your yacht shots, you're gonna have your yachts. They looked at me like I was crazy. And then I came back and drew it on the whiteboard and said, "I want a marina with yachts here, and we're gonna make it happen." And so we did.'

An area of solid vinyl 'water' was placed on the inside of turns 6, 7 and 8, and 10 luxury yachts were dry-docked among it to serve as super expensive hospitality units. It may sound easy, but it wasn't. In fact, the whole process of sourcing and transporting the yachts from the Port of Miami took around 10 months. Due to local permits, the yachts had to be transported at night, and special flooring was put in place so that the trucks wouldn't damage the track surface. The largest yacht took five hours to get into place.

But it proved to be worth it, even if only from a pure marketing perspective. The fake marina became a talking point at the track and a viral hit around the world during that first Miami Grand Prix weekend, with social media users going nuts over it. It was, of course, the butt of plenty of jokes, but Garfinkel welcomed the attention it brought to his race. 'I think we don't take ourselves too seriously,' he said. 'We're having some fun with it, right? I think people are enjoying it. I think the people on the back of those yachts watching the race will have fun, and I think the people that are sort of poking fun at it, I think it's funny, and it's great.

'We're not taking ourselves too seriously. We're trying to have some fun with it.'

11

IMOLA

Emilia Romagna Grand Prix
Autodromo Enzo e Dino Ferrari (Imola)
19–21 May 2023

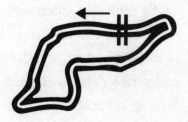

Imola is one of the more picturesque stops on the Formula 1 calendar, with the Autodromo Enzo e Dino Ferrari sitting on the banks of the Santerno, 40-odd kilometres from Bologna, in the beautiful Emilia-Romagna region of Northern Italy. That riverside location, however, proved extremely problematic in 2023.

In the couple of weeks following the Miami race, teams returned to their European bases ready to resume the European portion of the F1 season. By that point, Italy had already received a lashing from Mother Nature, with heavy rainfall in the country's north. On the Monday evening before the race weekend, the Department of Civil Protection issued a red alert for the Emilia-Romagna region. The alert covered Tuesday and Wednesday of that week, warning of high winds, heavy rain and thunderstorms that were likely to cause damage and flooding. The predicted figures were 100 millimetres of rain on Tuesday, which could swell to 150 millimetres on Wednesday. A meeting of the National Crisis Unit led to schools and roads being closed over fears they would end up under water. For the time being, though, Formula 1 remained confident the grand prix event would go ahead. In fact, it seemed like the perfect opportunity to give Pirelli's new wet tyre its competitive debut.

By Tuesday afternoon, however, things looked vastly different. The Santerno broke its banks as water began pooling in the F1 paddock and the TV compound at the circuit. Team and series personnel were evacuated from the track as the local government warned against travelling to, or around, the region. The following day, Imola was still a no-go zone, on what would usually be set-up day for the teams. Some of the Alpine crew members had to change hotels after their original accommodation became flooded. Still, while bracing for organisational chaos and disruption, the general feeling was that the weather would ease and cars would hit the track, as planned, on Friday.

But as Wednesday morning wore on, that sentiment began to change. Rain at the circuit did indeed begin to ease, but the damage was done. The mountains south of Imola had copped closer to 250 millimetres of rain, rather than the 150 millimetres that had been forecast. The Santerno was bulging, and the idea of being able to safely transport people in and out of the circuit – team crews, F1 staff, spectators – was becoming more and more far-fetched. And it wasn't only flooding at the circuit itself that was an issue. Running a major sporting event takes up a lot of response services – local police, ambulances and so on. Would a Formula 1 race really be the best use of those resources while people in the region were losing their homes and, in some cases, their lives?

Italy's deputy prime minister, Matteo Salvini, certainly didn't think so, taking to television channel Sky Italia to call for the race to be postponed. At that point there had already been five deaths due to flooding in the region, and Salvini wanted all services' efforts poured into relief work, not a grand prix. Formula 1 responded early on Wednesday afternoon by cancelling the race. 'It is such a tragedy to see what has happened to Imola and Emilia-Romagna, the town and region that I grew up in, and my thoughts and prayers are with the victims of the flooding and the families and communities affected,' read a statement from Formula 1 CEO Stefano Domenicali. 'I want to express my gratitude and admiration for the incredible emergency services who are working tirelessly to help those who need help and alleviate the situation – they are heroes and the whole of Italy is proud of them. The decision that has been taken is the right one for everyone in the local communities and the F1 family as we need to ensure safety and not create extra burden for the authorities while they deal with this very awful situation.'

It was the responsible call and, for once, made in a timely manner. It was a stark contrast to the Melbourne debacle in 2020, when both F1 and the Australian Grand Prix Corporation clung to the idea of running the race, despite the rapidly unfolding COVID-19 situation. In that case, the event was called off on the Friday morning of the grand prix weekend, while thousands of confused and angry spectators waited at Albert Park's locked gates.

The decision at Imola received unanimous support from the F1 teams and drivers. In the days that followed, Scuderia AlphaTauri driver Yuki Tsunoda was snapped on social media helping clean-up efforts in nearby Faenza, where both he and the team are based. Ferrari, meanwhile, donated a million euros to help those affected by the flooding. Formula 1 and its teams had banded together for the greater good . . . and a handy PR win.

Results Summary

Called off: No sessions held.

Emilia Romagna Grand Prix: A brief history

The 2023 Emilia Romagna Grand Prix wasn't the first time Formula 1 had run afoul of Mother Nature. In fact, as safety standards, and expectations, have risen, wet weather has become increasingly disruptive to the race schedule – despite Formula 1 still technically being an all-weather sport, unlike NASCAR, which traditionally avoids racing in the rain (although it has softened that stance recently, introducing a wet tyre for some circuits).

One circuit famous for its terrible weather is Spa-Francorchamps, nestled in the Ardennes in Belgium. The weather was actually fine and warm in the lead-up to the 1966 Belgian Grand Prix, to the point where qualifying had been delayed on the Saturday as fire fighters battled a blaze in the Burnenville hills. Then, on the Sunday, a sudden downpour soaked the field halfway around the opening lap. Only 7 of the 15 cars that had started the race made it to the end of lap 1.

Among those to crash out was Scotsman Jackie Stewart, who hit a telephone pole. With no help from officials in sight, he was extracted from his destroyed BRM car by fellow racers Graham Hill and Bob Bondurant, who laid him down in a nearby barn and removed his fuel-soaked race suit. He was later taken to the circuit's rudimentary medical centre, where his stretcher was left on a floor covered in cigarette butts, until he was eventually taken to hospital in Liege . . . but not before the ambulance driver got lost along the way. Because of his misadventure, Stewart would go on to become one of the most important safety crusaders in the sport's history, responsible for the introduction of full-face helmets, seat belts and so much more in F1.

Weather played havoc at Spa again in 1985. That year the issue started with too much wet and cold weather in the winter, which delayed planned circuit-resurfacing efforts. The resurfacing didn't take place until the immediate lead-up to the Belgian Grand Prix in the early summer. That wasn't enough time for the new surface to cure, though, and the Formula 1 cars started tearing chunks out of the road in practice sessions. Emergency resurfacing took place on the Saturday night, but it wasn't sufficient, and the race was rescheduled for September.

In 2021, the weather struck at Spa once more. With consistent downpours on race day, race control delayed the start from 3 p.m. to 3.25 p.m., at which point the field completed two formation laps. But the conditions were deemed too difficult, and the race was red-flagged before it could begin. It wasn't until 6.17 p.m. that there was another attempt to start the race – an attempt seen by many as cynical. The field followed the safety car for two full laps, which ensured that the race could be officially classified. After those two laps, the cars returned to the pit lane, where they stayed until the race was formally declared at 6.44 p.m. As less than two-thirds of the race had been run, half world championships points were awarded – laughable given there hadn't been a single lap of actual racing. Race control argued that the attempt to start the race was genuine and it was only when the rain increased once the field had been sent out for a second time that had made it impossible for the race to continue. Cynics, however, suggested that the two laps behind the safety car had only been completed so that Formula 1 could officially classify the race, voiding any obligation to provide refunds to the soaking-wet fans waiting trackside.

The farcical 2021 Belgian race – clocked at a total of 3m 27.071s – took over the record for the shortest grand prix of all time from Australia. Back in 1991, Adelaide was still the host of the Australian Grand Prix, then still the last race of the season. With Ayrton Senna having already locked up the world championship, the race was poised as a light-hearted dead-rubber event to see out the year. Senna qualified on pole and he looked set to put an exclamation point on what would prove to be his final title. Then, on the Sunday, the skies over Adelaide opened. The street circuit had dealt with water before – the 1989 race was hit with rain as well – but this was different. After just 14 laps, and multiple crashes, the race was called off. Senna was awarded the victory, while Nigel Mansell, who had crashed out of the race right before it was red-flagged, was reinstated in second place thanks to the count-back rule.

Perhaps the greatest anomaly in the race was diminutive Italian Gianni Morbidelli. Driver Alain Prost had been sacked by Ferrari for publicly criticising the team, and Morbidelli, who'd been racing for back-markers Minardi, was drafted into the Scuderia as a one-off. His career as a Ferrari driver would last 24 minutes of racing. He finished sixth and scored his first half world championship point. Adelaide would, four years later, yield the only podium of Morbidelli's Formula 1 career; he finished third for Footwork-Hart in a race where Damon Hill won by two laps and only eight cars made the finish line.

12

MONACO

Monaco Grand Prix
Circuit de Monaco
26–28 May 2023

There is no race in Formula 1 as famous, glamorous or prestigious as the Monaco Grand Prix. The streets of the principality
are iconic, bound to Formula 1 forever. And winning the race
instantly puts you among the motor-racing elite.

In fact, Monaco is part of motor racing's unofficial Triple
Crown, alongside the Indianapolis 500 and the 24 Hours of
Le Mans. McLaren even paid tribute to the Triple Crown with
a one-off livery for the 2023 Monaco Grand Prix. The rear end
of the car featured the classic McLaren papaya colour scheme,
a tip of the hat to Johnny Rutherford's victory in the 1974 Indy
500 in a McLaren M16C/D. The orange cut into an ice-white
middle section that formed the distinctive triangular shape
of Marlboro. The shape itself couldn't be marketed, of course,
thanks to modern tobacco-advertising laws, but McLaren

admitted that the white section was a homage to Alain Prost's 1984 Monaco GP win in the team's Marlboro-backed MP4/2. The front of the 2023 car was painted black, a tribute to the McLaren F1 GTR sportscar that won the 24 Hours of Le Mans in 1995 with JJ Lehto, Yannick Dalmas and Masanori Sekiya at the wheel.

Such is the principality's importance in motorsport, there's an old wives' tale that the royal family doesn't pay a race-hosting fee like the rest of the world, based on Formula 1 needing Monaco more than Monaco needs Formula 1. The rumour is not true, but at an estimated US$15 million per year, the figure is the lowest fee on the F1 schedule by far (Qatar is thought to fork out about US$55 million for its race).

Up until 2022, the first two practice sessions for the Monaco Grand Prix took place on the Thursday, followed by no track action on the Friday, which is the Monégasque Ascension Day public holiday. It was a unique Monaco quirk. The circuit would then be closed for more practice and qualifying sessions on Saturday, ahead of the race on Sunday. But thanks to Formula 1's rapidly expanding schedule, it was decided that Monaco would revert to a traditional three-day format in 2023. Regardless of the day, practice was underwhelming for Piastri. It wasn't his first taste of Monaco, a place he knew from the junior formulae. But tackling a tight, unforgiving street circuit in a Formula 1 car is always a challenge. And it wasn't a challenge that Piastri rose to. He finished more than a second off the pace on Friday, almost at the tail end of the field. 'It was a tricky day,' said a downbeat Piastri. 'In FP2 I improved in the areas I needed to from FP1, [so] now it is just [about] catching up in the rest of the places. Especially around here with all the low-speed corners, things can add up very quickly, so we will work on things overnight and see where I can do better.'

The early signs on Saturday didn't show much improvement. As practice came to a close with the third one-hour session, Lando Norris was in a smart fifth place while Piastri was second last. Lap times in practice are never truly indicative of performance thanks to different fuel loads and engine modes, but having been one of the final four drivers across all three sessions, and having gone backwards position-wise each time out, things weren't looking great for the rookie.

But that's the thing about Oscar Piastri. Glory runs in practice to pop up near the front of the pack aren't his style. He learns from the good and the bad. He takes his time. And when it matters, he just has a way of getting the job done.

In Monaco, when it matters is qualifying. The reality is that modern Formula 1 has long outgrown the classic circuit. It exists, undoubtedly, on the calendar through its legacy. And rightly so – tradition plays its part in sport, and the day Formula 1 forgoes its appearance in Monaco will be a devastating one. But at the same time, it's unrealistic to expect a deluge of amazing wheel-to-wheel racing to break out at this particular track. The delta advantage required to execute a pass around there is crazy. Strategy will always see a few positions change hands, as will human error, given how close the walls are. But if you really want to win, your best way to do it is to qualify on pole. Where you qualify will, very likely, reflect where you finish the race.

The first step for Piastri was, based on his practice form, to get out of Q1. He managed that much with a tenth of a second up his sleeve, thanks to a time of 1m 13.006s – his best of the weekend so far by almost a second. He found another six-tenths of a second in Q2 as he came within one position of securing a highly unexpected Q3 appearance, ending up 11th on the grid. Even the very measured Piastri admitted he was impressed by the gains he'd made on Saturday. 'I think by the end of qualifying I was quite happy with it,' he said. 'I think up until that point, it wasn't even really building up. I was consistently six- or seven-tenths off. And then I closed the gap quite a lot in qualifying. I made quite a big step, which I was very happy about. I think for the future, obviously, I want to be on the pace earlier than the first round of qualifying; it makes life a bit easier. But I was quite happy with how I performed in qualifying.'

When pressed on why he'd taken so long to show some pace, Piastri responded: 'We changed a few things on the car. We've been going back and forth a little bit through the weekend. But yeah, I mean, before qualifying there wasn't seven-tenths in the car. So I think I made quite a big improvement. I think the car also gave me a bit more confidence in qualifying. I probably pushed a little bit more as well, got a bit close to the walls. I think with the driving style and stuff like that, especially around a track like Monaco, it's taken me longer than I would have liked to get up to speed. I think I just started the qualifying session well . . . in all the practice sessions, I always started the first lap on the back foot, trying to catch up. I started qualifying a bit better this time.

And then just had a bit more confidence through the rest of the session.'

If you want any chance of success at Monaco, you need to survive the first lap of the race. Yes, that is stating the obvious. And yes, it's the case for every single race, not just Monaco. But Monaco has one of the more challenging opening laps on the F1 calendar, particularly if you're at the back of the pack. The reason for that is the legendary Fairmont Hairpin, one of the slowest corners in Formula 1. It's a single-lane corner; if you stray wide of the only line, you'll end up making a three-point turn. Given how narrow it is, and the fact that there is zero run-off, you don't even have to crash there yourself for your day to be ruined. It could be a car five positions ahead of you that gets the corner wrong, hits the barriers and blocks the track. It could be a car five positions behind you that brakes too late, nudges the car immediately ahead and causes a chain reaction that puts you into the wall. On that first lap, a mistake from almost any driver in the field can take any other driver in the field out of the race.

In 2023, though, it was a mostly tame start to the race, save for Lance Stroll running his Aston Martin high into the infamous hairpin. In fact, the first 50 laps of the race were pretty tame, particularly for the McLaren drivers. Norris, on medium-compound tyres, ran around the track in 10th place, with Piastri, using hard-compound rubber, about five seconds behind him in 11th. On lap 52, Norris made his pit stop to ditch the mediums and switch to hards, which reversed the positions of the two McLaren drivers. And then reports of rain started. Initially, it was Mercedes driver George Russell who called back to his pits to inform them it was 'spitting' at turn 3. The rain became more consistent, forcing the drivers on slick tyres to tiptoe their way from Massenet to Portier, eight corners into the lap. Most racing drivers will tell you that they like full dry conditions and don't mind full wet conditions. What they hate is when it's anywhere in between. A slightly damp track means that a wet set-up, and wet tyres, don't really help. Isolated rain is even harder to deal with. In this case, it was incredibly wet in one sector of the track – but the rest of the track was dry. So, if you switch to a super-soft-compound wet tyre, you'll tear it to shreds on the dry sections of the track. Oh, and street circuits make rain even more difficult to cope with, as there are painted white lines – which become incredibly slippery – heading in all sorts of directions.

As the rain continued, a number of drivers decided to roll the dice on intermediate tyres, a lightly grooved soft-compound tyre. Piastri hung onto his slick tyres until lap 55 when enough was enough and he decided to take on intermediates. Having not pitted earlier in the race actually worked in Piastri's favour, as that track position meant he was serviced first, while Norris had to wait behind him in the pit lane to receive intermediate tyres of his own. In the toughest of tough conditions, Piastri, unsurprisingly, couldn't keep the experienced Norris behind him. But when Norris was ahead once again, Piastri was able to mimic the progress of his teammate, the pair closing up on the back of Yuki Tsunoda, who was struggling with braking modes in his AlphaTauri. With 10 laps to go, Norris charged around the outside of Tsunoda into the first corner, Saint Devote. A lap later, Piastri pulled a carbon-copy move. Well, almost. There was a little lock of the brake as Piastri set the passing move into motion, something that can oh-so-easily end with a car in the wall. But Piastri eased off the brake just in time, finding the grip he needed to get around the corner and set up a double points finish for McLaren with ninth and tenth place.

A world championship point, only his second points finish in his career, left Piastri delighted off the back of what he felt was his toughest test in his brief time as a Formula 1 driver. 'On a personal note, after all the practice sessions, I wasn't very pleased with my driving, like, consistently six-tenths off,' said Piastri. 'It wasn't a very nice feeling ... The race itself was probably the most tricky of the year as well. But these are the weekends where you learn the most. I don't think it gets too much harder than Monaco in the rain on slicks, so [I'm] happy with that.'

When pressed on the challenge of snaking between the street circuit's walls in those mixed conditions, Piastri revealed that he did almost crash his car while momentarily splitting his attention between driving and speaking on the radio. At the same time, a stint behind reigning world champion Max Verstappen, even as a lap down, was a wonderful opportunity to learn. 'I don't think there were any touches [with the walls], but some very, very close moments, especially on the slicks,' Piastri said. 'I think one time I keyed up on the radio to talk and almost put it on the wall, like, mid-sentence. I won't do that next time. I think having Max right in front of me was actually quite useful in some ways, because that was my first time on slicks on a rainy track in an F1 car and having Max there, I obviously knew that if there's going to be anyone that's probably going to be okay, it's probably gonna be him. That was quite useful in some ways.'

Results Summary

Free Practice 1: 17th (1m 15.192s, +1.82s)
Free Practice 2: 18th (1m 13.673s, +1.21s)
Free Practice 3: 19th (1m 13.998s, +1.22s)
Qualifying: 11th (1m 12.395s, +1.03s)
Race: 10th

Monaco Grand Prix: A brief history

Monaco is a legendary Formula 1 circuit, but it's also the place that can make a Formula 1 legend. Alain Prost is undoubtedly a Formula 1 legend, but, just as undoubtedly, he took an interesting approach to success. His nickname was 'the Professor', thanks to his calculated, analytical approach to racing. The way he went about the business wasn't that spectacular. His driving style was smooth and efficient, and he would take every advantage he could find – on or off the track. If he needed to play politics, he would. Prost's ruthlessness had dimensions probably not seen in Formula 1 before.

Ayrton Senna, meanwhile, was different. He had that Brazilian flare. He was as razor sharp as Prost but more wrapped up in his own natural ability and bursting with flamboyance. Many believe that, as smart as Senna was, there was an element of naivety to his approach to Formula 1. Why play politics when you can simply be faster than the opposition? Senna would eventually learn that tactic doesn't quite work while teammates with Prost at McLaren later in his career.

Perhaps he should have learnt that lesson from the 1984 Monaco Grand Prix.

That year, Prost was a well-established F1 driver, part of the all-conquering McLaren team and a man destined to be world champion. Senna, meanwhile, was the reigning British Formula 3 champion – which at the time was the feeder series directly to Formula 1 – and an F1 rookie with the midfield Toleman squad. It was his first Monaco GP. And the weather wasn't playing nice. Sunday morning welcomed a drizzle in the principality. By the afternoon, around the start time for the race, that drizzle had turned into a downpour. Prost led early before being overhauled by Nigel Mansell. At the same time, Senna was on a charge from 13th on the grid. It took just 15 laps for him to be sitting in fourth place, having blasted past the likes of huge names Keke Rosberg, René Arnoux and Niki Lauda, the man who would later win the world title.

Senna would later become well known as a rain master, but at the time the display was mind-blowing. Back at the front of the field, Mansell's charge came to an end when he spun into the barriers on lap 16. That handed the lead back to Prost who, with a 32-second advantage over the field, looked perfectly situated to cruise to victory. Except for a pesky Brazilian in an unfancied Toleman. Suddenly, that 32-second margin was disappearing at a rate of two, three seconds a lap. Senna had only started in five other races, finished two, and yet here he was, reeling in an 11-time grand prix winner at an incredible rate. According to some on the ground, the rain actually began to ease around the lap 29 mark. At which point Prost began waving frantically to the pits each time he passed, clearly imploring the clerk of the course, Jacky Ickx, to call off the race on safety grounds. On lap 32, Prost's pleas that the conditions were too dangerous were rewarded when the red and chequered flags were consecutively waved to end the race. Prost slowed as soon as he crossed the line, just as Senna burst past. Senna thought he had won, but the rules fell in favour of Prost. He had lobbied for the race's early end, knowing he was a sitting duck to Senna. The timing was perfect. There were those out there who wondered if Ickx, being a Porsche factory driver in the World Endurance Championship, had made his decision to the purposeful benefit of Prost, who was driving a Porsche-powered McLaren. Not a claim that was ever substantiated, of course. At the very least, it was a beautiful example of Prost's ability to get things to swing his way.

Senna might not have won the race, but it signalled his arrival in Formula 1. He was clearly a talent worthy of racing's top tier, and the result was – realistically – as significant as if he'd actually won. The following year he was snapped up by Lotus and broke through for a pair of grand prix wins. In 1987, while still at Lotus, he finally won the Monaco Grand Prix for the first time. He would go on to become a six-time winner at Monaco, the most successful in the history of the event, with consecutive victories between 1989 and 1993. Accompanying him in the record books are Graham Hill and Michael Schumacher (five each) and Prost at four. On three wins are Stirling Moss, Jackie Stewart, Nico Rosberg and Lewis Hamilton – the best of those still competing in Formula 1.

The thing is, Senna could so easily have been a seven-time Monaco winner. The one that got away was 1988, the peak of McLaren's dominance in Formula 1, with the Gordon Murray– designed MP4/4 winning 15 of the 16 races that season in the hands of Prost and Senna. In Monaco, the Brazilian was by far the better of the two McLaren drivers. In qualifying, Senna took pole position with a margin of almost 1.5 seconds over Prost, who was second fastest on the day. It was a crushing effort, one that Senna would later explain was almost like an out of body experi- ence as he let instinct take over. And his trance-like form carried over into the race, where he pulled 55 seconds clear of Prost in the first 60-odd laps. Then, on lap 67, his trance momentarily broke and his McLaren smacked the barrier at Portier. A devastated Senna climbed from the damaged car and, instead of returning to the pits, walked home to his apartment. He didn't contact the team until later that evening.

Back in 2019, Murray spoke about that remarkable Monaco weekend to the *Guardian*. 'Everybody was stunned at his quali- fying,' Murray said. 'Everybody. Even the team who were used to him. Success at Monaco in particular is absolutely proportional to the courage. It's precision and courage. Commitment on the braking points and placing the car on the apex. Qualifying was a combination of those two things.' Expanding on Senna, Murray added: 'We became good friends. Although he was very intense about his racing, he was relatively quiet and almost religious sometimes outside the racing. We trusted each other and worked together very well. He loved setting the car up for qualifying. I would manage the session. We had a very simple system of me standing up on the wall with a stopwatch and watching for gaps to send him out.' And Senna's shock early exit from the race, while in such a commanding position? 'I knew Ayrton well and he would have been so angry with himself because his concentration and his precision and dedication was so intense,' Murray said. 'To do something like that would have destroyed him completely. He didn't want to face the team but not through embarrassment. I have told drivers, "If you do crash the car, don't come back to the pits because I don't want to see you." Drivers who do that a lot don't want to face the team, but not Ayrton. He would have been so upset with himself he would have wanted to contemplate that. He was that sort of guy.'

Adding to the pain was the fact that the rivalry with Prost was a bitter one, to say the least. But we'll cover that off later in the season . . .

13

SPAIN

Spanish Grand Prix
Circuit de Barcelona-Catalunya
2–4 June 2023

After one of the most anticipated races of the year in Monaco, the Spanish Grand Prix is, unfairly, seen as one of the most boring. It's not Spain's fault. It's not even the Circuit de Barcelona-Catalunya's fault. Well, actually, it kind of is. Between the circuit's central European location, Spain's relatively mild weather, and the diverse nature of the layout, Barcelona was for a long time *the* go-to testing track for Formula 1. So many pre- and in-season testing laps were turned around the Barcelona circuit. For so long, F1 fans were oversaturated with the place. As were the drivers. And the teams. By the time the grand prix weekend rolled around, everyone found it a little bit, well, boring. These days, the majority of the testing takes place in Bahrain, but the legacy of boring Barcelona kind of lives on . . .

But while the build-up to the 2023 Spanish Grand Prix was, generally, underwhelming, there was some excitement for McLaren fans. There was finally a firm date for the 'kind of B-spec car' that had been promised to arrive before the summer break. The significantly reworked design had been signed off at the Woking factory and would be introduced between the Austrian and British Grands Prix. 'The plan is we need to get the car more competitive,' said Andrea Stella. 'We've now released the package which should be available between Austria and Britain, and this is what should take the car to a more competitive level. It's progressing the car, evolving concepts we see as successful. It will be noticeably different to what we have at the moment. It will be the foundation for future developments next year. For the second part of the season there should be another major upgrade.' Given the Baku upgrades hadn't necessarily delivered, and the existing McLaren was a midfield car on even its best weekends, expectations were limited. But at least there was a date for the next wave of changes.

In 2022, Formula 1 made a fundamental change to its technical regulations. The complex aerodynamics of the cars had taken their toll on the ability for drivers to race. With a stepped floor and a series of winglets and wings all over the top of the car, incredible downforce figures could be produced. The cars were ridiculously fast. But all that surface downforce left a huge wake of what is known as 'dirty air', disturbed airflow that won't efficiently work on the wings of the car following behind. Even if you're faster than the car in front, eventually you'll hit an invisible wall of dirty air as you try to execute a pass. Your downforce will disappear, your tyres will overheat, and you've got no chance of getting past the car ahead of you.

So, Formula 1 resolved to improve the racing with a new set of regulations that limited dirty air. The answer to that was a technical phenomenon that was outlawed by Formula 1 back in the 1980s – ground effect. In simple terms, ground effect is the use of the floor of the car to generate downforce, rather than wings being depressed by surface air. If the floor has the right shape, and the air can effectively be trapped under the car, it then sucks the car onto the ground and remarkable downforce levels – with next to no drag penalty – can be created. Attempts at creating ground effect first appeared in Formula 1 in the early 1970s; however, it wasn't until the late 1970s that it was properly harnessed by Lotus. As the rest of the teams quickly embraced the concept, cornering speeds in Formula 1 skyrocketed – to the point where the technology became too dangerous. Circuit design and safety standards simply couldn't keep up with the speed of the cars. The reliance on ground effect was also risky because the instant 'contact' between the bottom of the car and the ground was lost, so was the downforce. If it happened mid-corner, a high-speed crash was unavoidable.

At the end of 1982, the FIA (or FISA, a motorsport-specific FIA body that existed at the time) banned ground effect and sliding skirts that would trap the air under the cars from Formula 1 and mandated flat floors. That remained the case until 2022, when the concept was revived to lower the reliance on surface aerodynamics and solve the dirty air problem. But when ground effect returned to F1, it brought an old friend back with it – porpoising. During the first ground-effect era, cars would often bounce on the track at high speed. As the air speed under the car increases, it sucks the car closer and closer to the ground. But once the car makes contact with the ground, the airflow stalls. That happens over and over again, causing the cars to bounce violently, an effect known as porpoising.

Porpoising came back with a vengeance on the 2022 cars. It affected some cars worse than others, with the likes of Mercedes and Ferrari badly hit by the problem. It was severe enough that there were concerns over the wellbeing of the drivers, and what effect the bouncing would have on their spines and brains. The issue could be alleviated by lifting the ride height of the car, but that came at a performance cost. A driver will sacrifice his spine if there is some lap time up for grabs. Porpoising was such a huge talking point across the 2022 season that, in response, the FIA imposed a 15-milli-metre lift of the minimum floor-edge height for 2023.

It seemed to work – at least until Formula 1 arrived in Barcelona. Suddenly, in Friday practice, drivers reported bouncing, most notably on the entry phase to the fast final corner of the track. That initially raised some concerns, although McLaren team principal Andrea Stella wasn't too worried. The good news, he said, was that all the cars, includ-ing the Red Bull, had been bouncing. Even at the worst of the porpoising in 2022, the Red Bull package had been 'robust', as Stella put it, against bouncing. So, the fact that it was suddenly an issue for the benchmark team suggested it was a circuit-specific issue, not a widespread return of the phenomenon.

In terms of performance, there wasn't much to write home about from the McLaren drivers. As was becoming a theme for Piastri, there were no practice heroics. The only real moment of excitement happened 15 minutes into Free Practice 2 when George Russell came flying up onto the back of Piastri's car into turn 10, seemingly assuming the slow-moving Australian would get out of the way. Piastri held his line through the tight left-hander and Russell was forced to take to the gravel. 'Who the fuck was that in the McLaren?' he fumed over the radio.

Somewhat unusually for Spain, weather affected Saturday's running. Conditions were mixed through Free Practice 3 before drivers faced a gloomy circuit, with damp patches, for qualifying. It was nowhere near damp enough for anything but a soft slick tyre, but there was a small river running across the track at turn 11 as the earlier rain drained across the circuit. That came as a surprise for Yuki Tsunoda, who gassed up his AlphaTauri on the exit of the corner and was immediately tipped into a high-speed spin. And then it happened to Valtteri Bottas. And then Nyck de Vries.

There were no such dramas for the McLaren drivers, though, with Piastri navigating the tricky conditions to log a 1m 13.691s, good enough for an easy passage to Q2. The second segment of qualifying was a little more tense, and both Norris and Piastri slipped into the drop zone as the clock ticked down. That left them both relying on their final runs to get through. Norris nailed his lap, going second quickest, just a hundredth of a second slower than Max Verstappen. A few seconds later,

Piastri crossed the line in sixth. Phew. After a very average showing in practice, the McLaren package had come alive with low fuel and in the cool conditions. To the point where Norris was able to stick his car third on the grid, a genuine shock result. Piastri could have been right there too, except for a costly mistake on his final run in Q3. He braked slightly late for turn 10, missed the apex and then found some of the patchy water that was sitting off the racing line. Game over, as he would later put it. He was six-tenths slower than his Q2 time and left starting on the outside of the fifth row on the grid. Still, for the McLarens, even reaching Q3 was somewhat surprising given every prior indication. 'I'm shocked to be here,' said Norris of his third place. 'We've not really brought anything to the car this weekend; the last upgrade we had was Baku with the floor and even that didn't give us a lot of performance, just a different direction to go in.' At the same time, Norris warned that the race could be a different story; there was a sense that qualifying had been helped by a perfect storm of conditions. 'Where we'll be in the race is a tough one. I think on average, we've been the fifth [or] sixth best team, so I'm not expecting a huge amount better than that, but we have a chance of racing the Alpines and some of the other cars. I don't think we're necessarily racing Astons. Ferraris will be tough, but we never know.'

The race was indeed a much tougher affair for McLaren. Any chance of Norris converting his sky-high starting spot into decent points disappeared within two corners. He left the door too far open for Lewis Hamilton on the run to turn 1, the Mercedes driver easing ahead in the transition to turn 2. In a moment of desperation Norris then dangled the nose of his McLaren inside the Mercedes, he and Hamilton making contact. 'I've got damage,' he immediately reported over the radio before pitting for a new nose and front wing. Piastri stayed out of trouble, but never had any pace. Saturday seemed like a distant memory as Piastri faded back to 13th, while Norris could only recover to 17th. 'It was just a long afternoon,' Piastri explained after the race. 'Just didn't have the pace to really do anything. Pretty poor first lap for myself as well, which didn't help things, but I don't think we really had the pace to stay in the points anyway. We'll have a look at why we struggled so much today compared to yesterday . . .

'I think yesterday was obviously not expected. I don't think we're, in normal circumstances, able to put the car that high up on the grid. Today was maybe a bit more back to reality. Probably a more difficult day than what we would have hoped, even considering.'

The worrying thing was that, cold-weather qualifying aside, Barcelona was a true test of pace for McLaren, a track without the weirdness of street circuits like Baku and Monaco. And things didn't look good. The second phase of the upgrades couldn't come soon enough.

Results Summary

Free Practice 1: 17th (1m 16.353s, +1.75s)
Free Practice 2: 12th (1m 14.583s, +0.68s)
Free Practice 3: 15th (1m 15.105s, +1.44s)
Qualifying: 10th (1m 13.682s, +1.41s)
Race: 13th

Spanish Grand Prix: A brief history

There have been some remarkable maiden F1 wins at the Circuit de Barcelona-Catalunya. Some have marked the birth of a legend. Others most definitely have not. The story of Pastor Maldonado falls into the second category.

The Venezuelan driver worked his way through Europe's junior open-wheeler ranks in the mid-2000s, eventually making it to GP2 in 2007. Three years later, he charged to the series title, which put him on the map in terms of Formula 1 interest. It wasn't only his dominance in GP2 that had teams at the less-classy end of the constructors' standings interested in him, though. It was the healthy backing he had from PDVSA, Venezuela's state oil company. The once dominant Williams team, which had been BMW's factory presence in Formula 1 until 2005, had by that point found itself bouncing around the midfield, using customer engines from Cosworth, then Toyota, and then Cosworth again. Even as late as 2010, the team could draw respectable driving talent. That year, the line-up was Rubens Barrichello – a race winner as recently as 2009 – and highly rated young German talent Nico Hülkenberg. But as funding seemingly became harder to obtain, the team decided to replace 'Hulk' with the well-backed reigning GP2 champ for 2011. It proved to be Williams' least successful campaign in Formula 1 history, with two ninth place finishes for Barrichello, and a tenth for Maldonado, as the team slumped to ninth in the constructors' standings.

For the 2012 season, Williams reunited with engine supplier Renault. The return of the Williams–Renault moniker conjured up memories of Williams' dominance that had yielded constructors' titles in 1991–94 and again in 1996 and 1997. There was even a return of perhaps the most famous name in Formula 1 history. Bruno Senna, nephew of the great Ayrton Senna, was signed in place of Barrichello to partner Maldonado. A great story, except that – with the greatest respect – Bruno was no Ayrton. The team denied it at the time, but, like Maldonado, it was a signing of financial convenience, given Senna enjoyed good backing from Brazil. But as much as it was a questionable driver line-up, there was a moment of magic for Williams in 2012. And it came from Maldonado.

There were some promising signs in the early races, including a sixth-place finish for Senna in Malaysia, and a double points finish (Senna seventh and Maldonado eighth) in China. But what happened in Barcelona was highly unexpected. For whatever reason, Maldonado was a front-running force. He initially qualified second for the race behind Lewis Hamilton, a sensational result on its own. Hamilton's car then stopped on his way back to the pits after his pole lap as it had run out of fuel, something the race officials deemed a no-no, as McLaren couldn't provide a mandatory fuel sample. Hamilton was sent to the back of the grid and Maldonado scored the first, and only, pole of his Formula 1 career.

Maldonado was joined on the front row by Ferrari superstar, and local hero, Fernando Alonso. When Alonso got the better of the jumps at the start and barged his way into the lead at turn 1, it seemed that the dream of a shock new winner in Barcelona was over. Except Maldonado was able to stay within touching distance of the race leader, and at times looked to be the faster of the top two. When Fernando Alonso found himself held up ever so slightly by backmarker Charles Pic before making his second stop, the advantage swung Maldonado's way. And as the laps ticked down,

Maldonado found himself leading the race, albeit under great pressure from Alonso and Kimi Räikkönen – drivers with three world championships between them. Maldonado held his nerve to score a freak, but in no way a fluke, first win. Adding to the drama, Maldonado made headlines twice that Sunday. Not even 90 minutes after the race, as Williams personnel partied in the garage, a faulty fuel rig sparked a fire. Maldonado – still in his driving suit – was photographed charging through the smoke with his 12-year-old cousin Manuel on his back. Manuel was recovering from a broken leg at the time and unable to run. Maldonado wasn't just a grand prix winner. He was a hero.

The nature of his win did cast doubt over Maldonado's 'pay driver' reputation. Maybe he was the real deal after all. Unfortunately (for him), it would prove to be his only win in Formula 1. And his only podium. He continued with Williams for the 2013 season before shifting to the struggling Lotus F1 team for a two-year stint in 2014 and 2015. It turned out that the 2012 Spanish Grand Prix wasn't the starting point of a Formula 1 legend after all.

The 2016 Spanish Grand Prix, however, is a very different story. That was the race that saw Max Verstappen make an utterly sensational debut for Red Bull Racing.

Verstappen had been ultra-successful in karting, before bursting onto the European open-wheeler scene as a teenager. In 2014, he, Esteban Ocon and Tom Blomqvist battled for the European Formula 3 title. Ocon won the title ahead of Blomqvist, but the Dutchman, just 16 going on 17, became the hottest property on the motorsport market. There were rumours at the time that Mercedes was sniffing around for a development deal, which probably would have seen Verstappen head to GP2 to be readied for Formula 1. Then, Red Bull made a far more attractive offer. 'Forget GP2,' they are rumoured to have said. 'Sign with us, and we'll stick you in a Formula 1 car next season.'

So, a 17-year-old Verstappen joined the F1 grid with Red Bull's junior team, then known as Toro Rosso, for the 2015 season. When he debuted at the Australian Grand Prix that year, he was exactly 17 years and 166 days old – the youngest ever grand prix driver. At the next race in Malaysia, he became the youngest ever driver to score world championship points. There were times in that rookie season when his inexperience was obvious, such as a classic rookie error in Monaco when he out-braked himself and piled into the back of Romain Grosjean. But equally obvious was his incredible speed. There's a theory in motor racing that you can calm a fast, flawed driver down, but you can't make a slow driver fast. What it means is, if you've got somebody super-fast, you can work with them, even if they wreck a few cars along the way. You can teach them to manage their limit and stop crashing. But being outrageously fast takes natural ability. Plenty of drivers are consistent and safe . . . but just not fast enough. And you can't fix that with coaching. Verstappen was clearly blessed with ridiculous natural ability and seemed set for a long, successful future in Formula 1.

Red Bull went into the 2016 season with Daniel Ricciardo and Daniil Kvyat in its 'primary' cars, but after a handful of rounds, it decided to make a drastic change. Kvyat wasn't necessarily showing signs of superstardom, and rival teams were starting to sniff around Verstappen again. Being stuck in the junior team might have opened the door for those rivals to make a play for the Dutch teenager at the end of the 2016 season. So, Red Bull pulled a proactive move and decided to switch Verstappen and Kvyat ahead of the Spanish Grand Prix. It allowed the energy-drinks giant to tie Verstappen up in a longer-term deal and remove any risk of defection.

By that point, Ricciardo was already a proven race winner. He'd successfully gone up against four-time world champion Sebastian Vettel at Red Bull Racing in 2014, winning three races to the German's zero, so the arrival of a teenager probably didn't set off any alarm bells for the Australian. At least until their first race as teammates.

On the day of the 2016 Spanish Grand Prix, Verstappen was 18 years and 228 days old. That probably shouldn't have mattered, given how dominant Mercedes was that season. Ricciardo and Verstappen had qualified third and fourth for the race respectively, but anything except a win for Mercedes teammates, and fierce drivers' title rivals, Lewis Hamilton and Nico Rosberg seemed impossible. Until, of course, Hamilton and Rosberg collided while fighting for the lead at turn 4 on the opening lap of the race. Both Mercs were out of the race, one of several significant moments in what became a bitter battle for the 2016 world title. The pair had once been close friends in their junior racing days. But the fight for the top prize in world motorsport took its toll on the relationship.

With the Mercs out of the race, Red Bull Racing was suddenly in the box seat for a race win. Initially, Ricciardo led the way, with Verstappen playing rear gunner. When Ricciardo made his first pit stop of the race, Verstappen – on what was thought to be the less-ideal strategy – stayed out on the track to become the first Dutch driver to lead a grand prix. It only lasted a lap until he made a stop of his own, but it was the first moment of significance on a history-making afternoon. When the next round of stops arrived, again Ricciardo was the first of the Red Bulls to pit. But instead of following suit a lap later, Verstappen stayed out. Suddenly, Red Bull was hedging its bets between a three- and a two-stop strategy. When Ricciardo made his third stop of the race, Verstappen took over the lead ahead of what was expected to be a long, tough final stint. Except it was Ricciardo who struck trouble on the run to the chequered flag, not Verstappen. Having been undercut by now-Ferrari driver Vettel, Ricciardo struggled to get past him to chase down Verstappen. Eventually a puncture put paid to any hopes of victory. Out front, Verstappen was soaking up the pressure from another Ferrari driver, and fellow two-stopper in the race, Räikkönen. But while the Finn was within DRS range, the teenage sensation just wouldn't blink. He crossed the line as not only the youngest ever winner in F1 history, but as the first Dutch driver to win a Formula 1 race.

Unlike Maldonado, there was nothing one-off about Verstappen's Spanish magic. Now the apple of Red Bull motor-racing supremo Dr Helmut Marko's eye, Verstappen's star continued to rise. In 2017, Ricciardo managed to finish the season ahead of Verstappen in the drivers' standings, but Verstappen won two races to Ricciardo's one. The following year, the pair shared two wins each, but it was Verstappen who finished two places clear of Ricciardo in the standings. At the end of 2018, Ricciardo's Red Bull Racing contract was up. The team wanted to keep him, but Ricciardo wasn't sure if he wanted to stay. That Red Bull was quickly becoming 'Max's team' was painfully obvious. When Renault flashed some cash Ricciardo's way, along with the promise of leading an ambitious factory team, he decided to jump ship for 2019. It was an admirable, and entirely understandable, decision. Ricciardo felt that, if he really wanted a shot at a world title, it wasn't going to happen at Red Bull. That chance would go to Verstappen.

Unfortunately, Renault never really provided the hardware during Ricciardo's two-year stay at the team. He decided to move to McLaren for 2021, which in hindsight proved to be a terrible decision. There was one victory at Monza in somewhat fortunate circumstances, but Ricciardo struggled to deal with the fickle McLaren package and was largely upstaged by newcomer teammate Lando Norris. His underperformance would ultimately lead McLaren to go looking for Oscar Piastri as a replacement for 2023. So, Ricciardo returned to the Red Bull family, first as test driver and, after another mid-season swap in 2023, as a race driver with its junior team AlphaTauri. Verstappen, meanwhile, is still at Red Bull Racing and is a three-time world champion. And counting.

14

CANADA

Canadian Grand Prix
Circuit Gilles-Villeneuve
16–18 June 2023

In the immediate lead-up to the Canadian Grand Prix, Oscar Piastri sat down for a three-on-one interview with journalists from Motorsport.com, AutoHebdo and the *Frankfurter Allgemeine Zeitung*. During the chat, he was asked about the lack of damage he'd inflicted on racing cars, not just in Formula 1 but throughout his time in the junior categories as well. There were so few documented occurrences of Piastri spinning into the gravel or smacking a wall and significantly damaging a car. He responded, 'I've had a couple of spins in an F1 car, but the last time I hit a wall or got stuck [in the gravel] … yeah, that was probably Formula Renault in 2019, so it's been a while.'

Piastri explained that his 'softly, softly' approach to a race weekend was entirely on purpose, although he also admitted that, at some point, he needed to start taking a few more risks, particularly in races.

In other words, he wasn't expecting his damage-free run to last forever.

'I think in some ways that is quite helpful, building it up slowly through the weekend,' he said. 'I think in general, especially at circuits we've been to like Saudi Arabia, Baku and Monaco, building through the weekend is useful because you find the limit at the right time, and you don't go over it. And I think that's sort of been something I've tried to do through my whole career as well.

'I just think in the races themselves, I try to be quite sensible in some places, maybe even a bit too cautious at times. In Saudi Arabia I had contact because I was too cautious, I think. So, in some ways I can be a bit more aggressive, but obviously I'm new to F1 and trying to build up as much [experience] as I can. There's been some close calls, definitely, and some big moments, but no, there's not been any crashes yet. It will happen one day, but for now I'm just trying to get there slowly and maximise my track time as well.'

The weirdness at the Circuit Gilles-Villeneuve started before cars hit the track for the first practice session of the 2023 grand prix. When the teams all plugged in their tyre blankets ahead of Free Practice 1, the power supply to the pit lane – which is specially adapted from the standard North American frequency of 60 Hz to the 50 Hz used in Europe – overloaded, and then cut out. Teams had to scramble to fire up generators to get their rubber up to a safe operating temperature before sending the cars out for what should have been an hour of running.

A little over three minutes into the session, Alpine driver Pierre Gasly keyed up his radio. 'I've lost the drive shaft,' he reported back to the pits as his car rolled to a complete stop between turns 7 and 8. 'Let me know what to do. No gears.' Race control understandably red-flagged the session so that the stricken Alpine car could be recovered and pushed safely behind the barriers. Once that was done, the teams expected the session to simply be restarted. Mercedes even sent its two cars to the end of the pit lane to wait for the red light to turn green. And there they sat, waiting at the red light. After a few minutes, a handful of Mercedes mechanics jogged to the pit exit and pushed the two cars back to the garage. Gasly's car was well out of harm's way, but there were no signs of the session getting back underway. TV pundits speculated that the delay was due to Alpine lobbying race control to allow a truck to bring Gasly's car back to the garage. But 20 minutes into the session, the FIA came clean about the hold-up. 'The session restart has been delayed due to issues with the local CCTV infrastructure around the circuit,' read a statement. 'The local organisers are working to resolve the issue and until that time we can't restart for safety reasons.' Another 20 minutes passed before the FIA issued a second statement. 'The delay will be longer as the CCTV is not synced correctly and until the issue has been fixed, we cannot run on track,' it read. 'This system is a local installation and they are continuing to work to resolve the problem. The clock will continue to run down on FP1 and the session won't be extended as there must be 2.5 hours between FP1 and FP2. We are looking at options to extend FP2.' In modern Formula 1, a functioning CCTV system is considered critical to safely running a session. It has nothing to do with TV coverage, but rather it is a method of reviewing on-track incidents that may pop up and require input from the stewards. With 10 of the scheduled minutes of FP1 remaining, another update from the FIA confirmed that the session wouldn't resume, but FP2 would start 30 minutes earlier than scheduled and run for 30 minutes longer.

The second practice was significantly more orthodox, but far from easy – particularly for a rookie. Piastri was suddenly facing an incredibly green, slippery track that he was unfamiliar with, knowing he'd had less practice time than usual. Adding to the stress was a constant threat of rain. With a little under a quarter of an hour to go, Piastri, sitting in 11th place, rode his luck coming through the famous turn 12 to 13 section, a.k.a. the Wall of Champions. His McLaren drifted wide on the exit and dragged along the way, hard enough that a flurry of sparks bounced off the concrete. 'I clipped the wall on the exit of the last corner with the rear right,' he reported over the radio. 'Feels okay so far.' It was a lucky escape for a young driver yet to have any sort of significant crash in a Formula 1 car.

Come Saturday there was no more guesswork on the conditions. The rain set in early and was expected to continue throughout the day. Knowing that the track would be, at the very least, damp for qualifying, a wet FP3 became a critical hit-out for the drivers as they tried to work out where the grip was hiding. The highly experienced Carlos Sainz got it very wrong with 25 minutes to go when he brushed his right-rear wheel over a white line while braking into turn 1. That tipped his Ferrari into a high-speed spin and a crunching impact with the barriers. It all happened so fast and so easily. There were no such issues for Piastri, though, who had put his Friday brush with the wall behind him and was back to looking every bit like a safe pair of hands.

The rain eased a little heading into qualifying, with the track damp rather than soaking wet, making intermediates the tyre of choice. At the same time, there were dark clouds circling the venue, which meant getting a time on the board while conditions were potentially at their best was incredibly important. That led to a mad rush at the start of Q1 as everyone tried to get out on track. Within seconds, Sauber's Zhou Guanyu was on the radio reporting that he didn't have any drive. He limped the car around the circuit before eventually giving up and pulling to the side of the track. Race control red-flagged the session, at a time when Logan Sargeant, Alex Albon and Valtteri Bottas were the only three drivers to have logged a time. Everyone else was praying it wouldn't rain before they had a chance to get on the board. Including Piastri, who'd already had a little excursion across the grass between turns 1 and 2 after locking a front brake at the end of the front straight. Once the session went green again, conditions actually improved rather than worsened. In fact, as Q1 drew to a close, race engineers were starting to ask drivers if they would consider a slick tyre, given there were now significant stretches of dry track. Nobody was quite brave enough to try it, but as the chequered flag flew to end Q1, the crossover point was very, very close as the track evolved rapidly. For a moment, the flurry of improvements had left Piastri at risk of being bumped from Q1. That was until he jumped into the top 10 on his very last lap of the segment.

As the field rolled out for Q2, the dry line was obvious, and it was just a matter of time before somebody rolled the dice on a soft-compound slick tyre. Dry lines are the ultimate game of risk versus reward. If you survive the lap, you'll be faster than those running intermediates. But if you stray a millimetre wide of the line onto a damper section of the track, you're almost definitely going to spin. Albon was the first to take the gamble, and he timed it to perfection, jumping to the top of the times. Most of the field, including Piastri, followed suit – right as light rain started to fall. It takes more than light rain to steal the grip away from a hot slick tyre, but any level of rain takes its toll on driver confidence. It beads on a driver's visor, right in front of their eyes, and will generally look heavier than it really is. Nobody could run down Albon's time, but Piastri was among those to stick with the slick and brave it through to the third and final segment of qualifying.

The drizzle persisted through the break between the second and third qualifying segments, forcing the last 10 drivers left in the fight for pole back onto the intermediate tyres. And, with the rain increasing, there was another rush to get out on track and bank a time as soon as the light went green at the pit exit. By the time the final session got going, the track was truly wet again and only getting wetter. There was no time to ease into it. Pole would likely be decided on the first run. Unfortunately for Piastri, he didn't make it through the first run. After a very conservative sighting lap, he started to push on his second flying lap. On the way out of turn 6 he pushed slightly too hard, lighting up the rear tyres and backing his car into the wall. It wasn't a ridiculously hard impact, but hard enough to damage the right-rear suspension. As the car sat there, its left-front hanging sadly off the ground, Piastri radioed back to the McLaren pit. 'It's broken, sorry,' he said. 'Sorry about that . . .'

In his typically analytical style, Piastri wasn't overly disheartened by the crash. After all, he had flagged that a crash was inevitable, at some stage, before the weekend – a point he reiterated as he reflected on his qualifying mishap. 'It's my first sort of major mistake and I had to get the first crash out of the way at some point,' he said. '[I was] just too aggressive on the throttle and that was all. It is easy to do, and obviously a shame. I'm sorry to the mechanics who now have more work than they need. But yeah, all in all, I'm still reasonably happy with how the weekend has gone.'

The rain disappeared on Saturday night, with the drivers greeted by nice, dry conditions for the race on Sunday. Piastri made a hugely promising start, charging into seventh place on the opening lap. He then latched onto the back of Nico Hülkenberg, liberating the German of sixth place right before an early virtual safety car, where the field is neutralised by way of an electronically enforced speed limit should a minor issue need to be rectified by trackside marshals. Not long after, George Russell fired his Mercedes into the wall on the outside of turn 9, forcing race control to throw a real safety car. Most of the field pitted, with Piastri shuffled back to 10th in the order for the restart. From there, the race turned into something reminiscent of Barcelona. His pace was average, particularly on the hard tyre, and he drifted just outside of the points. The McLaren package was clearly only good enough to be mired in the midfield battle on race days, and it was proving to be frustrating as the wait for upgrades continued. 'We're looking forward to the upgrades that are coming soon,' said Piastri on Sunday evening in Montreal. 'I think at the moment we're, on our good days, probably at the top of the midfield. We need to get out of that midfield and start being able to focus on the top four teams. Yeah, [I'm] looking forward to that.'

Results Summary

Free Practice 1: 6th (1m 21.496s, +2.77s)
Free Practice 2: 11th (1m 14.533s, +0.81s)
Free Practice 3: 12th (1m 25.191s, +2.08s)
Qualifying: 9th (1m 31.349s, +5.49s)
Race: 11th

Canadian Grand Prix: A brief history

There aren't many race circuits that can trace their existence back to an underground railway and a successful bid to host a world's fair.

In the late 1950s, Canada made a play to host an official World Exhibition in 1967 to celebrate the country's centenary. The North Americans went up against Austria and Russia in the bidding process – and lost out to Moscow. Two years later, when the Russians binned their plans for an expo, then Montreal mayor Jean Drapeau urged the Canadian federal government to bid again. It did, successfully, and Expo 67 was born. Drapeau decided the best location for the expo was Saint Helen's Island, in the middle of the Saint Lawrence River. Except the island wasn't big enough. So, the Canadians used all the rock that was being excavated to build the Montreal Metro to make Saint Helen's Island bigger, and then to create a neighbouring man-made island. Fifteen million tonnes of rock were used to create Notre Dame Island, or Île Notre-Dame, just to the east of Saint Helen's Island.

Expo 67 was a raging success in terms of attendance and interest. Three years later, Canada and the city of Montreal mounted a successful bid to host the 1976 Summer Olympic Games. Notre Dame Island was revamped for the games to become the hub for rowing and canoeing. The Olympic Basin is still a hot spot for man-powered boat sports, to this day. With the Olympics done and dusted, attention turned to what else Notre Dame Island could be used for. And it turned out that the access roads around the island could be transformed into a race circuit. Canada, with its European flair, had been a staple of the Formula 1 schedule for a decade. But there were some safety concerns over the Mosport Park circuit near Toronto that was used for the grand prix at the time. So, in 1978, the Canadian Grand Prix shifted to the brand-new Circuit Île Notre-Dame. The circuit made a perfect debut when Canadian superstar, and Quebec native, Gilles Villeneuve won the first race in his Ferrari. In 1982, Villeneuve was killed during qualifying for the Belgian Grand Prix – and his home track was renamed Circuit Gilles-Villeneuve, as it is known today.

The track is much like Melbourne's Albert Park in that it's technically a street circuit but presents more like a parklands circuit. It's reasonably fast and tree-lined in some sections, and it features a tight right-hand hairpin that leads onto a long back straight. At the end of that straight is a right-left combo onto the front straight, the exit of which is a wall. And that wall is known as the Wall of Champions, because it has caught out some of the biggest names in the history of the sport. What makes the complex so tricky is that it connects two long straights – and maximising straights is critical in F1. A driver sheds an incredible amount of lap time by braking too early at the end of the back straight on the way into the corner, which leaves themselves vulnerable to being passed at the end of the front straight if they don't get a good run out of the last corner. So you have to be fast in, and fast out, right on the limit. And if you overstep the limit by the tiniest fraction, you end up in the wall.

The Wall of Champions story technically starts in 1997 thanks to Jacques Villeneuve, son of the great Gilles Villeneuve. The younger Villeneuve had cut his teeth in the US open-wheeler scene, winning the Indy 500 and the IndyCar World Series in 1995. That scored him a call-up to Formula 1 in the all-conquering Williams squad, with Villeneuve taking pole position at his first race, the Australian Grand Prix, in 1996. He finished second in the title race that year before winning the world championship in just his second Formula 1 season in 1997. But there was no fairytale win on home soil. Villeneuve was running second at that year's Canadian Grand Prix, behind Michael Schumacher, when his car snapped into oversteer as he tackled the right-hander, rotating and clipping the wall.

In that moment, Villeneuve wasn't yet a champion and the concrete hadn't been christened. That happened in 1999, when four drivers hit the turn 13 wall, three of whom were world champions. The first of the champions to clobber the wall was 1996 title winner Damon Hill, now driving for Jordan, who hit the wall on lap 15. On lap 30, race leader Michael Schumacher (1994 and 1995 world champion) launched his Ferrari into the wall and out of the race. Then, five laps later, Villeneuve became the third champion to hit the wall. The coronation of the Wall of Champions was complete. It wasn't until 2005 that the wall claimed another scalp, and, like Villeneuve's 1997 effort, it came before the driver – Jenson Button – had actually been crowned champion. Button was running third in his Honda and, under immense pressure from Schumacher, hit the wall. Four years later he would win the world title. The most recent champion to hit the wall is Sebastian Vettel, who crashed his Red Bull during practice in 2011 while defending his 2010 crown.

Next time you're watching the Canadian Grand Prix, keep an eye on TV camera shots of the famous hairpin. In the background you'll see a huge, eerie dome structure that looks like something from a sci-fi movie. That's the Biosphere, built as the pavilion for the US's display at Expo 67 on St Helen's Island. These days, it's a museum – and both a somewhat bizarre backdrop to Canada's Formula 1 race and a reminder of the circuit's unique history.

15

AUSTRIA

Austrian Grand Prix
Red Bull Ring
30 June–2 July 2023

McLaren may not have publicised its plans, but internally, the team had been working towards the British Grand Prix to introduce the full B-spec version of its 2023 car. A handful of the upgrades, however, were ready to go a little earlier than expected. In the age of limited testing, the sooner you can get new parts on the car, the sooner you can evaluate them and, potentially, benefit from their performance. Of course, design and production schedules mean it's not always possible to produce enough parts to cover off both cars. When that happens, traditionally it's the lead driver that gets them first. In McLaren's case, Norris was considered the lead driver – and he therefore got his hands on the 'A-point-5-spec' car for Austria, while Oscar Piastri continued with the A-spec car with the Baku upgrades.

According to McLaren, Norris's upgrade was a 'fully revised floor', which featured 'updated fences, floor edge as well as diffuser shape'. It also included updated mirrors, halo fairing, sidepods and engine cover. This was the team's first big swing at eliminating the lack of aerodynamic efficiency that had held the car back all year. '[The upgrade] was all meant to come for Silverstone, so the fact we've got some of it [for the Austrian Grand Prix] is already going to be a good step forward', said Norris. 'Especially with it being a sprint race and maybe some opportunity to get points twice if we can, if it's enough of a step, which is why we pushed everyone so much and the team were able to deliver on getting some bits earlier.

'This is our first upgrade of the season, really, for performance. We obviously had an upgrade in Baku, but it wasn't a performance deliverer. It feels like it's been a very long time, but at the same time, the team has done a good job. We wanted to make sure things were done correctly and done in the right way. So, I want to say I have confidence that it's a decent step.'

Introducing a significant update to the car was a risk with the Austrian Grand Prix being a sprint weekend. As Norris had pointed out, yes, there were more points on the table than usual. But instead of three hours' worth of practice, there was only one hour of practice to familiarise himself with the upgraded car. And it was a far from promising hour, at least from the outside. Norris cut just 20 laps and was out of the car well before the end of the session, as the team tinkered with the front wing. That meant he missed the soft-tyre runs and ended up dead last. Meanwhile, Piastri put in a performance typical of the old-spec McLaren: smack bang in the midfield.

Next up was qualifying for Sunday's grand prix, and all of a sudden the updated McLaren came alive. Both cars got through Q1, Norris four spots and around half a tenth of a second ahead of Piastri. Not much in it, but encouraging for Norris given his practice woes. In Q2, Norris burst out of the blocks with a 1m 05.038s, more than half a second quicker than Piastri's first run. On his second run, Piastri improved significantly, moving into the top 10 and within two-tenths of Norris. At least until he was pinged for a track-limits infringement at turn 9 and stripped of his lap times.

Track limits are a funny thing in motor racing. The modern trend of circuit design is acres of bitumen run-off, rather than the old deterrents like grass and gravel outside of the racing surface. The thing about bitumen run-off is that, given it has roughly the same grip as the racing surface, it's a benefit for drivers to run wide. You can carry more speed through the corner if you let the car drift wider on exiting the turn. There are white lines on the track to indicate exactly where the racing surface starts and stops, and the rules clearly state that you need to have at least some part of your car inside those white lines to be legally driving around the circuit. It's hardly a controversial concept. In football, a white line decides whether the ball is in or out. But in motor racing, it causes all sorts of problems. At any of these circuits with bitumen run-off, track limits become a problem. Drivers suddenly forget how to judge the edge of the racing circuit and they often run wide, and because there's no wall or grass or gravel to slow them down, they keep going and finish their laps – usually very quickly. But if race control spots that they've gone over the line by even a millimetre, the lap time is deleted. Drivers argue that it's unfair. Why lose your best lap when you've only gained the tiniest of tiny advantages? The counterargument is that you need to specify what is 'in' and what is 'out' of bounds. Now, if there was gravel on the outside of the white line, there would be no arguments, and the majority of drivers wouldn't dare drop so much as a tyre pimple on the wrong side. But that's how racing drivers work. They live for grip. They won't see the white line if there's bitumen on the other side; they'll just see grip and speed.

And that's why the rise of modern circuits has led to an explosion of track-limit controversies. The fact that Piastri had used too much road in Austria was undeniable, and his lap was gone. He was out of Q2, while Norris took the new McLaren to fourth on the grid by the end of qualifying.

The performance from the Briton, in the updated package, should have been cause for celebration at McLaren. So rarely do mid-season updates deliver what looked to be this level of improvement. But Andrea Stella wasn't ready to believe just yet. To him, the update was worth the difference between Norris's Q2 lap and Piastri's deleted Q2 lap. 'If we see the lap time that was deleted of Oscar in Q2, it's actually not too far from Lando, just a few tenths. This is pretty much in line with what we expected from the package.' Stella added that he was also concerned that Austria could be like Barcelona, where Norris's qualifying form wasn't representative of the team's real pace, but rather was a product of the cool, cloudy conditions that seemed to suit the McLaren. 'I'm a little prudent because Austria is a track a little bit like Barcelona,' he explained. 'We were P3 in Barcelona. Obviously the gap was bigger [in Spain]; here I think we are more competitive, looking at the gaps. Positive indications, but it needs to be confirmed in other tracks. Austria, with the big braking and the high speed, is another one that suits us, and there was no sun.'

The benefit of the sprint format was that McLaren could put its new design philosophy to the competitive test the very next day. Given the question marks over practice pace, another qualifying session and a race would allow McLaren to properly assess whether Norris's newfound pace was in any way genuine. For the second consecutive race weekend, the weather played a role in Saturday's running. The sprint shootout kicked off on a damp track with a mostly dry line. A few drivers started out on the intermediate tyre, but the soft-compound slick quickly became the tyre of choice. The nature of the drying circuit meant rapid evolution, helping Piastri go fastest on his first flying lap, before he was shuffled back down the order as the track got faster. With around three minutes to go, Piastri was still just on the right side of the bubble when, on another soft-tyre run, he came across a slow-moving Charles Leclerc at the final corner, which ruined his lap. 'Got massively impeded by the Ferrari,' he reported over the radio. He pressed on for another lap and jumped all the way up to fifth place, 10 spots clear of the drop zone with exactly 75 seconds left on the clock. But things change quickly in Formula 1, especially on a drying, heavily evolving track.

By the time the chequered flag was waved, Piastri had been pushed back to 17th and bundled out of the session. Leclerc was later fined 5000 euros and given a three-place grid penalty for his role in Piastri's SQ1 exit, not that it did Piastri much good.

The good news was that Norris didn't just make it through the first qualifying segment, he went on to put the updated McLaren third on the grid for the sprint race. Maybe there was something to this new floor and aero after all.

The weather kept everyone guessing ahead of the sprint race as well. Half an hour out from the start, as the cars had to leave the pits and form up on the grid, light rain was falling but the track wasn't quite wet. The majority of the field played it safe and left the pits on intermediate tyres. Valtteri Bottas was the only driver to roll the dice on slicks, starting way down in 19th place. It was a brave choice. A little too brave, as it turned out. By the time the race got going, it was way too wet for a slick tyre and Bottas pulled into the pits to switch to intermediates at the end of the formation lap.

Out front, things looked incredible for Norris for a brief moment. He sat behind the squabbling Red Bulls through turn 1 as Sergio Perez got past Max Verstappen. He then tried to follow Verstappen past Perez as the field compressed for the tight right-hand turn 3. But then it all went south. A tiny lock of his rear brakes at slow speed sent his engine into anti-stall, a software mode designed to keep the engine running when it is about to run out of puff. By the time he got the car out of anti-stall, he had been swamped and pushed back to 10th place, one spot behind where he would ultimately finish.

Piastri, meanwhile, spent most of the race cruising around where he'd started towards the back of the pack. Until, with six laps to go, he and McLaren decided to take a slick-tyre gamble on what had once again become a drying track. George Russell had already taken the plunge and looked pretty quick in his Mercedes. Given there were unlikely to be any points on offer, why not have a go?

The trip to the pits dropped Piastri to 20th and last place . . . but not for long. As others followed suit and switched to slicks, he floated back up to 17th in no time. And the move to the soft slick brought the old-spec McLaren to life, with Piastri able to blast past the likes of Leclerc and Alex Albon in the closing laps to finish 11th in the sprint. The move on Albon was particularly impressive, Piastri driving into a McLaren-shaped hole at the apex at turn 4. Forceful, aggressive, but still measured. A little touch of the wheels between the two cars as Albon realised he was being mugged. Perfect. 'It's always fun going through the field instead of backwards,' said Piastri after the sprint. 'I think getting past Leclerc and Albon in two corners was definitely the highlight. So yeah, it was a fun afternoon. A shame it wasn't for anything apart from some fun, but that's half the battle sometimes.'

Race day was dry, making tyre choice easy, but the conditions didn't overly suit the old-spec McLaren. Piastri battled away on the wrong side of the points places until his race unravelled entirely on lap 23. His demise actually started three positions ahead of him, when Yuki Tsunoda charged down the inside of Lance Stroll into turn 3. That ran Stroll wide, and forced Kevin Magnussen to brake suddenly behind the Aston Martin driver. Piastri, meanwhile, was hot on Magnussen's heels and had nowhere to go except into the back of the Haas. It was light contact, but enough to damage Piastri's front wing and force him into the pits for a new nose. From there, 16th place was as good as it was ever going to get. 'There was like three cars in front of me, having their own incident,' Piastri explained post-race. 'They all slammed on their brake mid-corner and I didn't have anywhere to go. That was frustrating. But I think even apart from that, our pace wasn't great. It was a much better day for the team and Lando on their side, so encouraging for next week.'

Norris came fourth in the new McLaren, with both drivers set to get their hands on the next stage of upgrades for the B-spec car ahead of the British Grand Prix.

Results Summary

Free Practice 1: 12th (1m 06.809s, +1.07s)
Qualifying: 13th (1m 05.605s, +1.21s)
Sprint Shootout: 17th (1m 07.106s, +2.66s)
Sprint: 11th
Race: 16th

Austrian Grand Prix: A brief history

There are two traditional styles of Formula 1 team owner – a carmaker, or a privately run specialist race team. Enzo Ferrari used to call the latter the 'garagistas'.

Given the huge dollars required to fund and run a Formula 1 team, let alone a successful one, there have been notable distortions to the model over time, usually involving big businesses looking to leverage the sport for marketing purposes. Of course, the most common way to do that is to sponsor a Formula 1 team. But there are examples where sponsorship hasn't been enough and the companies want ownership.

The most prominent modern example is Benetton. The famous fashion label sponsored the likes of Tyrrell, Alfa Romeo and Toleman in the early 1980s, before buying the Toleman team ahead of the 1986 season. The team quickly became a force in Formula 1, particularly after appointing the flamboyant Flavio Briatore to lead the way. That aggressive play to secure Michael Schumacher in 1991 was another turning point, with the German winning world championships for Benetton in 1994 and 1995. Later, during less successful years, Benetton even brought one of its other fashion brands, Playlife, into the mix. Between 1998 and 2000, the Benettons were powered by Supertec V10 engines rebranded as Playlife engines. Benetton sold the team to Renault in the early 2000s and it still exists in Formula 1 to this day, as Alpine.

The 1999 season saw the debut of British American Racing (BAR), which was owned by – surprise, surprise – British American Tobacco (BAT). BAT had enjoyed great success in motorsport by sponsoring Subaru's world rally team with its 555 brand and decided to give Formula 1 a good shake. The team lured 1997 world champion Jacques Villeneuve from Williams and paired him with Brazilian rookie Ricardo Zonta. BAR's plan was to split its liveries and have Villeneuve in a Lucky Strike–branded car and Zonta in a 555-branded car. After the launch, however, the FIA quickly interjected and insisted that, according to Formula 1 rules, the two cars had to look the same. So for 1999, the BARs ran the infamous 'zipper livery', which featured the red, white, silver and gold of Lucky Strike on one side, the blue and yellow of 555 on the other, and a zipper right down the middle.

The BAR experiment never really flew, and the team was sold to Honda at the end of the 2005 season. It then went through Ross Brawn's hands in 2009 before becoming the Mercedes factory team.

In 1995, Swiss Formula 1 team Sauber showed up with prominent Red Bull signage. Austrian businessman Dietrich Mateschitz had discovered the genesis of the energy drink while in Thailand in the mid-1980s and had created a version of it aimed at major markets such as Europe and the US. Red Bull GmbH, headquartered in Austria, targeted extreme sports for its global marketing push, including Formula 1. The company backed the Sauber squad until the end of 2004, when Ford put its struggling Jaguar Formula 1 team up for sale. Mateschitz pounced on the team, and Red Bull Racing (RBR) debuted in 2005. By then, Red Bull already had its huge driver development program, and soon bought a second Formula 1 team, perennial backmarkers Minardi, to act as a junior team at the end of 2005. Scuderia Toro Rosso debuted the next season.

Suddenly, Red Bull had a huge presence in Formula 1. And it would soon become a highly successful presence. In 2008, Red Bull scored its first Formula 1 race win – however, it came via Toro Rosso, not RBR. The winning driver was Red Bull junior Sebastian Vettel, who was promoted to the main team for the following season off the back of his Monza triumph.

In 2009, Vettel had another breakthrough win, this time for RBR, and went on to finish second in the world championship.

Between 2010 and 2013, the German won four world titles on the trot, cementing Red Bull as a major force in Formula 1. The start of the hybrid era was a little tougher for RBR as it struggled to match Mercedes until 2021 when, armed with the explosive Max Verstappen, it won another title. And it has absolutely dominated since then.

But Red Bull's presence in Formula 1 isn't limited to team ownership. It also owns the circuit that hosts its home grand prix. The Österreichring was originally built among the Styrian hills in 1969 and hosted the Austrian Grand Prix between 1970 and 1987. Its narrow, fast nature was eventually deemed unacceptable for the wild, turbo-powered Formula 1 cars of the mid- to late-1980s, with the average speed of Nelson Piquet's pole lap in 1987 an eye-watering 256.621 km/h. Formula 1 decided enough was enough and didn't return in 1988. The circuit was operational until 1995 when the calls for better safety standards grew too loud, and Hermann Tilke was called on to give it an overhaul. The costs of the redesign and rebuild were footed by Austrian mobile phone network A1, so the circuit was renamed the A1-Ring.

Formula 1 returned to Austria between 1997 and 2003 before the circuit was sold to Mateschitz in 2004, who quickly set about demolishing much of the existing infrastructure. His plans, known as 'Project Spielberg', were to build a world-class facility, but getting the approvals to get the job done proved tricky. It wasn't until 2008 that the 70-million-euro revamp of the circuit really started, but by 2010 the eyes of world motorsport returned to the newly christened Red Bull Ring when it hosted a round of the DTM series. In 2014, Mateschitz finally convinced Formula 1 to return to Spielberg to give Red Bull a proper home grand prix.

16

BRITAIN

British Grand Prix
Silverstone Circuit
7–9 July 2023

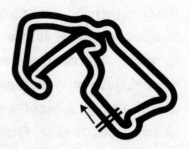

It was tough to get a proper read on how happy the team was with the almost-B-spec upgrade that went on Lando Norris's car in Austria. Yes, he'd been quick and finished near the front. But the public-facing reaction from McLaren was very cautious. 'I was a bit nervous coming into the [Austrian] race, that the race pace was going to let us down, but actually it was better than I was expecting, which was a good surprise,' Norris said. 'It's still not great, Fernando [Alonso] was clearly quicker a chunk every lap, and I am almost crashing in every corner.

'The car just goes quicker around every corner, but the way you have to drive is exactly the same, which is our next issue to tackle,' he added. 'Things that we've been complaining about all year that are still the same but just at a higher level, so I feel I can be really confident [in the car] if we can tackle these issues. I feel like they are letting us down a lot at the minute, so it is not just about downforce, it is about handling and how you handle the car. More technical things that we need to tackle and understand. When we do that, I am confident we can fight the quicker cars ahead of us.'

Added to the Austrian Grand Prix updates was a new front wing as the team neared its proper B-spec car, although once again Norris got the wing and Piastri didn't. Piastri did at least get the upgrades that Norris had run in Austria. There wasn't much to split them in the first practice session at Silverstone. Norris was 8th fastest, Piastri 10th, a hydraulic issue having cost him a few minutes at the end of the hour. In Free Practice 2 Piastri was 9th and Norris 14th. Solid, but not spectacular. The new McLaren hadn't necessarily outperformed what the old McLaren could have done if the conditions had suited it.

The British weather lived up to its reputation on the Saturday of the grand prix weekend, with grey clouds circling Silverstone as Free Practice 3 kicked off. That put a premium on the early running while the track was still dry. Most of the field took off on either soft- or medium-compound tyres, but Piastri opted for a race run on the hard-compound tyres. He was still belting around on the slowest of the tyre compounds when he keyed up the radio and said, 'There's lightning towards turn 15, outside of turn 15.' Within 10 minutes, umbrellas started popping up in the grandstands, usually the earliest indication that it is raining. Piastri had missed the boat for a soft-tyre qualifying lap; not a disaster, but an explanation for his lowly 17th position in the session's standings.

The question marks over track conditions continued into qualifying. Right as Q1 went green, the umbrellas started appearing in the crowd again. In the short term, though, the track remained too dry for a wet tyre. So, out went the field to tackle the dauntingly fast Silverstone layout, with aggressive qualifying set-ups and slick tyres, in damp conditions. It was an immense test. Even on a damp track, the turn-in speed at Copse is the best part of 300 km/h with just the lightest lift off the throttle. Lewis Hamilton showed how difficult the conditions were when he dropped his Mercedes midway through Stowe and spun into the gravel. The threat of heavier rain persisted throughout the first segment of qualifying, but never materialised. In fact, after a late red flag, the track was at its best for a single-lap sprint to the chequered flag. Piastri didn't quite nail his lap, but it was good enough to sneak into Q2. Norris, meanwhile, was fastest of everybody.

As the 15 cars left in contention for pole lined up at the end of the pit lane for the start of Q2, something remarkable happened. A burst of sunshine broke through the clouds. That seemed to cause even more confusion over conditions. McLaren reported to its drivers that there would be no more rain. Red Bull Racing's forecast was a very light sun shower that would last around five minutes. Either way, the tyre choice was clearly a soft slick, and it was going to take a big commitment to get through to Q3. With five minutes to go, Piastri went fastest of the pack, before being pipped by Hamilton, to the audible joy of the British crowd. Seconds later, Norris made it a British one-two as he beat Hamilton's time. The track evolution wasn't done there, though, the grip ramping up as the seconds ticked down. Right at the flag, Max Verstappen blew everyone away with a time of 1m 27.702s. The only other driver to join the Dutchman in the 1m 27s bracket? Oscar Piastri, who pulled off a blinder of a final lap in the closing seconds of Q2.

The conditions were nearly perfect for the final phase of qualifying, although it was in those improved conditions that Piastri made his first mistake of the session as he straddled the exit kerb on the way out of Becketts. 'Check the floor,' he asked the team over the radio. 'I went off at turn 13.' Piastri was still third fastest on that lap, behind Verstappen and Hamilton. But there was a final run to come. Norris went first of the two McLaren drivers, jumping to the top of the times. It was only a brief moment in time before Verstappen crossed the line to pip the hometown hero, but long enough to draw another huge cheer from the crowd. Piastri went third fastest to make it a McLaren two-three. Was this B-spec McLaren the real deal? Or was it another case of the conditions suiting the McLaren and masking the car's weaknesses? 'There's definitely a pattern,' said Andrea Stella. 'High-speed corners, cold conditions, soft tyres and, by the way, the same [tyre] compound. So, we like these conditions, our car likes it. The rear end kind of finds naturally some good grip, which we may be missing over continuous laps, or when it's hotter. So conditions come to our favour. But, at the same time, I think, in this result, some contribution is coming from the improvements we've made to the car. We measure these improvements in terms of downforce, and we see that in some of the low speed, we are decently competitive now.'

Race day would be the big test. In Barcelona, where the conditions had also suited the McLaren in qualifying, both drivers struggled in the race. The question was, would the McLarens sink like stones through the field this time around as well?

The race at Silverstone couldn't have got off to a better start. Norris recorded a reaction time 0.003s better than Verstappen as the lights went out, which helped him sweep into the lead. Piastri clung onto the back of the reigning world champion, and even showed his nose down the inside into Copse at the start of the second lap. There was an inevitability that Verstappen would take control of the race, but for a few thrilling laps he was stuck in a McLaren sandwich. On lap 5, Verstappen made his move, cruising past Norris into Brooklands with the help of the drag-reduction system. Given there was a decent gap between the three frontrunners and Charles Leclerc in fourth, McLaren made a strategic decision – its drivers weren't to fight each other. Norris and Piastri were told to focus on following Verstappen clear of the field, not battling each other over second place. The plan was working to perfection until lap 33 when Kevin Magnussen's Haas stopped on the Wellington straight, flames licking out from under the engine cover. Piastri had just made his pit stop under full green conditions. Now there was a safety car, which meant a cheap pit stop for the likes of Verstappen, Norris and Hamilton. That helped Hamilton jump Piastri for third place, the pair remaining in that order until the finish.

A bit of bad luck had cost Piastri his first podium finish in Formula 1. But at least the McLarens hadn't gone backwards in the race. Second and fourth, even if a little disappointing for Piastri, was a mega result for the team. 'The race pace is clearly where we've made a massive jump,' said Piastri. 'You know, I think going into the race, I was maybe slightly cautious that we might hit reverse a little bit like we have done previously. But if anything, it was even stronger than Austria, so that was super exciting. Yeah, it hurts a little bit to be P4 when we were looking on for a podium for so long and a bit unlucky with the safety car timing. But I'm just so happy that I'm disappointed with fourth place instead of what we've been disappointed with earlier in the season . . .'. Indeed, what had looked to be a solid rookie campaign for Piastri suddenly had a hint of the spectacular about it.

Results Summary

Free Practice 1: 10th (1m 29.658s, +1.06s)
Free Practice 2: 9th (1m 28.926s, +0.85s)
Free Practice 3: 17th (1m 29.437s, +2.02s)
Qualifying: 3rd (1m 27.092s, +0.37s)
Race: 4th

British Grand Prix: A brief history

Both Silverstone and the British Grand Prix represent the pinnacle of traditionalism in Formula 1. In fact, when Silverstone hosted the British Grand Prix in 1950, it was the very first world championship Formula 1 race. Up until then, grands prix were mostly standalone races, or part of European or regional championships. But in 1950, a proper world championship for cars built to a specific rule set known as Formula 1 was formed. Giuseppe Farina etched his name into the history books by winning that first ever world championship race in his Alfa Romeo.

Silverstone was originally a Royal Air Force bomber station that featured three runways. Between those runways and the access roads around them, it had all the makings of a race circuit. A group of friends who lived in Silverstone village were first to work it out, and they started holding impromptu, unofficial races there in 1947. The Royal Automobile Club caught on a year later, and the circuit's era of official racing came to life. Since then, Silverstone has been redeveloped several times, although the track has consistently retained its fast, flowing nature. Over time it has become the home of British motor racing, not only because of its history with Formula 1, but also because so much of the industry is based at or around the circuit. The Aston Martin Formula 1 team calls the circuit home.

But as traditional as Silverstone is, we're in a new era of Formula 1. The *Drive to Survive* era of Formula 1. And that's why when the 20 regular grand prix drivers walked into the drivers' briefing before the 2023 British Grand Prix, preparing to tackle one of the fastest, most brutal circuits on the planet, they were joined by Brad Pitt.

The Hollywood megastar wasn't a celebrity guest simply there as an interested observer. He wasn't at Silverstone to party in the Paddock Club. He was there to take part in the British Grand Prix – as a driver. Well, sort of.

Midway through 2022, Apple Original Films announced plans for a blockbuster movie centred around Formula 1. Joseph Kosinski was signed on to direct and Jerry Bruckheimer to produce, alongside Lewis Hamilton. Pitt was signed on as the lead actor. The story revolves around Pitt's character, a successful but ageing racing driver who returns to Formula 1 with a fictional backmarker team called APXGP, competing alongside a rookie driver played by Damson Idris.

Now, the quality of racing films varies greatly. Given it is such a niche sport, and such a technical sport, it's hard to get right. Early examples such as *Grand Prix* and *Le Mans* were always seen as a successful representation of motor racing. *Days of Thunder* is a classic. *Driven*, which came out in 2001, was terrible and set the genre back decades. *Ford v Ferrari*, the most recent racing-related film, was very much a step in the right direction.

Work on this latest F1 film by Apple happened throughout the 2023 season, but the high point of visibility was Silverstone. It was there that Pitt and Idris actually spent time on track, with other cars around them. Real Formula 1 cars.

Now, the two actors didn't drive Formula 1 cars themselves. Instead, Mercedes helped convert two Formula 2 cars to look exactly like Formula 1 cars, so they were a little cheaper to run and a little easier to drive. APXGP was set up as a proper 11th team for the Silverstone weekend, with a garage and all the usual driver signage for Sonny Hayes (Pitt) and Joshua Pearce (Idris). The actors were in the drivers' briefing, took part in a number of dedicated filming sessions over the race weekend, appeared in full race suits as part of the pre-race formalities (including the national anthem), and they even appeared on the grid and formation lap among the actual F1 cars and drivers. Although, by that point it was racers-turned-stuntmen Craig Dolby and Luciano Bacheta in the APXGP cars.

Only time will tell how the film stacks up in terms of authenticity, but at the very least, Pitt won over some fans by showing some genuine interest in, and understanding about, motor racing while speaking to commentator and former driver Martin Brundle before the race. 'I've got to tell you, as a civilian, I had no idea what it takes to be a driver, and the aggression and dexterity,' said Pitt. 'They're amazing athletes. I've got so much respect for everyone out there in all classes. I'm going to be here till they kick me out. Because I'm loving it. I think it's every guy's dream. My character would have raced in Le Mans, he would have raced in Daytona. I saw you won Le Mans, you won Daytona. I just thought it was stellar. Again, I have so much respect for what you guys do, and I've been enjoying your stuff for years.'

And as for what the F1 drivers, superstars in their own right, thought? 'I think it's one of those [things], when you see a worldwide superstar for the first time, it's quite surreal,' said George Russell. 'And then it's only when you get to be with those individuals, whether it was Tom Cruise, Brad Pitt or Roger Federer, whoever we've been fortunate enough to meet, you recognise they're just normal human beings. He was joking around and having a good time and just kind of one of the boys really.'

17

HUNGARY

Hungarian Grand Prix
Hungaroring
21–23 July 2023

At Silverstone, Oscar Piastri had delivered another standout rookie performance. He'd looked every bit like a driver that belonged in Formula 1. In fact, as the performance of the car improved with each upgrade, he was making the transition to Formula 1 seem kind of . . . easy.

But of course, it isn't. As of the end of the British Grand Prix weekend, there were only two drivers who hadn't scored a single world championship point for the season. They were Nyck de Vries and Logan Sargeant, the two other rookies in the field.

Two days after Silverstone, the Dutch media was sent into a spin. According to *De Telegraaf*, Red Bull's motorsport advisor Dr Helmut Marko had lost patience with de Vries and was ready to oust him from the AlphaTauri line-up ahead of the Hungarian Grand Prix. Within a day, the shock move was official, as AlphaTauri confirmed that de Vries was out on the spot, and Daniel Ricciardo would take his place. The same Daniel Ricciardo who had, in oversimplified terms, been shuffled out of McLaren to make way for Piastri. Not that the de Vries/Ricciardo shuffle had any real impact on Piastri, except to highlight what an exceptional job he was doing in his rookie season – and maybe ease the pressure from some factions of the Aussie supporter base that were still dirty on McLaren for ousting Dan in the first place.

The significance of Piastri's efforts compared to his fellow rookies wasn't lost on Andrea Stella. After Silverstone, he explained that not only was the team thrilled with what Piastri was delivering, but that they could see Norris responding to the challenge. 'Oscar's performance is just outstanding, if you think he's a rookie,' Stella said. 'This allows also some synergies between the drivers because both can see where you can improve from each other. And this elevates the performance of both drivers. So, not only are we impressed, but there's a net benefit in having two competitive drivers because both can benefit.'

The Ricciardo news wasn't the only bombshell announcement in the lead-up to Hungary. In early July, Alpine CEO Laurent Rossi outlined a management shake-up for the Formula 1 team. Bruno Famin, who had been in charge of the engine department, was named as vice president of Alpine Motorsports. Team principal Otmar Szafnauer would now report to Famin. Then, on the eve of the Hungarian Grand Prix, Rossi was moved out of the CEO role and replaced by

Philippe Krief. At the same time, there was mounting pressure on Szafnauer as the team continued to lack any sort of decent form, a plight exacerbated by a double DNF at Silverstone. By the race, Piastri's decision to choose McLaren over Alpine was looking better and better.

The Hungaroring, on the outskirts of Budapest, couldn't be more different than Silverstone. The latter is fast and flowing, the former tight, twisty and technical. A common comparison is that the Hungary circuit is just like Monaco, but without the walls. That was potentially concerning, given what Lando Norris had said about the new and, potentially, improved McLaren after Silverstone. 'We do have a poor car, and when I say poor, I would say pretty terrible, in the low-speed corners,' he had explained. 'It's extremely difficult to drive. I feel [people] getting excited and I accept that, but we're going to go to a couple of tracks coming up where I'm sure people are going to be saying, "What have you done now? How has it got so bad all of a sudden?"' McLaren did take the exact package from Silverstone to Hungary as well. There had been plans to complete the B-spec upgrade on Norris's car with the third round of upgrades, but they were shelved due to production delays. Piastri, however, finally got the same suite of upgrades that were fitted to Norris's car in England, which meant they were now both on a level pegging for the first time since before the Austrian Grand Prix.

There wasn't too much to learn about the low-speed competitiveness of the McLaren in Free Practice 1 of the

Hungarian Grand Prix. The session started in dry conditions, and nobody had put a lap down before Sergio Perez flung his Red Bull into the barriers at turn 5. The session was red-flagged, and by the time it restarted, rain had begun to fall. The good news was that the McLaren was at least quick in wet conditions, with Piastri and George Russell trading fastest times until the end of the session, the Mercedes driver just winning out in the end. It was hot and dry for the second hour-long session, with Norris doing some soft-tyre running while Piastri looked to focus on the medium tyre and race runs. That left Piastri right at the bottom of the timesheets, while Norris was second fastest in what was a promising sign for qualifying.

By Saturday evening, any concerns over the McLaren's pace, at least over a lap, was put to bed. Norris lost a lap to track limits in Q1, but he managed to clamber out of the drop zone on his final run, as Piastri cruised on through to the second segment. Norris made much lighter work of Q2, leading the way as, once again, Piastri looked untroubled as he progressed. All of a sudden, it was as normal as anything for both McLaren drivers to make it through to Q3 – an incredible turnaround from the start of the season. The good times continued in the third segment, Norris qualifying third while Piastri was right behind him in fourth. And at a track where the drivers had been sure the low-speed weaknesses of the car would be costly. Piastri wasn't even all that happy with the lap that ended up putting him on the second row of the grid. 'Turn 1 wasn't amazing, turn 5 was pretty average,' he said afterwards. 'The rest of the lap wasn't too bad, but I think

I was already a tenth and a half down after turn 1, so a bit of a shame. It would have taken quite a lot I think to get into the top three, but you know, for my own sake, I want to make sure that I can deliver . . . when I really need to.

'I think today I got off lightly still being fourth with a lap like that. But you know if it was a tenth or a tenth and a half to pole, I'd be kicking myself. So I need to make sure I improve on that. It'll come with time, I'm sure, but something I want to improve on. But it's much nicer to have that kind of lap and stay fourth, instead of have that kind of lap and stay 14th . . .'

As Stella had pointed out heading to Hungary, there are great benefits that come from having two drivers relatively equal on speed. The competitive nature of a racing driver means teammates always want to beat each other, and two fast drivers means two drivers pushing each other. At the same time, it does create complications. When a team has a clear team leader and a number two, and there is an obvious speed discrepancy between them, life is pretty simple. All of the team's energy, and its prime strategy, is focused on one car.

For the first time that season, the strategic complications of having two cars at the front of the field landed at McLaren's door on Sunday in Hungary. The issue, really, was some clever driving by Piastri at turn 1 of the grand prix race. A fast-starting Norris found himself alongside Hamilton and Verstappen on the run to the first corner. When Verstappen got next to Hamilton on the inside of the tight right-hander, he, cleverly, made sure he ran both Hamilton and Norris wide. Piastri could see it all unfolding in front of him and held a tight line through turn 1. That put him ahead of not just Norris, but Hamilton as well as the rookie swept into second place.

Piastri led Norris across the first stint of the race, until the first round of pit stops rolled around. And that's when things got interesting. Generally, pit priority – which means whatever the team believes to be the best strategy – between teammates goes to the driver with track position. In this case, that was Piastri. So, it was somewhat surprising when, on lap 17, McLaren called Norris into the pits first and left Piastri out. In Formula 1, what's known as the undercut is to benefit from the speed of a brand-new tyre after a pit stop. If you are following a driver, you pit before they do and use your superior tyre grip, and the clean air ahead of you, to lap faster than them until they decide to pit, helping you leapfrog them out on track. If you can undercut somebody in a single lap, that's perfect. You gain track position without a great difference in tyre life, which could leave you vulnerable to an overcut (where the other driver with better tyre longevity re-passes you) later in the stint. Pitting Norris was clearly a move to cover off Hamilton, who had pitted a lap earlier. But the question was, why did McLaren pit Norris first? The team pulled Piastri in the very next lap, but the damage was done. Norris swept past Piastri as his teammate came into the pits. Hamilton, the supposed threat, was miles back. Once in front, Norris was clearly the quicker of the two McLaren drivers. The experienced Brit managed his tyres well over the next two stints to end up best of the rest, albeit more than half a second behind race winner Verstappen. Piastri, meanwhile, struggled with the management of the hard- and medium-compound tyres and fell into the clutches of Sergio Perez and, later, Hamilton, leaving him to finish in fifth place.

After the race, Andrea Stella played down the idea that there had been any favouritism towards Norris when he was given the opportunity to undercut Piastri in the first stint of the race. 'In terms of the undercut that we had at the first stop, you just go really with the sequence that is natural, because you cover with the car that is more at risk, and then you cover with the other car,' he insisted. 'Lando's out-lap was just super, super quick, which meant Oscar lost the position. To be honest, our approach to these situations is to think about the team first. We think as a team, and then we deal with the internal situation. I think when you are fighting against other competitors outside your team, you need to be very careful that you don't engage in an internal battle that will cost the team.'

Piastri, in his calculating, analytical style, was more worried about his own shortcomings on tyre management than the undercut. 'At the end of the day, it didn't change my race. I clearly didn't have the pace to stay with Lando or challenge him. I think for myself, the biggest takeaway is to look into the tyre degradation and tyre management. You can do the best starts and first stints in the world, but if you can't hang on for the next two, then it doesn't matter.'

Meanwhile, fresh off the back of Rossi's exit from Alpine, the team recorded its second successive double DNF. This time, it was all over on lap 1. In fairness, it wasn't the team's fault. Zhou Guanyu made a woeful start to the race, which meant he was swamped on the run to the first corner, where his Alfa Romeo then hit Ricciardo, who in turn hit Esteban

Ocon, who in turn hit his Alpine teammate, Pierre Gasly. Both cars were too damaged to continue.

Results Summary

Free Practice 1: 2nd (1m 39.154s, +0.36s)
Free Practice 2: 19th (1m 19.117s, +1.43s)
Free Practice 3: 14th (1m 18.598s, +0.79s)
Qualifying: 4th (1m 16.905s, +0.30s)
Race: 5th

Hungarian Grand Prix: A brief history

In the early 1980s, then Formula 1 supremo Bernie Ecclestone set himself the ambitious goal of taking the sport behind the Iron Curtain. Plan A was the USSR itself, with Ecclestone hoping to get a race going in Moscow. According to the archives of long-time Formula 1 photographer Keith Sutton, Ecclestone approached Leonid Brezhnev, the General Secretary of the Central Committee of the Communist Party of the Soviet Union, by means of a letter in 1982. 'In politics, the prestige of a Formula 1 grand prix is comparable with Olympiad,' wrote Ecclestone. 'Each grand prix is televised and transmitted through approximately 40 countries to 300 million viewers live and to another 400 million on delayed transmission or by other media . . . and what is more, you do not have to deal with foreign Federations of State but with very serious and independent sportsmen who think only of the sport and do not get involved in politics.

'All the technologically and economically advanced countries have a Formula 1 grand prix. For example, the USA has three, two of which, Long Beach and Detroit, are held in the streets of the town, suitably equipped, as will be in Moscow. A Formula 1 grand prix is also run on the streets of Canada (Montreal), not forgetting the most famous of all grands prix, the one held in Monte Carlo. It is therefore quite surprising to note that a country as large as yours does not have a Formula 1 grand prix. In a city such as Moscow, which is so vast, it would be appropriate to have the premier event in motorsport, which involves the highest of technology used by such large manufacturers as Ferrari, Renault, Alfa Romeo, Talbot, Lotus, etc.'

The story goes that Brezhnev, a known car fanatic, loved the idea. Ecclestone reportedly threw in some sweeteners, such as offering to fund the whole thing, as well as offering a third car run by his own Brabham team for a Soviet driver for the Moscow race. Moscow even featured on the provisional calendar for the 1983 Formula 1 season with a scheduled date of 21 August.

And then Brezhnev died, as did Ecclestone's hopes of getting a signed contract to hold his Soviet race.

Some say it was in a helicopter flying over Budapest on return from an unsuccessful trip to lobby Moscow. Others say it was while killing time during a rain delay at the Monaco Grand Prix. Either way, at some point after the Soviet Grand Prix idea died, Ecclestone and his close friend, Brazilian Grand Prix promoter and Hungarian native Tamas Rohonyi, decided on the next target to get Formula 1 behind the Iron Curtain. '[Ecclestone] said Moscow was depressing and the bureaucracy made it near impossible anyway,' Rohonyi told *Reuters* in 2015. 'I told him, why not try Budapest?' With his typical decisiveness, Bernie said, "Well, let's not talk about it. Why don't you go to Hungary and ask them?'"

Hungary was already one of the more progressive Eastern Bloc countries, allowing things like McDonald's and casinos within its borders. And Formula 1 appeared to be the perfect way to advertise to the world that it was a Western-thinking nation. When talks became more serious and Ecclestone visited Budapest, he too liked what he saw. There were plenty of hotels and the airport was big enough to support an international event. The dream of a race on communist territory was becoming a reality.

Ecclestone's preference was for a street race in Budapest itself, but the city council rejected two separate proposals. So, the government bought a parcel of land 15 kilometres east of Budapest and decided to build a permanent circuit instead. The Hungaroring was built in a record eight months and the Hungarian Grand Prix was included on the 1986 Formula 1 calendar. Local authorities helped the Formula 1 circus get through the Iron Curtain by allowing teams to skip the brutal visa process, while a dedicated gate was set up at the Austrian border so race-team trucks could enter Hungary with nothing more than a sticker.

On 10 August 1986, history was made when the Hungaroring hosted the Hungarian Grand Prix, won by Williams driver Nelson Piquet. More than 200,000 people flocked to the track for their first glimpse of this Western spectacle. They came from Czechoslovakia, Romania, Bulgaria and other countries under communist government at the time, while TV figures in all of those countries, as well as in Russia and Poland, pushed the global audience close to a thousand million.

The Hungarian Grand Prix has been a mainstay of the calendar ever since.

18

BELGIUM

In Hungary, Alpine team principal Otmar Szafnauer had responded to Alpine's management shuffle and what was perceived by many as mounting pressure on his job. His response was that he trusted Renault Group CEO Luca de Meo's promise to give him 100 races to start winning, despite Laurent Rossi's axing as Alpine boss. 'Yes, [Rossi] did hire me, but Luca also hired me, and it was Luca de Meo who ultimately sat down with me and convinced me to join his project,' said Szafnauer. 'And the project was the Alpine project with the 100-race plan, and I think we are 30-something races into that. So we still have some 60-odd races to go, and that is another three years to go to start winning.

'It takes time. It has taken everybody time. I know Luca is a man of his word, and he gave me his word on 100 races to

219

start winning, and sometimes you take a half-step backwards to take two steps forward. So I have no concern that Luca will be true to his word and give me the 100-races time that is required.'

Four days later Szafnauer was out of a job.

According to the announcement, Szafnauer's exit was by 'mutual agreement'. He would stay on for Belgium and then leave the team during the summer break, along with sporting director (and Benetton/Renault/Alpine legend) Alan Permane, leaving vice president of Alpine Bruno Famin to take over the team-principal role in an interim capacity. 'We were not on the same line or timeline on how to recover or reach the level of performance we were aiming for; we decided to split our ways,' Famin said of Szafnauer.

Spa-Francorchamps is a daunting, difficult circuit. It's long and fast and unforgiving, a real drivers' circuit where bravery makes a difference. More often than not, the weather adds to the challenge. Piastri came into the Belgian Grand Prix weekend with plenty of experience there from his time in the junior open-wheel categories ... but at a circuit like Spa there's a difference between experience, and experience in a Formula 1 car. Oscar Piastri's first taste of Spa in a Formula 1 car came in full wet conditions. The rain came and went over the single hour of practice, but there was no talk about slick tyres at any point. Not that Piastri seemed to mind as he splashed his way to second place. Practice doesn't count for much, but it was still a hugely impressive showing for a rookie.

Being a sprint weekend, that sole practice session on Friday was followed by qualifying for Sunday's grand prix. Talk about a baptism of fire. At least the conditions Piastri had flourished in during practice carried over to the start of qualifying. The track was soaked, although, weirdly, there was sunshine as well. Piastri was lightning quick in the wet, going fourth fastest as Lando Norris struggled and even threw his McLaren off the road at one point, but still managing to sneak through to the second segment. As the sun continued to shine over Spa, the changeover from wets to slicks came midway through Q2. Piastri was one of the first drivers to gamble on a soft-compound slick tyre and promptly topped the segment.

The track continued to dry during Q3, which usually would make things easier for a driver. But up until that third qualifying session, all of Piastri's F1 experience at Spa had been in wet conditions. And he'd been quick in the wet. So, the drier the track became, the more the odds were stacked against Piastri. The fact that, in just his second session at Spa in a Formula 1 car, he qualified sixth and ahead of his teammate Norris was remarkable. Even if he still felt he'd left too much out on the track. 'I felt very comfortable when the conditions were really tricky,' said Piastri after qualifying. 'I think in some ways, the track drying up and becoming closer to normal was a hindrance for me because I've not done a dry lap around here in an F1 car. Braking points and stuff like that, especially when off line it's wet, you never want to brake too late. And I think that's where I left quite a bit on the table, unfortunately.'

Saturday brought back Piastri's preferred conditions at Spa, with heavy rain delaying the start of the sprint shootout.

Once the session finally got going, there were eerie parallels to Friday as the sun shone through the clouds and down on a wet track. This time, however, the wetter conditions proved less encouraging for the McLarens, Piastri coming 11th and Norris 13th in SQ1. But they got through SQ2. And then Piastri put his star power beyond doubt by finishing SQ3 in second place, a one-hundredth of a second slower than Max Verstappen. To almost match the reigning world champion, who is in the best car in the field by a mile, at Spa, in front of tens of thousands of Verstappen's loyal Dutch fans (who traditionally make the trek across the border to Belgium) was something remarkable. The best finish to an official, competitive Formula 1 session for the rookie – at the toughest track on the calendar in very tough conditions.

Like the sprint shootout, the start of the sprint race was delayed by the weather. That extended Piastri's first experience of starting a Formula 1 race, even if it was just a sprint, from the front row of the grid. That empty view down to turn 1 – what every racing driver dreams of. The rain did ease, but with the default setting one of conservatism at Spa these days, for reasons outlined later in this chapter, it was decided to start the race behind the safety car – robbing Piastri of the opportunity to sit on the race's starting grid, on the front row, with nobody except the polesitter ahead of him. To add to the peculiar nature of Piastri's first front-row start, he didn't actually take his first front-row start. Once the safety car had pulled in, and Verstappen made his decision to get things going, Piastri swung straight into the pit lane, instead of following the Dutchman down the front straight. He'd decided that the extreme wet tyres were the wrong choice and that he needed a set of intermediates. It was a risk the race leader simply couldn't take at the start, but Verstappen also realised very quickly that he was on the wrong tyre. He pitted at the end of the first lap for the inters, but Piastri had the jump on him, sweeping down the front straight to start the third lap as Verstappen pulled out of his pit box. For the first time in his short career, Oscar Piastri was leading a Formula 1 race.

Holding off Verstappen was never going to be easy. Realistically, it was never going to be possible. Another safety car was triggered after a spin from Fernando Alonso, and when the race did restart, six laps from home, Piastri decided to hit the loud pedal early. In hindsight, it allowed Verstappen to be too close as they came out of the first corner. From there, in the powerful Red Bull, Verstappen was able to tuck under Piastri through Eau Rouge and then cruise into the lead down the Kemmel Straight. Inevitable, but finishing the sprint second was still a standout result for Piastri. Not quite his first podium – the sprint isn't a grand prix – but impressive all the same. On the Saturday evening, Stella was asked if Piastri's rapid evolution, to the point where he was able to give Max Verstappen any sort of headache, was surprising. He said Piastri was, fundamentally, living up to what the team expected of him . . . but that didn't mean there wasn't an element of surprise. 'Where he is at the moment is part of the gradient that we saw right from the start at testing and the first races,' said Stella. 'When you have a gradient, you very much have an expectation. But when you see this expectation becoming material, then you're always a little impressed. And the interesting point of Oscar is that he's making all this look simple. You know, he's making it look simple that in these conditions you pit, you lead the race and you go from inters to dry and you never make a mistake. And all this is achieved with a pretty unique approach in terms of how calm he is, and considerate.'

At the start of the grand prix on Sunday, for the first time all weekend, tyre choice was easy. The clouds were persistent, but the track was dry. In sixth place, Piastri was in what should have been the clean part of the field – but the tight hairpin that is the first corner at Spa is tricky. He made a good getaway as the lights went out and found himself duelling with Carlos Sainz as they came into La Source, the tight right-hand first corner. Sainz had a small lock-up in the braking zone and looked to limit the damage with an early turn into that first corner. But Piastri was right beside him, and they touched. Piastri didn't do much wrong, although in hindsight he could have been more aggressive. If he'd pushed the McLaren another third of a car length up the inside of the corner, then the contact wouldn't have hurt him. As it was, Piastri found himself in no man's land, which led to being sandwiched between Sainz's Ferrari and the wall. The impact left his car badly damaged. Devastating. 'I don't know what he was doing,' reported Piastri over the radio as he limped the car down towards Eau Rouge (with other cars whizzing by at the best part of 300 km/h). 'I was there, and he just turned in like I didn't exist.'

Moments after retiring from the race, a deflated Piastri faced the media. 'I think I had a front puncture; I think the right front was broken as well,' he said of the damage. 'I got up Eau Rouge with about 180-degrees of [steering] lock and [I was] still going straight, so something was clearly broken.

It wasn't fun, that's for sure. I think I was quite lucky that everyone got around me before Eau Rouge.' He had, however, walked back on his radio message that Sainz was at fault for the crash, now describing it as 'quite firmly in the category of a lap 1, turn 1 incident'.

'I think looking back on it we both could have done things a bit differently,' he explained. 'I think from Carlos's point of view, the move to the right surprised me a bit. I think from there I was quite limited. Maybe I could have braked a bit later and been further alongside, but it's very easy to say that with hindsight. I think once I was in that position it was quite hard to either go forward or go backwards, and I was kind of stuck.' Sainz had a slightly different take. He felt Piastri should have yielded . . . an interesting opinion given he was the one that was hurrying to the apex with a brake locked. 'At some point someone needs to back out and he's the guy who is alongside my rear-right that I think needs to back off and move, not me,' said the Spaniard.

Norris managed to climb up to seventh at the finish thanks to some solid late pace on soft-compound tyres to score points for McLaren, but it was still a case of what could have been.

Results Summary

Free Practice 1: 2nd (2m 03.792s, +0.58s)
Qualifying: 6th (1m 47.365s, +1.20s)
Sprint Shootout: 2nd (1m 49.067s, +0.01s)
Sprint: 2nd
Race: DNF

Belgian Grand Prix: A brief history

Once upon a time, there was no sport as life-endangering as motor racing, and Formula 1 in particular. The biggest part of the battle to become a professional racing driver in the 1960s and 1970s, as the cars got faster and faster, was being prepared to die each time you got into one. That's just how it was.

These days, motor racing is safer. There are many reasons for that. Safety-equipment standards have risen enormously. Suits, gloves, boots, helmets – all much safer than ever, thanks to improvements in technology and materials. And the introduction of a head-and-neck-support (HANS) mandate has been about as important as anything since the inclusion of seat belts. Before these changes, too many lives were being lost to seemingly innocuous front-on impacts. As someone who competed in open-wheel racing cars without a HANS device, I simply can't believe we ever did it. We didn't know better, but now we do.

The cars are so much safer now too, with crash structures that protect the drivers, wheel tethers that stop wheels flying into other cars (or marshal posts, or even spectators) and the halo, which offers unprecedented protection for the driver's head. In comparison with what we now know about head trauma from high-speed, contact ball sports, such as the rugby codes, the NFL and the AFL, motor racing is far less dangerous.

Except for the very rare occasions when it's not. And the Belgian Grand Prix stands as a very modern reminder of that.

Tragedies at the race track are usually distant memories. Every trip to Imola invokes an outpouring of remembrance for Ayrton Senna. For some in the paddock that is still a very personal loss, but, through nothing but the inevitability of time, those directly connected to Senna are dwindling in numbers. None of the current drivers on the F1 grid, for example, were close to Senna. In fact, only six – Fernando Alonso, Sergio Perez, Daniel Ricciardo, Valtteri Bottas, Kevin Magnussen, Nico Hülkenberg and Lewis Hamilton – were even born before Senna died.

Suzuka is a little different, because of the crash that ultimately cost Jules Bianchi his life. That one continues to resonate hard, particularly for Charles Leclerc, who was Bianchi's godson.

And then there is Spa-Francorchamps.

The daunting Eau Rouge/Raidillon is one of the most infamous stretches of road in world motor racing. It used to promote a daring game of chicken with the throttle for a driver as he or she tried to not lift. In a modern open-wheeler, it's pretty much easy flat, which means the speeds through the section have sky-rocketed in recent years. That's all well and good, except for the fact that visibility on the climb up the hill is limited from the cockpit of an open-wheeler. In 2019, the mix of low visibility and very high speed led to tragedy. On the second lap of the Formula 2 race, French driver Anthoine Hubert was involved in a high-speed crash with two other cars. He had arrived unsighted to cars slowing for another incident ahead, and he clipped one that sent him into the wall, before he bounced back onto the track and into the path of another car that was arriving at full speed. The horrifying impact cost Hubert, just 22 years of age, his life, while Juan Manuel Correa, the other driver involved in the crash, sustained serious leg injuries.

Lewis Hamilton was conducting a TV interview at the very moment that the crash happened. Midway through a sentence, he looked up and saw the replay on a screen nearby. It visibly rattled him. 'Oh wow,' he said with a stunned expression on his face. 'I hope that kid's good . . .' The interviewer tried to continue the conversation, but Hamilton's mind was clearly elsewhere. 'That's terrifying,' he added, before walking away from the media pen.

Given Hubert was young and known by most of the current F1 drivers, his death sent shockwaves through the paddock. It was particularly painful for Pierre Gasly, a close friend of Hubert's.

Changes were made to that part of the Spa circuit ahead of the 2022 grand prix, with redesigned barriers to try to stop drivers bouncing back onto the circuit following impact. But, in July 2023, tragedy struck again during a Formula Regional European Championship race. Once again, it was the exit of the Eau Rouge/Raidillon complex, and once again, it was a stranded car hit by another travelling at speed. This time, weather was an additional factor, with the race taking place in torrential rain. Eighteen-year-old Dutch driver Dilano van 't Hoff lost his life.

When Formula 1 arrived at Spa nearly a month later, there was clearly an uneasy feeling among the driver group. Racing in the rain has become a big talking point in Formula 1 in recent years, particularly as these new ground-effect cars throw up a lot of spray, further complicating any wet-weather race. It's not so much the lack of grip that worries the drivers, but rather the lack of visibility when following another car. And with such fresh, tragic examples of how badly things can go wrong in low-visibility conditions, it's no surprise that the drivers were left on edge at Spa. Particularly when the Saturday sprint race took place in the rain. 'If Oscar or Max [crashed] in the middle of the straight, I would've been straight inside him,' said Gasly about the sprint race. 'I couldn't even see 10 [to] 20 metres in front of me and even when we were all warming up the tyres and stuff, it was just . . . you were just hoping for the best. I didn't feel safe. When they restarted, I was really hoping no guy gets off the track or collides and gets stuck in the middle of the straight because we know obviously what's happened . . .'

Between wet-weather visibility and high-speed sections of race tracks, Formula 1 is nearing some sort of crossroads. Once upon a time, the sport was marketed on its danger. Loss of life was accepted as part of the show. But, rightly, that is no longer acceptable. Before too long, decisions will have to be made about racing in the rain. Does Formula 1 simply ban the idea? Or does it need to innovate through technology to make racing in wet conditions safer? Spray guards were trialled at Silverstone following the 2023 grand prix, something Oscar Piastri took part in. On an artificially dampened track, he provided the benchmark in a McLaren without spray guards. Mick Schumacher drove a Mercedes fitted with the guards. Part of the running saw Piastri following Schumacher and reporting back regarding the amount of spray. Given the aerodynamic intricacies of a Formula 1 car, making such changes is not a straightforward process. But at least the process has started.

The other philosophical question facing Formula 1 is whether a circuit like Spa, with that fast Eau Rouge/Raidillon complex, is suitable at all for the modern era of sport. By its nature, it's dangerous, which suggests not. But if we take all of the danger away, does the romance of the sport, and the titans who compete in it, disappear too?

It's a hell of a question. And one that will need answering.

19

THE NETHERLANDS

Dutch Grand Prix
Circuit Zandvoort
25–27 August 2023

Spa had undoubtedly been a reality check for McLaren. The upswing in form had looked so good, but the team had, eventually, paid the price for its radical upgrade program. The focus on the upgrades and fixing the high drag on the standard aerodynamics package had come at the expense of a proper low-drag rear-wing solution, critical for the faster circuits. In the wet conditions at Spa, it wasn't an issue, given top speeds are down anyway. But in the dry, the car struggled on the long straights. 'The car is improved in some areas. This was confirmed,' said Andrea Stella. 'But, at the same time, [the Spa] weekend confirmed the areas that we haven't addressed yet. [It] gives us a reality check that there's more work to do and, to some extent, confirms that those areas, they need to be addressed quite urgently. This urgency, for instance, comes from the fact that a second race after [the European summer] shutdown is Monza. You can't go racing in Monza like [we did in Spa]. So, there's urgent work that needs to happen at McLaren to fix the situation.'

Before Monza, however, was the Dutch Grand Prix. The Zandvoort circuit is a unique, old-school layout that snakes through the dunes next to the North Sea. It's almost the complete opposite to most modern Formula 1 circuits. Forget track limits – if you run wide here, you're probably going to crash, either into a wall or the gravel. Before the Dutch Grand Prix weekend, Piastri's experience of the circuit was limited to a handful of practice laps in a Formula Renault. 'I've done a few laps around here, I'd say like maybe 15 or 20 in a Formula Renault in a practice session a few years ago,' he said on the Thursday. 'So it's not completely new. The speed at which all those corners come at me is going to be new, but it's an old-school track. I think it'll probably take all Friday to get close to being fully up to speed. [I'll] sleep on it, process it, then hopefully by Saturday, it's okay. But around here, you get it wrong, you pay a big, big price, which in some ways is nice.

'There's talk about track limits and stuff like that. It should be pretty obvious if you've exceeded track limits, because you'll probably be in a gravel trap somewhere. But yeah, it looks like a really cool track and especially in an F1 car, I'm sure it'll be a lot of fun.'

The unforgiving nature of the fast, banked circuit was highlighted in Free Practice 1 when the ultra-experienced Nico Hülkenberg dropped his Haas at turn 13. The rear let go midway through the fast right-hander, Hülkenberg bouncing through the gravel and nudging the wall. The red flag to recover the stricken Haas was followed by a flurry of fast times, Piastri keeping his nose clean and ending up a respectable eighth fastest.

Ten minutes into Free Practice 2, the wall outside of the Hugenholtzbocht corner turned into a magnet for Australians. Karun Chandhok was midway through a monologue on how well Piastri was dealing with the unique challenge of Zandvoort in a Formula 1 car when the camera cut to his McLaren facing the wall and clearly damaged. Classic commentator's curse. As the camera switched to another angle, Daniel Ricciardo's AlphaTauri was spotted a few metres up the road, sporting even more damage. The McLaren pit wall radioed through to Piastri. 'Is the car possible to come back?' was the question. 'No, no. Sorry,' was the very clear response from Piastri. It turned out that he had simply lost the rear on the change of direction into the left-hander and, as he overcorrected, he hit the wall with the front of the car. Seconds later, Ricciardo arrived on the scene. The distraction of the stranded McLaren was enough for him to miss his turn-in point and clatter into the wall as well. 'Sorry, I didn't see the McLaren,' he reported back to his team over the radio.

Piastri emerged from the crash with a dent in his pride and facing a loss of critical practice running. It seemed that would go for Ricciardo as well. But the next radio transmission between the Western Aussie and the AlphaTauri team hinted that all wasn't well. 'Are you okay?' Ricciardo was asked. He swore and then said, 'My hand . . .'

After the session, Red Bull confirmed that Ricciardo had been taken to hospital in Haarlem for checks on his left hand. A while later, it was announced that Ricciardo had broken a metacarpal and was out of action for the foreseeable future. Liam Lawson, young Kiwi and Red Bull reserve driver, was drafted in as a last-minute replacement.

The rain rolled in on Saturday, the field running full wets as they splashed around for the third and final practice session. Despite Piastri's Friday crash, there were some good signs from McLaren. Lando Norris had topped FP2, and in the third and final practice, Piastri led the way for the team with the seventh-fastest time. Q3 beckoned, no matter what the weather gods had up their collective sleeves.

Not for the first time this season, those gods kept the paddock guessing. Q1 started in wet, but improving, conditions. At the same time, more rain was expected. For a hot minute, true to his wet-weather form, it looked like Piastri might top the first segment of qualifying, only for Williams driver Alex Albon to provide an even bigger shock as he maximised the conditions and led the way into Q2. For Piastri, third was just fine. He was in the mix for Q2 as well, leading the way as the chequered flag came out . . . until he was bested by hometown hero Max Verstappen by a lazy half a second. In Q3, the lost track time from Friday finally caught up with Piastri. Like Spa, the drying conditions worked against the rookie. He lacked the experience to really piece together his final run, to find the limit as the conditions evolved. Even a slight lack of track knowledge will do that. He ended up eighth on the grid while Norris charged to second. 'I was hoping it would stay a little bit wet, because in those conditions it's the same for everybody and it's new conditions for everybody,' said Piastri. 'When it was dry, not getting those laps in yesterday, through what was my own fault, made a difference today.'

It was slick tyres for the start of Sunday's grand prix, but not for long. Drivers pitted for intermediates within two laps, although Piastri was among those to brave out the mixed conditions on the soft slick tyre. The strategy did come back to benefit Piastri as the field had to switch to the slicks once again. For a while, the sun was shining. But by the latter stages of the race, dark clouds had gathered. Eleven laps from home, just as the race had settled into a rhythm, the heavens opened again. The field dived into the pits for intermediate tyres, but it was the wrong choice. The rain was too heavy and the extreme wet tyre was the only rubber to be on. Someone was going to pay the price for the conditions, and it ended up being Zhou Guanyu, who buried his Alfa Romeo in the barriers at turn 1. Red flag. Through all the madness, Piastri ended up ninth, only two spots behind teammate Norris. A solid result given so much had gone against him across the weekend.

Results Summary

Free Practice 1: 8th (1m 12.658s, +0.81s)
Free Practice 2: 19th (1m 12.901s, +1.57s)
Free Practice 3: 7th (1m 22.892s, +1.26s)
Qualifying: 8th (1m 11.938s, +1.37s)
Race: 9th

Dutch Grand Prix: A brief history

The Dutch sure are patient when it comes to success in Formula 1.

Seventeen drivers from the Netherlands have competed in the world championship. Five of them have scored world championship points. Two have stood on a Formula 1 podium. Only one has been a race winner. Only one has been world champion.

The first Dutch driver to score world championship points was Jonkheer Karel Pieter Antoni Jan Hubertus 'Carel' Godin de Beaufort. Carel Godin de Beaufort was one of the last true amateurs to succeed in Formula 1. He competed under the Ecurie Maarsbergen banner, a nod to the village near Utrecht where the Beaufort family were royalty of sorts. His cars, mostly Porsches, ran in classic Dutch orange. He scored a grand total of four world championship points, scored a single point at a time with sixth-place finishes in the Netherlands and France (1962) and Belgium and the US (1963). In 1964, he was killed in practice for the German Grand Prix.

The next Dutch driver to score world championship points was Gijs van Lennep. Like Beaufort, he too was a 'Jonkheer', part of the Dutch nobility. Van Lennep's professional career started in sports-cars as a Porsche factory driver. He and Dr Helmut Marko combined forces to win the 24 Hours of Le Mans in 1971 in a Porsche 917K. Dr Marko, of course, would go on to play a very significant role in the career of the greatest Dutch driver of all time. Van Lennep scored two world championship points in his career, one with a sixth-place finish for Williams at the Dutch Grand Prix in 1973 and another for a sixth-place finish for Ensign at the German Grand Prix in 1975.

Next up on the list of Dutch world championship points scorers is Jos Verstappen. 'Jos the Boss' is your classic Formula 1 journeyman. He spent eight seasons in Formula 1 and managed, somehow, to cycle through seven different teams.

Verstappen was signed on as test driver for Benetton in 1994 but found himself thrust into a race seat when JJ Lehto was injured during pre-season testing. His career got off to a spectacular start when he flipped during the Brazilian Grand Prix. He made a second start before being benched once Lehto was fit. At least temporarily. Lehto lasted exactly four rounds before he was benched and Verstappen came back into the line-up alongside Michael Schumacher. Benetton was a good team at the time (Schumacher won the world title in 1994 and 1995) and Verstappen was able to finish third in Hungary and Belgium. Perhaps the most famous moment of his grand-prix career came at the German Grand Prix in 1994 when his car was engulfed in flames during a pit stop. Verstappen and the crew were uninjured, but photos of the inferno made front pages around the globe.

Looking to secure the manufacturers' title, Benetton opted to bench Verstappen in favour of the experienced Johnny Herbert for the last two races of the 1994 season. The Benetton team boss Flavio Briatore then decided to farm Verstappen out to the uncompetitive Simtek team for 1995. That union lasted a whole five races, before Verstappen returned to Benetton as test driver. Briatore could have kept Verstappen for 1996 but decided against it. So, Verstappen moved to the Footwork Arrows outfit. There was a point for a sixth place in Argentina, but for the most part, Verstappen failed to make the finish line. For a long time, it seemed that another season with Arrows beckoned – until it became clear that world champion Damon Hill was on the market. Arrows snapped Hill up and Verstappen was, once again, without a seat. He moved to Tyrrell for 1997 but was shuffled out when British American Tobacco bought the team at the end of that year. That left him on the outer for the 1998 season, until Stewart Grand Prix drafted him in as a mid-season replacement for an underperforming Jan Magnussen. For 1999 he teamed up with Honda for its planned factory entry to Formula 1, which didn't get beyond the testing phase. In 2000 Verstappen returned to a race seat with Arrows, the surprisingly efficient A21 helping him to a fifth place in Canada and a fourth in Italy. He stayed with Arrows for 2001, scoring points again with sixth in Austria. The final stop on his F1 journey was a pointless campaign with Minardi in 2003.

Between all that jumping from team to team, Verstappen and his partner Sophie Kumpen, a gun karter and racer in her own right, welcomed Max Verstappen to the world. The younger Verstappen was ultra successful in karting and, after a brief stint in the junior open-wheel categories, was handed a shot at Formula 1 as a teenager by Red Bull. As we all know, Red Bull's gamble paid off. And so did the patience from Dutch Formula 1 fans. It might have taken years, but you'd have to reckon Max Verstappen was worth the wait. Not only is he the only Dutch driver to have won a Formula 1 race as of 2023, he's also the only Dutch driver to have won a world title. He has three titles to his name at the time of writing and is probably going to win a lot more. It's hard to see how he won't go down in modern Formula 1 history as one of the greatest drivers of all time.

The younger Verstappen's success has been wonderfully embraced by the Dutch fanbase. Even before the Dutch Grand Prix was revived, having fallen off the schedule in the mid-1980s, Dutch fans would descend on a number of the central European grands prix with their orange flares, most notably the Belgian Grand Prix, being so easily accessible from the nearby Netherlands. Since 2021 there's been a proper Dutch Grand Prix back on the schedule. And as of 2023, Max Verstappen is unbeaten at Zandvoort.

20

ITALY

Italian Grand Prix
Autodromo Nazionale Monza
1–3 September 2023

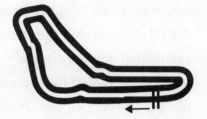

McLaren's high-speed woes at Spa were a wake-up call for Monza. The Temple of Speed, as it is known, is one of the fastest circuits on the Formula 1 schedule. But unlike other high-speed layouts, such as Silverstone and Jeddah, there is little in the way of fast corners. Monza is all about long straights interrupted by big stops and slow corners. Traditionally, teams bring a special aerodynamics package to Monza to maximise top speed. And, based on what McLaren had seen from its car at Spa, a revised rear wing was critical. Given the significant resources that had gone into the B-spec car, there wasn't scope to develop a rear wing specifically for Monza, with the team instead reworking its existing low-downforce package by trimming and removing parts of the rear wing to improve it.

*

239

Friday at the Italian Grand Prix was a day of solid, but far from spectacular, running for the McLarens. Norris kicked off the first practice session with a huge aero-monitoring rig attached to his car as the team continued to assess and validate its updates. Piastri had a bit of an off at turn 1 at some point, which is an easy thing to do at Monza. The long front straight leads into a painfully slow chicane, so it's critical to brake as late as possible and maximise the time spent at top speed. And given the cars are carrying so little downforce, getting them stopped into turn 1 can be quite a challenge. Norris was seventh and Piastri eleventh after the first hour of running. There was some excitement for Piastri early in the second practice session when he arrived at the Seconda Variante chicane at full speed to find Lewis Hamilton crawling through the corner. Piastri was forced to take evasive action and abandon his lap. 'Yeah, nice from Hamilton,' he reported over the radio. Soft-tyre runs helped the McLaren drivers climb up the order as the session wore off, Norris sitting second and Piastri fourth when the red flag flew a few minutes from the end. The culprit was Sergio Perez, who'd sent his Red Bull into the gravel at the Parabolica. The session did get going again but there were no significant improvements near the top of the times.

On the Saturday, McLaren celebrated its 60th birthday. Six decades to the day since the famous team was founded by New Zealander Bruce McLaren in 1963. Since then, the team has racked up 8 constructors' titles and 12 drivers' titles in Formula 1. While there had been signs in recent races that the team was clawing back its powerhouse status, there was no great confidence over any sort of birthday surprise at Monza. The team decided to limit Piastri's running in the third and final practice session, 15 minutes passing before he turned a lap. A soft-tyre run helped him jump into the top six, before he made a mistake on his next run midway through Seconda Variante and bounced through the gravel on the exit. That necessitated a trip back to the pits to ensure the floor hadn't been damaged. There was more action for Piastri as the session came to a close. Looking for a final run, he arrived at the first chicane to find a slow-moving Carlos Sainz. The Ferrari driver then swung across in the middle of the chicane, resulting in light contact between the pair. In Piastri's now typical laid-back radio style, he keyed up and said, 'Mate, is Carlos blind, or what?' Sainz was shown the bad sportsmanship flag, but not before taking a swipe at Piastri on his own radio transmission, where he suggested the contact was 'on purpose' from the Australian. It was almost like he thought it was some sort of carryover from their first-lap clash in Belgium . . .

There wasn't a sense that McLaren was in the fight for pole in Italy, but getting both cars into Q3 had become the new normal for the squad. Between the usual track evolution and trying to score a tow, timing was everything in all three segments of qualifying. With three minutes to go Piastri found himself stuck in the drop zone, before heading out once more and going 12th fastest . . . at least for a few seconds. That time was promptly wiped for a track-limits infringement, dropping Piastri back to 19th with less than a minute remaining in Q1. It took a Hail Mary effort right at the flag to progress to the second segment.

In Q2, it was Norris's turn for a scare, the Briton sneaking through in 10th place by just 0.013s. Piastri's passage was comparatively easy as he finished up eighth.

Piastri continued to lead the way for McLaren in Q3, jumping Hamilton to qualify seventh, two spots clear of Norris. Piastri was satisfied with his Q3 effort, but realistic about any hopes of moving forward in the race, given the McLaren's ongoing straight-line speed deficiency. 'We're lacking a little bit of pace to the front guys this weekend,' he said, before adding that even Alex Albon wasn't a realistic target. For context, the Williams driver was the surprise of the session based on his car's impressive top speed. 'We will not be going past [him], not on a straight at least, anyway. We'll see what we can do. I think we know that this track, with such long straights, is still not ideal for us. We're starting in the points, and we'll try and finish there too.'

If Piastri thought Sunday would be a tame affair at the back end of the points, he was badly mistaken. The drama started before the lights had even gone out, when the engine in Yuki Tsunoda's AlphaTauri expired on the formation lap. That meant an aborted start, one of the great frustrations for a race driver after they've meticulously worked through the pre-race procedures, only to have to do it all over again. When the race finally did get going, Piastri made a very positive start by clearing Albon on the opening lap. But, in keeping with Piastri's own predictions, Albon was able to blast back into sixth place between the first and second chicanes only a lap later. Piastri spent the rest of the first stint running just ahead of Norris, McLaren opting to run both cars long without stopping. As the race leaders all cycled through the pits, Piastri found himself leading a proper grand prix for the first time in his career. It was only due to the pit sequence, but a nice moment all the same.

That's where the niceties stopped, though. Once again, it was Norris who was put on the preferred strategy when McLaren pulled him into the pits on lap 22. Piastri pitted a lap later, giving Norris the slightest of undercuts. Piastri left the pit lane and blazed down to turn 1 on the right-hand side of the road. To his left, Norris arrived in the braking zone at speed. Norris was slightly ahead as the pair swung into the right-hand part of the chicane. As the track swung to the left the two McLarens made light contact, Norris emerging from the chicane with track position. Few things are frowned upon like contact between teammates, even if there isn't any lasting damage.

With their positions reversed, Norris and Piastri carried on in seventh and eighth place. Norris did his best to attack Albon ahead, while Piastri eventually came under fire from Hamilton behind. The Mercedes driver had run longer than anybody in the first stint and then switched to a set of medium-compound tyres when the rest of the lead group were on hards. That meant he was quicker than the cars ahead, but on a tyre that may run out of grip before the end of the race. Hamilton's cause was helped by the fierce Albon–Norris battle, which created a bottleneck for Piastri. With 10 laps to go, Piastri's attention had been firmly taken off Albon and Norris as he found his mirrors full of Hamilton's Mercedes. Initially, Hamilton played a smart game as he looked to get past Piastri, biding his time through the first chicane before using his superior tyre grip to get better drive and pull alongside him heading into the second chicane. Then, the seven-time world champion made a slight error in judgement as they raced side-by-side into the braking zone. Piastri, seemingly resigned to the fact that Hamilton was going to get through, was as far right as he could go on the approach to the left-hander. Suddenly, the Mercedes veered right to open up the corner, and they made significant contact. 'He just turned across me under braking,' reported a bemused Piastri as he limped back to the pits for a new front wing. Hamilton seemed to escape any serious damage, but he couldn't escape the wrath of race control as he copped a five-second penalty. Not that it mattered: Hamilton was able to run down both Norris and Albon and then pull five seconds clear of them both to finish sixth. Piastri, meanwhile, survived another hairy Seconda Variante moment with Liam Lawson before finishing 12th.

To Hamilton's credit, he sought out Piastri after the race to apologise for their crash. 'I apologised because it was obviously my fault,' said Hamilton. 'And it naturally wasn't intentional. I got up alongside and just misjudged the gap that I had to the right [and] clipped him. It could happen anytime. But I knew shortly afterwards, it must have been my fault. I wanted to make sure he knew that it wasn't intentional. That's what gentlemen do, right?'

Meanwhile, the stewards may have overlooked the contact between the two McLarens midway through the race, but Andrea Stella didn't. He made his disappointment in his drivers very clear. 'There should never, ever be contact between two McLaren cars,' he said. 'There was a contact, which doesn't fit the way we go racing at McLaren. What is important is to have clear parameters as to what you deem acceptable and what you deem unacceptable. You deal with racing in a similar way.

This is very clear that for any driver, there's something bigger than them. It's the team.' When asked if the team had contributed to the awkwardness by giving Norris the opportunity to undercut, Stella pushed the onus straight back on the drivers. 'If the contact is due to the fact that there was pressure because of the undercut, then we have something to review,' he said. 'Because it means drivers put their team at risk because of affirming themselves. This is not acceptable.'

In truth, neither driver was at any sort of major fault. There were two main contributing factors: one, the way the first chicane jinks right and then left, meaning the preferred line changes in an instant; and two, that there was just so little to split between the McLaren drivers in terms of pace. Stella did, however, hint at who may have received the more severe dressing down behind closed doors with a reference to a driver on cold tyres maybe needing to take a bit more caution.

'My role is to give [the drivers] principles and a clear parameter within which they can race,' he said. 'In terms of how you stay within the parameter, it's not for us to say because we are not the drivers. It's actually within them to have the skillset to say, "The tyres are a bit cold, maybe I need to take more margin." They need to appreciate that there is no way the line should be crossed.'

The driver on cold tyres was, of course, Piastri. There are moments even the most measured of rookies, and the most promising of talents, falls on the wrong side of the split-second decision-making process.

Still, even a missed opportunity to score points and a rap across the knuckles from the boss was decent in comparison to Alpine's Monza weekend. Pierre Gasly and Esteban Ocon were bundled out of Q1 on Saturday. On Sunday, Ocon had to retire his car mid-race due to steering issues, while Gasly battled to 15th. McLaren's form had seen it pull clear of Alpine in the constructors' standings, the two teams sitting fifth and sixth respectively. In fact, McLaren's target was quickly becoming running down fourth-placed Aston Martin. The plucky squad, led by Fernando Alonso, had done the opposite to McLaren and had nosedived in form compared to the start of the season. McLaren was less than 100 points behind as of Monza – and looking the much faster of the two teams.

Results Summary

Free Practice 1: 11th (1m 23.446s, +0.79s)
Free Practice 2: 4th (1m 21.545s, +0.19s)
Free Practice 3: 14th (1m 22.302s, +1.39s)
Qualifying: 7th (1m 20.785s, +0.49s)
Race: 12th

Italian Grand Prix: A brief history

The slipstream. It's always been the holy grail at Monza.

In open-wheel racing, drivers are always looking for what is either called the slipstream or the tow. Both terms refer to tucking in behind another car and letting that car do the hard work in terms of the airflow. The lead car cuts a nice hole in the air and the car behind can go faster, without that resistance.

Back in what were technologically simpler times, the tow was the key to close racing, as it penalised whoever was leading, fostering lead changes. The tow was a huge benefit at nearly every circuit in the world.

But few places provided epic slipstream battles like Monza.

The Formula 1 cars of the 1960s and early 1970s were ideal for slipstreaming. The classic cigar shape, with the radiator at the front to facilitate a slim, sleek body, and the engine right behind the driver. Even once rudimentary aerodynamics started to come along in the sport, they would be ditched for the flat-out blast around Monza.

The 1967 Italian Grand Prix is a classic example of an epic Monza slipstreaming effort. It may not have been, given the pace the legendary Jim Clark showed in his Lotus early in the race. He looked to have successfully 'broken the tow' – a term that describes pulling just clear of the slipstream effect – before a slow puncture brought him back to the field. Clark eventually needed to pit for a new wheel and returned to the race more than a lap down. Once he got going again, Clark began to tow teammate Graham Hill clear of the pack. In fact, he towed Hill nearly a lap clear of the chasing pack, led by Jack Brabham. When Hill's engine expired, Clark had caught back up to leaders Brabham and John Surtees – and blasted past them into the lead. Until his Cosworth engine coughed on the last lap, starved of fuel. Surtees burst back into the lead and crossed the line 0.2s ahead of Brabham in a wild slipstreaming battle. Clark had to settle for a distant third.

The 1969 race was even wilder. It was a race-long, four-strong battle between Matra drivers Jackie Stewart and Jean-Pierre Beltoise, Lotus driver Jochen Rindt, and Bruce McLaren in the car bearing his name. There were countless lead changes as the quartet duked it out. The thing about an amazing slipstream battle is that it's all about timing. Sometimes, the lead is the worst place to be until the final moment of the race. In this case, all four drivers were in the mix to win as they came out of the Parabolica for the 68th and final time. Stewart ended up winning the race by 0.08s over Rindt. Beltoise was third, a whole 0.17s behind the winner. McLaren was 0.19s back in fourth. Imagine missing out on a podium finish by 0.02s . . .

The ultimate Monza slipstreaming battle, however, was 1971. To this day the race stands as the closest finish in Formula 1 history, with 0.01s separating first and second. The top five were separated by just 0.61s. Incredibly, the five drivers who did battle for victory were all drivers who were yet to win a grand prix. BRM driver Peter Gethin was the man who crossed the line first, ahead of Ronnie Peterson (March), François Cevert (Tyrrell), Mike Hailwood (Surtees) and Howden Ganley (BRM). At an average speed of 242.615 km/h, the race held the record of the fastest in Formula 1 history for 32 years.

In modern Formula 1, the slipstream is a little complicated. Thanks to the dirty air that comes off the back of the high-aerodynamic cars, and the sensitivity of the aero and the tyres when you're following, the tow isn't worth what it once was. That's why the Drag Reduction System (DRS) was invented. DRS is a system where drivers can open a slot in the rear wing in certain, dedicated parts of a circuit when within a second of another car. It is quite literally an artificial reproduction of the slipstream.

These days, it takes a circuit like Monza, where aero levels are slashed to the bare minimum, for the tow to have any great value. And that's why we see awkward scenes in qualifying where drivers effectively line up, refusing to start their run without someone first going ahead of them.

Of course, Monza is more than its long straights. It's a place where the passionate support for motor racing is unparalleled.

As is the support for the Italian manufacturers. The 'tifosi' is the name given to the fanatical local support. It was never originally tied to Ferrari, the term applying to local fans of a number of sports, and a number of Italian manufacturers in different disciplines of motorsport. But over time, the term 'tifosi' has become synonymous with the Ferrari Formula 1 team. Each year, the tifosi flock to Monza to support Ferrari. The support for the team comes ahead of any Italian drivers on the grid. A Ferrari driver is an adopted Italian anyway. This preferential treatment was first made obvious at the 'second' Italian Grand Prix, the San Marino Grand Prix, in 1983. Despite its name, a way around the rule that a nation could not technically host two grands prix, the San Marino race was held at Imola in Italy. Italian Riccardo Patrese, driving for Brabham, was in the box seat for victory before he crashed a handful of laps from the end. That handed victory to Frenchman Patrick Tambay in the Ferrari. Despite the Italian driver's loss, the tifosi went wild.

Another example of the tifosi's oddball support is a Frenchman named Jean-Louis Schlesser . . . who is neither Italian, nor a Ferrari driver. But who was a tifosi favourite, nonetheless. Why? Well, in 1988, McLaren was unstoppable. Between its drivers Ayrton Senna and Alain Prost, the team won 15 of the 16 races on the F1 schedule. The only race it didn't win was the Italian Grand Prix. For that race, Schlesser, Williams' test driver, was drafted into the race line-up to deputise for the unwell Nigel Mansell. Fast forward to the closing stages of the race, and Senna was in control ahead of Ferrari driver Gerhard Berger. Until he went to lap Schlesser and they made contact, which left Senna beached in the gravel. Berger went on to win the Monza race and send the tifosi into a frenzy, cementing Schlesser as a hero among the local fans.

21

SINGAPORE

Singapore Grand Prix
Marina Bay Street Circuit
15–17 September 2023

The Italian Grand Prix marked the end of the European season, with Formula 1 embarking on its stretch of flyaway races through Asia, the Americas and the Middle East to round out 2023. After the relative straightforwardness of Monza, the Marina Bay circuit on the streets of Singapore offered a significantly more technical test, with a far wider range of corners spread out over a very long lap. The form that McLaren had been showing since Austria was remarkable, given where the team had started the season. But unless they are winning, drivers are never happy, and having struggled with outright top speed at Monza, the team's attention turned back to the low-speed weakness of the McLaren heading to Singapore.

Another suite of upgrades was applied to Lando Norris's car, while Piastri received a few bits and pieces but would

250

have to wait until Japan for the full package. The upgrades included an eye-catching new sidepod design, described as a 'waterslide' channel. There was also a revised engine cover, a new floor and diffuser shape, and a new front wing and endplate geometry. 'Probably since Austria, it is the thing that we believe will help us move forward the most since then,' said Norris on the eve of the event in Singapore. 'Obviously, we've not run it on the track yet, and so we don't want to say too much until we've actually got it to work properly, but it's a good step. The team have worked hard to get it on one of the cars here, and then we'll have the rest in Japan too. So it is an exciting couple of weekends for us. If we can fix a little bit of this slow-speed [weakness], if I can get a bit more what I believe the car needs to take that next step – a bit of it is what we hopefully will have this weekend, a bit of it will be what I want from a driving style point of view – that's when I'm confident we can take the fight to the majority of the teams, including Red Bull.'

Things certainly looked rosy for Norris and his new McLaren in Friday practice as he went fourth fastest in the first session and sixth fastest in the second. Piastri, in a very stark contrast, was 19th and 15th in the first two sessions respectively. Not that the gulf between the teammates was solely down to the upgrades – Piastri admitted on Friday evening that, in classic Piastri style, he'd spent the day building up his pace and that there was plenty of speed left up his sleeve. 'It's difficult,' he explained. 'I mean, it's hot. It's a technical circuit. It's bumpy. There's a lot going on. It was also very dusty in FP1. It's a difficult circuit. I enjoyed it, though. It's been a lot of fun. But we need to see if we can find a bit more speed. I think the gap from [FP1] to [FP2] obviously shrunk a lot. So I feel like I'm improving and learning all the time. It's going to take a bit of time.'

Come Saturday, Piastri was clearly more comfortable on the long, complicated city circuit. In the third hour-long practice session, he charged to seventh place, four spots behind Norris. Yet another double helping of McLarens in Q3 seemed very much on the table. Qualifying kicked off at 9 p.m. local time under the bright lights that line the track. Initially, things seemed to be going to plan. Both McLarens were well inside the top 15 on their banker runs (the conservative effort to get a time on the board) and only needed to evolve with the track, and the rest of the field, on their final runs to ensure passage to the second segment of qualifying. The radio chatter between the pit wall and the drivers was that a time of 1m 32.5s would, roughly, be the cut-off to make it through to Q2. After the early runs, only five cars were under that number, highlighting how much track evolution the boffins were predicting. Piastri's banker was 1m 32.902s, well below what was going to be needed to progress.

Usually, being further back in the order is better when it comes to the track conditions, as there's more rubber going down on the racing line. The danger, however, is that something completely out of your control can derail your plans. As the times of the drivers ahead of him in the queue improved, Piastri was shuffled into the Q1 drop zone. No drama yet, though, given he was on his critical final lap. So was Lance Stroll, a bit further down the road. Also needing to improve to have any shot at progression, the Aston Martin driver was pushing. On the way out of turn 17, the third last corner, Stroll needed a ton of opposite lock to avoid the wall. He nailed the apex of turn 18 and then ran just wide on the exit of turn 19, the run onto the start/finish straight. His car straddled the exit kerb, which spat him into the wall at a frightening speed. The destroyed Aston Martin bounced back to the middle of the circuit, facing the wrong way. Race control immediately threw a red flag, as Stroll confirmed over the radio that he was okay. Good news for him, but the red flag was bad news for Piastri. Unable to finish his lap, he was left stranded in 17th place and out of qualifying. 'I would have been able to get through if it wasn't for that,' said Piastri. 'I don't have anything else to say about that. These are obviously things that are gonna happen at times. I wished it had happened about 15 seconds later . . .'

While Stroll had emerged relatively unharmed from his crash, it was later decided that his weekend was done. Between some lingering soreness from the impact, and the state of his car, both the team and driver elected that he take the rest of the weekend off.

Starting 17th on a street circuit is hardly an enticing prospect. From that far back, on a layout not ideal for overtaking, it's hard to envisage getting a points result. Throw in the fact it will be a hot, brutal affair with drivers literally sweating out kilograms along the way, and Piastri can be forgiven for not being overly excited heading into the Singapore Grand Prix.

Given his starting position, the team had two options when it came to strategy. Be super aggressive to try to swing things Piastri's way, knowing that such a tactic could come back to bite them in any number of ways (including a destroyed car). Or take the complete opposite approach – demand that Piastri keep his nose clean, and see if, somehow, the race came to them. When Piastri rolled out to start the race on the medium-compound Pirellis, rather than the more aggressive soft tyres, the plan was clear. Despite the more cautious approach, Piastri made a promising start to the race by climbing to 14th in the first couple of laps. A well-timed safety car around 20 laps in allowed Piastri to jump Nico Hülkenberg for 13th, before he cleared Liam Lawson for 12th shortly after the restart. When Kevin Magnussen out-braked himself, Piastri moved into 11th place. When Sergio Perez pitted on lap 39, Piastri moved into 10th, which then became 9th when Max Verstappen stopped two laps later. A little under 20 laps from home, Esteban Ocon's Alpine rolled to a stop on the inside of turn 2. 'No, no!' shouted the Frenchman, who'd been poised for a good haul of points. That elevated Piastri to eighth place. Then, Fernando Alonso served a painfully long pit stop that included a five-second penalty for an earlier breach of the pit entry line, and a delayed tyre change. That moved Piastri into seventh. He dropped back to eighth briefly when Verstappen charged back through field, before reclaiming seventh place when George Russell hit the wall.

And that's where he finished the race. The slow-and-steady approach had worked beautifully. 'We were discussing since yesterday,' explained Andrea Stella. 'Do we want to be sort of aggressive with a strategy, you know, like you pit lap 1, and then you tried to undercut everyone? Or we just let the race come to us by staying out of trouble. We knew we had pace in the car. Not the pace of the new car, but I think even the old car was good enough for points. And we opted to go for the second option. I think it looks easy, but it requires no mistakes, capitalise your opportunities, overtake when you are in condition to do so . . . and when the tyres get difficult, just cope with it. That's what Oscar did. And for a rookie, it is quite impressive.'

Meanwhile, Norris finished the race second behind Ferrari's Carlos Sainz, marking McLaren's third podium of the season, and the first since Hungary back in July. The upgraded McLaren was clearly another step forward.

Results Summary

Free Practice 1: 19th (1m 35.474s, +2.12s)
Free Practice 2: 15th (1m 33.461s, +1.34s)
Free Practice 3: 7th (1m 32.730s, +0.66s)
Qualifying: 17th (1m 32.902s, +1.92s)
Race: 7th

Singapore Grand Prix: A brief history

Singapore is one of the more, if not the most, peculiar stops on the Formula 1 calendar. The Southeast Asian hub first joined the schedule in 2008 thanks to the work of former Formula 1 boss Bernie

Ecclestone. Wanting to take advantage of the huge (and pre-Netflix) popularity of the sport in Asia, but not wanting to sacrifice another race to a non-Europe friendly time zone (such as Australia, Japan, China and Malaysia), Ecclestone decided to make the new Singapore Grand Prix a sensational night race. Not only would it showcase the vibrancy of Singapore and have the marketing pull of being Formula 1's first race under lights, but it would also mean sessions could comfortably straddle a number of time zones. Not too late for the huge fan base in Asia, not too early for the huge fan base in Europe.

Upon the first visit to Singapore in 2008, the Formula 1 paddock clocked on to something important. Given it was a night race, geared to cater to the European time zone, why fight jet lag? It was unavoidable for the other Asian races on the calendar and for the Australian Grand Prix, where the track action takes place during the day. But in Singapore, there was no reason to be awake in the daylight hours. There was no reason to be jet-lagged. Every driver and team member could just follow their body clocks and stay on European time.

The Singapore race generally starts at 8 p.m. local time, which equates to 2 p.m. European Central Time. The practice and quali-fying sessions also shift to later in the day and evening, so they ultimately relate to the main race in the same way they would for any other grand prix. For the night-race weekend, drivers will gener-ally work on a schedule of going to bed at 5 a.m. local time, before waking up at 2 p.m. local time. Pre-weekend media sessions are scheduled for late afternoon, while the post-race media sessions run until midnight. Hotels are warned to not try to clean rooms occupied by drivers and team staff during the day, and accommo-dation with the best black-out curtains are most popular among the F1 paddock. Piastri summed up the weirdness of the whole situation perfectly when, a day after arriving in Singapore for his first race there in 2023, he tweeted, 'I love a lie-in but breakfast at 14:30 local time is even a new one for me.'

It's not only the nocturnal existence that makes the Singapore event a little kooky. The ultra-urban setting spooked Red Bull Racing in 2008 when the gearbox on Mark Webber's car failed at turn 13 during the inaugural race. Team boss Christian Horner declared that the issue had stemmed from the underground railway running under the roads used for the track. 'A tram line runs beneath the track at that corner and it seems as if static from a passing tram at the very moment Mark was in the corner passed through the ground [and was to blame],' Horner claimed. It sounded legitimate enough, until the SMRT Corporation, which operates Singapore's MRT underground railway, interjected. 'There is no MRT track beneath turn 13,' a spokesman later countered. 'The nearest MRT tunnel is about 200 metres away, with a depth of about 10 metres. In addition, train wheels and running rails are made of metal and therefore do not generate static electricity charges during train operations.'

Another peculiarity of Singapore is the huge monitor lizards that, from time to time, happen to wander out onto the track. The first sighting of a rogue lizard came in 2016 thanks to Max Verstappen. 'Woah,' he reported over the radio during a session. 'There's a giant lizard on the track.' His race engineer Gianpiero Lambiase calmly responded with, 'Face to face with Godzilla then, mate . . .'

The gag was reprised in 2023 when practice was interrupted by another curious reptile. Verstappen was once again right on the scene. 'There's a lizard again on the track,' he excitedly told Lambiase over the radio. 'A smaller one this time.' Lambiase responded in his dry style, 'Okay, understood. Maybe Godzilla had a kid.' There were reports, however, that Godzilla Junior didn't make it to safety and instead succumbed to Fernando Alonso's Aston Martin . . .

Singapore was also the scene of one of the great modern Formula 1 controversies, a.k.a. Crashgate. Alonso, the alleged lizard killer, made history in 2008 for winning the inaugural Singapore Grand Prix. At the time he didn't realise just how historically significant the win would be. Alonso was driving for the Renault team, then under the control of Flavio Briatore. The Spaniard started the Singapore race way back in 15th place in a car that wasn't overly competitive. But, in what seemed like a fortuitous piece of timing, he pitted at the exact right moment before his teammate Nelson Piquet Junior fired into the wall, which brought out the safety car. That filtered Alonso up to the front of the queue and, once in the lead, he was able to hold off the faster cars within the tight confines of the street circuit. There wasn't much thought given to the whole thing at the time. Piquet Junior was re-signed by Renault on a one-year deal for the 2009 season, before being axed nine races in, without a single point to his name.

And then Piquet Junior claimed that he had been asked to crash in Singapore the previous year so that Alonso could win the race.

The FIA investigated the matter and reached the conclusion that Renault, led by Briatore, had indeed conspired to fix the result. The team was handed a two-year suspended ban. Both Briatore and engineering boss Pat Symonds left the team, the former handed an indefinite ban from any FIA-sanctioned event, while the latter was banned for five years, although the severity of both bans was later downgraded. Alonso, meanwhile, escaped punishment after it became clear they neither he nor his crew knew about the sinister plan to secure his unlikely, and highly illegal, win.

22

JAPAN

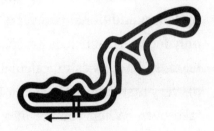

When McLaren lured Oscar Piastri away from Alpine, it did so based on a two-year commitment covering 2023 and 2024. By late September, that commitment felt awfully short-sighted. Piastri was living up to every bit of his potential, driving more like a seasoned star than a rookie as he pushed Norris and scored points. And McLaren was looking every bit like a front-running team (even if Red Bull Racing was still a fair way down the road). Somewhat unsurprisingly, a couple of days out from the Japanese Grand Prix, McLaren confirmed that Piastri's existing contract had been torn up, and he'd signed a brand-new agreement that locked him in as a McLaren driver until the end of 2026. Andrea Stella explained that while Formula 1 is 'a highly professional business, highly competitive', it is also underpinned by human beings. And to get the best out of human beings, you have to give them confidence by showing trust in them. 'That was one of the reasons we wanted to show [Oscar] very early [that] we don't need any more reassurance,' said Stella. 'We are totally happy that we want our future to be with Oscar, we are ready to commit. And we were delighted when he said, "You know what, I agree. I'm thinking the same." It was an easy conversation.'

Piastri's on-track performance had spoken for itself and was clearly the major factor in McLaren's decision to sign him up for an additional two years. The major factor, but not the only factor. As much as his speed had endeared Piastri to the team, so had his calm, calculated nature. His ability, even in his very first year as a Formula 1 driver, to not let his emotions take over. 'When you are in a pressurised environment like Formula 1, it becomes very important to be a calm, considerate person,' Stella added. 'He doesn't have nervous reactions. He doesn't have unnecessary irritation. He doesn't add tension in his comments. His comments are a genuine report of what happens with the car or a genuine report of what happens in a situation that wasn't ideal. You can trust what he's saying; he's not adding anything speculatively because he needs to promote himself. He is trustworthy and calm. And to be honest, calmness is a quality I generally try to strengthen as much as possible throughout the team. There's already enough reasons to be tense. Nobody should create additional [tension], just through behaviours or the way you speak to your colleagues. He is calm, he is very considerate with his words, he is very considered with the way he presents himself. And he's a totally trustworthy person.

'Twice this year [we had] a situation where we needed to make a call as to who [gets] the new upgrades. And both times they went to Lando, because we thought that's the best thing for the team. Well, both times the conversations with Oscar were calm, rational, constructive conversations where it was easy for me to say, "I'm talking in the name of the team." And it was easy for him to understand that. At no point during the Singapore weekend [was there] any reference to any annoyance, any comment like, "I am a little slower but obviously the other [driver] has the new parts." Like, not even indirectly. Leaders, and drivers are definitely leaders in a Formula 1 team, they lead by example – and with Oscar, you can trust he is going to do it even when he is at a disadvantage.'

There was something special about the McLarens on the Friday in Japan. Max Verstappen, fresh off the back of a rare loss in Singapore, was as usual in a league of his own. But the McLarens were well in the game on the fast, flowing Suzuka circuit. Both of them. Even the usually slow-starting Piastri was inside the top 10 in both Friday sessions in his now fully upgraded McLaren.

In Saturday's final hour of practice, the form guide became clear. Verstappen was back to being the driver to beat, but he had company at the front of the field. And that company was Lando Norris and Oscar Piastri. Based on the qualifying simulation runs in Free Practice 3, there wasn't much in it between the three drivers over a lap. Both McLarens came within three-tenths of the rapid Dutchman. By comparison,

Sergio Perez, fourth fastest on the day, was more than seven-tenths slower than his Red Bull teammate.

Those qualifying sims proved accurate as well. The McLaren drivers breezed through the first two segments of qualifying. In Q1, Norris was second and Piastri fifth. In Q2, the two McLarens were so confident in their pace that they stayed in the pits on the final runs, to keep a set of tyres up their sleeve for the final segment of qualifying. The only other driver with that level of confidence was Verstappen. Piastri ended up sixth and Norris ninth overall in the second session.

There'd been bugger all between the McLaren drivers on the Saturday in Japan, and the battle over fractions of a second continued into Q3. Both went quickest on their first runs, Piastri 0.035s faster than Norris over the 90-second lap. Three-hundredths of a second – that was the margin that sealed Piastri's first front-row start in a proper Formula 1 grand prix. At a circuit he'd never been to before. Of course, Piastri played it cool. 'The first lap was pretty solid,' he said, referencing the very run that put him second on the grid. 'I was quite happy with it, [although at] the last chicane I could have done a better job. But yeah, it was a good lap. Then the second lap, my first sector was good. And the next few sectors not so good.'

For some time, Nicole Piastri, Oscar's mum, had been developing quite a following on X, the social media platform previously known as Twitter. When Oscar's new McLaren deal was announced, she posted, 'What!! So we are doing this for another three years???' – a post that was seen by a million people. When McLaren posted about Oscar qualifying second at Suzuka, Mama Piastri responded on X with, 'Anyone got a cheap flight to Japan?' The request reached McLaren CEO Zak Brown at his Saturday-evening media session. 'I'm very happy to buy her airline tickets,' he said. 'If you can get here, Mrs Piastri, we want to see you tomorrow.' Nicole Piastri wussed out, though. 'Thank you for the kind offer,' read her X post, 'but I think it's best that I have my anxiety attack in the comfort of my own home.'

On Sunday afternoon at the Japanese Grand Prix, Piastri found himself sitting on the grid, waiting for the start of a Formula 1 race, with absolutely no cars ahead of him. Nothing but clear track on the run to the first corner. Even if the view was from second on the grid, not pole, it was still a momentous occasion. Unfortunately, he didn't get to enjoy it for long.

The outside of the front row, second place, is actually the inside of the front row at Suzuka, with the driver on pole getting the grippier racing line. As the lights went out, Verstappen swung immediately left to cover Piastri. A slightly smarter start from the Red Bull driver meant he could do so successfully, forcing Piastri to back out on the way into the fast right-hand first corner. Norris, meanwhile, in third, was left with a nice big hole on the fastest line and, momentarily, swung past both Verstappen and Piastri. Verstappen was able to wrangle the lead back immediately, while a cautious Piastri was relegated to third place. Verstappen clearly had the McLarens covered for speed, but there was little between Norris and Piastri. On lap 12, Sergio Perez locked a brake into the hairpin and tagged Kevin Magnussen into a spin. Shards of carbon fibre went flying in every direction thanks to the impact between the Red Bull and the Haas.

For a couple of laps, the race continued under green-flag conditions despite the crash, McLaren electing to pit Piastri for a set of hard Pirellis. It was good timing; Piastri hit his box right as the race director called a virtual safety car to clean up the debris at the hairpin. It made for a very cheap pit stop for Piastri, even more so when the safety car ended before any other drivers from the lead group managed to get around to the pits. That stroke of fortune helped Piastri jump Norris, and not by a little bit – he ended up more than four seconds down the road. Norris undoubtedly had the better pace of the two drivers and was able to whittle down the margin. By mid-race, there was almost nothing separating the McLarens, creating an awkward situation for the team. Particularly as George Russell was attempting an ambitious one-stop strategy, which was keeping McLaren on its toes.

Eventually, Norris had enough of sitting behind Piastri and decided to start lobbying the pit wall for a swap – one of the more annoying occurrences in modern Formula 1. Knowing that contact with your teammate is a no-no, and based on the massive differences in speed required to execute a clean pass, drivers will often campaign to be waved past them. Sometimes there is bargaining involved. 'Let me through and if I don't pass the guy down the road, we'll swap back' – that sort of thing. In this case, Norris simply wanted a free passage past Piastri. 'The longer I spend behind now, the worse you're going to make the race for me,' he told his engineer. 'Understood,' was the response. A lap later, he got half a run on Piastri down the front straight, before Piastri swung across to cover into turn 1. It wasn't overly aggressive, but Norris had clearly been expecting to be let through. 'What's he doing?' asked Norris. 'It's just ruining the race, now,' the Briton continued. 'If he wants George to beat us, then . . .' The next response from the garage was simple: 'I'm working on it.' The lobbying paid off. Norris had just given one more spray on his radio – 'I'm way quicker, I'm just in the dirty air' – before the drivers were told to swap positions. Piastri let Norris take second place into turn 1 the next time by.

The McLarens later took their second pit stops and resumed in the same order, although both were now behind the one-stopping Russell. Norris was able to quickly blast by, but Piastri, who'd lost a good five seconds across the second stint due to some poor tyre management, took a bit longer to catch the Mercedes. By lap 42, Piastri had caught Russell, and he tried a cheeky move around the outside into the slow final chicane. That didn't work, and initially it looked as if Russell had got a good enough run onto the straight to hold position until the finish. But Piastri tucked in behind the Mercedes, opened his DRS and pulled one hell of a ballsy move around the outside of Russell into turn 1.

It was the move that sealed Piastri's first podium in grand prix racing. 'Well done, everyone, I'll remember that one for a long time,' he radioed back to the crew on his cool-down lap.

You'd think getting your first proper podium in a Formula 1 race, an achievement that so few people on the planet ever realise, let alone in their rookie season, would be cause for mass celebration. But Piastri doesn't quite work like that. As he sat in the official FIA press conference on a Sunday afternoon for the first time, a privilege reserved for the podium finishers in each grand prix, he couldn't get past the fact that he hadn't managed his tyres all that well in the second stint of the race. 'It probably wasn't my strongest Sunday,' he admitted. 'From that side of things, there's still a few things I want to work on.' When asked to expand on what he could have done better, Piastri added, 'I just wasn't quick enough at certain points of the race. These high-deg races are probably the biggest thing I need to try and work on at the moment. I think it's still quite fresh for me; obviously in all the junior racing, there's no [high-deg] races like this. So the only way you can learn is by just doing the races. It's exciting to know that we can finish on the podium, even if I feel like there's more to come.'

Nicole Piastri enjoyed the festivities, though. As she watched her son hoist a Formula 1 trophy for the first time, she posted a photo of a handful of old karting trophies on X. 'Nice work today, Osc,' she wrote. 'Does this mean I can get rid of some of these, finally?'

Results Summary

Free Practice 1: 7th (1m 32.713s, +1.07s)
Free Practice 2: 8th (1m 31.662s, +0.97s)
Free Practice 3: 3rd (1m 30.555s, +0.29s)
Qualifying: 2nd (1m 29.458s, +0.58s)
Race: 3rd

Japanese Grand Prix: A brief history

Sure, there was a little bit of tension between Oscar Piastri and Lando Norris at Suzuka. But in the grand scheme of McLaren teammate woes in Japan, it was nothing.

McLaren was the powerhouse team of the mid- to late-1980s, its cars instantly recognisable by the red and white of its sponsor Marlboro. The cool, calculated and incredibly fast driver Alain Prost joined the team in 1984 and won titles in 1985 and 1986. That achievement elevated him to number-one status within McLaren – until the team signed flamboyant Brazilian Ayrton Senna ahead of the 1988 season. It was a blockbuster line-up: two driven, focused and ultra-competitive drivers, with entirely different philosophies and approaches to both life and racing.

So, of course, the combination was explosive.

Fuelling the fire was the dominance of the McLaren. In 1988, the car was peerless, as Senna and Prost won 15 of the 16 races of the season between them (the only loss for McLaren being the tifosi special recounted in Chapter 20, the brief history of the Italian Grand Prix). Senna won the drivers' title that year, and Prost complained that engine supplier Honda had been favouring him ... which Honda reportedly admitted to doing, based on its enjoyment of Senna's aggressive driving style.

Things really came to a head the following season. The rivalry had been simmering for a while, before boiling over at Imola. Senna and Prost had agreed to not race each other until after Tosa (the third corner) to avoid any contact and/or damage. Senna got the better getaway at the start and Prost dutifully tucked in behind his teammate. When Gerhard Berger was involved in a fiery crash at Tamburello, the race was stopped. When it restarted, Prost was quicker off the line, only for Senna to pass him . . . into Tosa. Prost was livid that the agreement had been broken.

As the season wore on, Prost built a solid case for the drivers' title. He also got sick of McLaren and Senna and announced, ahead of the Italian Grand Prix, that he was moving to Ferrari for 1990. Unfortunately for Prost, that left McLaren firmly on Senna's side when it came to the intra-team battle for the 1989 title.

By the time they got to Japan, Senna needed a win to keep his title hopes alive, and he took pole at Suzuka by a whopping 1.7s margin. But it was the Frenchman who got the better start of the two McLarens and led the race. Cleverly, Prost had opted for a low downforce set-up ahead of the Japanese Grand Prix. It meant that, even though Senna was faster over a lap, he didn't have the top-end speed to execute a pass. Seven laps from home, Senna decided to shoot his shot. He got a run into the last chicane and looked to have the move done. But Prost was never going to let it happen and turned into his fellow McLaren driver as they got to the corner. They collided and ended up off the road. Prost was out of the race on the spot, but Senna urged the marshals to give him a push start, weaved around the barriers and carried on. In one of the more remarkable drives in Formula 1 history, he stopped for a new front wing and still managed to hunt down Alessandro Nannini to win the race.

Until he was stripped of the win by the stewards for, laughably, gaining an advantage by short-cutting the chicane after the clash with Prost. It basically handed the 1989 world champion title to Prost. Senna was adamant that the penalty was conspiracy work between French hero Prost and the head of the FIA, Frenchman Jean-Marie Balestre. McLaren appealed the decision, effectively going against its own driver Prost, and the FIA responded by ramping up the penalty for Senna to a six-month ban and a US$100,000 fine.

Incredibly, the pair found themselves locked in an equally bitter title fight when they got to Suzuka again 12 months later. At least this time they drove for different teams, Senna still at McLaren while Prost drove for Ferrari. By Japan, the penultimate round of the 1990 F1 season, the picture was clear. Prost had to beat Senna to stay in the running for the drivers' title. If neither scored in Japan, Senna would be world champion. The Brazilian took pole position, after which he lobbied to Balestre that the grid should be reversed and the pole put to the grippier outside line of the track (as is the case at the time of writing in 2023), rather than the slippery, dirty inside line. Balestre refused, to the surprise of few. A year earlier, when crashing had favoured Prost, it was very arguably the Frenchman who had sparked the collision. This time around, it was Senna who had vowed to lead into turn 1 . . . no matter what. When the race started, Prost, unsurprisingly, got the jump from the outside of the front row. But as he swung across to assume the lead, Senna didn't yield, the contact taking them both out of the race. Senna was world champion and Prost was furious.

Oscar Piastri may have been born 11 years after that 1990 clash of the titans at Suzuka, but it is so entrenched in Formula 1 folklore that he couldn't help but think about it at the start of the 2023 race. Not that there was any bitter title battle in play, but as a slightly faster-starting Max Verstappen swept in front of him into turn 1, Piastri, for a single moment in time, realised that if he didn't lift, he could have 'Senna'd' Verstappen into the gravel. 'I mean, looking back on it now, I was in the perfect position to emulate Senna and Prost,' he joked in the post-race press conference. 'Like, literally, perfect.'

23

QATAR

Qatar Grand Prix
Lusail International Circuit
6–8 October 2023

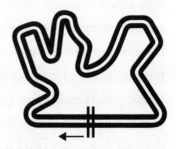

As accomplished, credentialled and highly rated as Lando Norris is as a race driver, he's never actually won a Formula 1 race. Not a sprint, not a grand prix. At least, he hasn't at the time of this book being written, anyway. He's been close. At the Russian Grand Prix in 2021, he was leading the race when a late rain shower wreaked havoc on the Sochi circuit. Norris elected to stay out on slick tyres while the rest of the field pitted for intermediates. The gamble didn't pay off, the win slipping through his fingers as he slid off the road on the penultimate lap. Later that same season, McLaren found itself in a winning position again at the Italian Grand Prix, helped by Max Verstappen and Lewis Hamilton taking each other out of the race. Unfortunately for Norris, that proved to be one of the few weekends a largely out-of-form Daniel Ricciardo had the upper hand, with

Norris forced to settle for second place in what was McLaren's first one-two finish in 11 years.

Fast forward two years and Norris was forced to watch another Australian take a race win in a McLaren before him.

Being a sprint weekend, there was only the single hour of practice on the Friday of the 2023 Qatar Grand Prix. Both of the McLaren drivers opted against a soft-tyre run at the end of the session, instead ranked on an earlier medium-tyre run, when track conditions weren't yet at their best. Still, Oscar Piastri ended up ninth fastest, one spot ahead of Norris.

A short while later that Friday evening, qualifying for Sunday's grand prix started under the Lusail lights. Heading into the session there were predictions that, thanks to the vast tarmac run-off, track limits would be a big issue. As soon as the session went green, laps were being deleted. Norris went fastest early in Q1, only to have the time scrubbed when it was judged he'd run too wide at turn 5. Piastri himself would lose a lap a few minutes later. Both McLarens did eventually log legal laps that comfortably got them into Q2. In the second segment of qualifying, Norris was second fastest and Piastri third; there were just three-hundredths between them after Piastri gave Norris a small tow.

From there, it all got a bit messy.

Norris went fastest on his first run, only to have his time deleted for running wide again at turn 5. Not that the lap itself would have been good enough for pole, but it was a great banker. Piastri might have been slightly slower than his teammate, but at least his lap was legal . . . which proved to be important. As the field fired in their critical final runs, Norris charged back into second place, behind a checked-out Max Verstappen. Piastri improved too, slotting into fourth behind George Russell. It all looked great for McLaren, until Norris let slip over the radio that he was in strife. 'I'm so shit sometimes,' he said on his in-lap. It turned out that he'd had a huge dose of oversteer on the way through turn 10, the correction of which carried him well over the track limits. He knew his final lap was going to be deleted and, without a banker, he would drop all the way back to 10th on the grid.

Initially, there was nothing from race control. Norris was directed into parc fermé, where the top three cars are held after qualifying, as if he'd qualified second, despite the inevitability that he would be stripped of the lap. Eventually, the confirmation came. It was a little awkward, but nothing compared to the awkwardness that Piastri had to deal with. Norris losing his lap promoted Piastri to third on the grid, so he had to front the cameras and give his thoughts to millions of people around the world, live on TV. The first cringeworthy moment was when presenter Naomi Schiff, clearly not having been told about the Norris penalty, asked, 'What's happened, why am I talking to you, Oscar?' Piastri grabbed the microphone and explained, 'I swapped out with the other one.' Piastri then described his session ('It was a very, very scruffy last lap') and answered another question from Schiff about the upswing in McLaren's form. Piastri was onto his third answer, 1 minute and 10 seconds into a live TV interview, when a graphic showed up on the screen advising everyone that he had also lost his final lap of qualifying due to exceeding track limits. Piastri, still answering a question, had no idea. 'I think we're just hearing that you had a track-limits infringement,' said Schiff. 'Is that accurate? Did you know something was under investigation for your track limits as well?' Piastri, cool as you like, said, 'Ah, I didn't know. This is fun, isn't it?' When Schiff told him he'd be starting sixth instead of third, Piastri gave the camera a big thumbs up: 'Wonderful'.

Saturday got off to an odd start in Qatar, with an unexpected 10-minute practice session. Friday's running had exposed some issues with the tyres as they rattled across the new 50-millimetre-high 'pyramid' kerbs used around the Lusail circuit. A decision was made to move the track limits inwards by about 18 centimetres at turns 12 and 13, so drivers wouldn't use quite as much of the exit kerb. So, the sprint shootout was pushed back, and the drivers were given an additional 10 minutes on track to get a feel for the new limits.

Despite those extra minutes of running, track-limit issues dominated the sprint shootout. Thankfully, this time, it wasn't an issue for Piastri, who cruised through SQ1 with the seventh-fastest time. In SQ2, he was eighth fastest. Comfortably through to the final segment, but nothing spectacular. In SQ3, however, Piastri found himself scrapping with Norris and Verstappen for pole. Verstappen's efforts were hampered by first losing a lap to track limits, and then failing to outpace the speedy McLaren drivers when he did lay down a legal marker. Norris, meanwhile, was slightly quicker than Piastri on his first attempt, but he ran wide on his second run and had to abort the lap. A mistake-free Piastri improved on his own time to take pole for the sprint race. It won't go down in history as an actual pole position, as it wasn't for the grand prix.

But still, an incredible achievement for a rookie. Following the shootout session, Piastri faced Schiff and the TV cameras once more. 'Oscar, I'm so glad that we get to do this again,' she opened with. 'Yeah, I'm very, very happy,' replied Piastri. 'I might just give the FIA five minutes first to make sure I'm actually on pole . . .'

For the second race meeting in a row, Piastri found himself staring at clear track ahead of him. And this time he was on pole, which meant starting on the clean side of the track. The start itself couldn't have gone better, Piastri rapid off the line as Norris and Verstappen were swamped behind him. He led into the first corner and had a nice little first-lap break when the safety car was called to recover Liam Lawson, who was left beached in the gravel on the outside of turn 3. As the field was neutralised, Piastri found George Russell and Carlos Sainz sitting behind him. Those two had gambled on the soft-compound tyre, using the additional grip to clear the rest of the lead group. Now they were right behind Piastri, who was on the medium-compound tyre – and in danger of being run down by those on the faster, but more fragile, rubber. A few corners after the lap 3 restart, Russell used his superior grip to barge past Piastri and into the lead, right before Logan Sargeant spun his Williams into the gravel and prompted a second safety car. Once the race went green, Russell was able to skip away at the front, while Piastri came under fire from Sainz in the Ferrari behind him.

The key for the rookie was just holding on long enough for the sting to come out of the soft tyres. 'We know it will come to the medium,' came the coaching from the pit wall to Piastri over the radio. On lap 9, Piastri set a new fastest lap of the race. The engineers were right. The race was coming to him. As the pair raced down the front straight to start lap 11, Piastri activated his DRS and breezed past Russell to retake the lead. A lap later there was a third safety car after Nico Hülkenberg and Sergio Perez collided. By that stage, Verstappen was up to third place and looking to seal his third world championship with a race win. He didn't need to win the race to win the title, but it's always the preference for a driver. Wild celebrations when you haven't actually won the race do look a little odd. Verstappen was suddenly in a menacing position behind Piastri, but at the same time was feeling the pressure from the race leader. As the field sat behind the safety car, Verstappen's race engineer asked him to start taking better care of his tyres. 'I'm starting to see some surface damage, look after them,' was the message. 'I know, I'm trying, I'm trying. Piastri is pulling,' said Verstappen. The clearly frustrated response from the Red Bull Racing wall was, 'Forget about Piastri. We need to get to the end. I told you about this. Let it come to you.'

Eventually there was a five-lap dash to the chequered flag, Russell providing a nice buffer for Piastri at the restart. It took Verstappen a whole lap to clear Russell, by which point Piastri was 2.6 seconds down the road. That left Piastri in the box seat, but winning would require a flawless final few laps. Forget that there's a now three-time world champion chasing you down. You cannot make a single mistake.

Piastri, of course, didn't blink. He still had two seconds up his sleeve when he crossed the line to take a sensational – and near unbelievable – sprint race win. As a rookie. For a team that had looked like a midfield outfit, at absolute best, for nearly half the season. Verstappen might have been the world champion, but Piastri stole the headlines that day. He couldn't call himself a grand prix winner, yet. But he was a Formula 1 race winner.

After such a breakthrough Saturday, starting back in sixth place for the grand prix itself was a bit of an anticlimax for Piastri. Until it wasn't.

As the Qatar Grand Prix kicked off and the field descended on the fast right-hand first corner, Verstappen had a nice little lead. But behind him, it was tight. Too tight. Lewis Hamilton, starting on the soft tyres, got a good jump and tried to sweep around the outside of teammate Russell. But there wasn't quite enough room. The two Mercedes made contact, and both were sent into a spin. Like in Hungary, Piastri had elected for a tight line through the first corner. And again, it paid off. Charles Leclerc and Fernando Alonso both had to take evasive action to avoid getting caught up in the Mercedes crash. And sixth became second for Piastri. The strategic picture was simplified by the ongoing tyre issues, Pirelli having mandated an 18-lap maximum stint per set due to the ongoing concerns. That meant a three-stop race for everyone, which, given the high ambient temperatures in Qatar, made it a stern physical test for the drivers. In brutal heat, the flat-out nature of the desert race pushed drivers to their limits. Some didn't even make the finish line, Logan Sargeant retiring his Williams and emerging from the cockpit a man clearly out of sorts in the hot conditions. Piastri struggled like everybody, but he was up for the challenge. He didn't put a wheel wrong as he executed his three-stopper and came home second in a race of physical attrition. He was now a two-time podium finisher and a sprint race winner, all in his rookie season – achievements that some drivers don't reach over the course of their entire careers. 'Turn 1 was nice; that was definitely in the game plan before the race,' said Piastri of his rapid start. 'Yeah, really impressive pace – [but] definitely the hardest race I've had in my life. It was hot. With the three stops it was basically flat-out. It was 57 qualifying laps. Which I definitely feel like I've done . . .'

Lando Norris capped off a solid day, and weekend, for McLaren with third place, giving the team another double podium. Not that he was entirely happy with his end result. During the final stint of the race, Norris had been instructed by the team to not challenge Piastri and to hold position, with fears that should the two start to battle, it could bring George Russell back into the podium equation. The message from the pit wall to Norris was clear: 'We're going to hold position. Bring it home.' Norris's response was equally clear: 'Why do you want to do that? We have a big gap [to Russell]. I'm clearly a lot quicker.' Andrea Stella later explained that, as part of the team's protocols, Norris was within his rights to question the decision . . . so long as, as soon as the situation was clarified to him, he dropped the matter. 'When we give drivers an instruction, we tell them to challenge us because we want to make sure we understand their point of view,' he said. 'So [we tell them], "Challenge us, tell us exactly what you think. We will reassess the situation and come back to you. But once we come back to you, just respect it." This is exactly what happened, and that's what you heard.'

In typical Piastri style, there were no hysterics about his Qatar weekend as he faced the media in the post-race press conference. But he did use some strong language that suggested what it meant to him. Words like 'exceptional'. Phrases like 'close to perfect'. Fair enough, given he'd just had the sort of weekend that dreams are made of. The sort of weekend that solidifies your Formula 1 career.

'Yeah . . . it's been pretty exceptional to be honest,' he said. 'Friday was difficult. [I was] obviously a bit disappointed after qualifying on Friday, but [Saturday] went as close to perfect as it could have. And [Sunday] I think second was probably the most we could have done. I'm very, very happy. Exciting weekend. A lot of progress made. And I'm just very proud that, as a team, and also for myself personally, that we've managed to get the most out of what our car has been capable of.'

Results Summary

Free Practice 1: 9th (1m 28.380s, +0.95s)
Qualifying: 6th (1m 24.540s, +0.76s)
Sprint Shootout: 1st (1m 24.454s, -0.08s)
Sprint: 1st
Race: 2nd

Qatar Grand Prix: A brief history

The history of Formula 1 in Qatar sure is brief – as was the lead-up to the first Qatar Grand Prix in 2021. The Lusail circuit was drafted in as a late replacement for the Australian Grand Prix that year, which was first postponed and then cancelled due to the COVID-19 pandemic. There was an empty slot in the F1 schedule, and Qatar had an FIA Grade 1 circuit that could fill it. In late September, the inaugural Qatar Grand Prix was announced and in mid-November it happened.

As quickly as Qatar appeared on the calendar, it disappeared. With the summer months too hot for racing in the desert, and November and December a little busy with Qatar's (controversial) hosting of the FIFA World Cup, Qatar slipped off the F1 schedule in 2022 . . . only to return in 2023 with a monster 10-year deal.

In the short history of the event, the 2023 grand prix definitely stands out, thanks to both the on-the-fly track changes and the searing heat that left drivers either at, or over, their physical limits. As mentioned, Williams driver Logan Sargeant couldn't finish, the American retiring from the race due to heat stroke. His teammate Alex Albon had to go to the medical centre after the race for treatment of what the team described as 'acute heat exposure'. Fernando Alonso, struggling with something getting very hot next to his seat, at one point asked the team to throw a bucket of water over him during a pit stop. 'The seat is burning, man,' he shouted over the radio. 'Anything we can do in the pit stop? Throw me water or something . . .' Given that whatever was burning Alonso's backside was probably electronic, Aston Martin made the wise decision not to douse him with water. Meanwhile, Esteban Ocon vomited inside his helmet during the race as he battled with the heat, and Lance Stroll parked next to the ambulance after the race, stumbling out of his car and in clear need of help.

The conditions sparked an uproar from many of the drivers. George Russell, whose role as head of the Grand Prix Drivers Association is to deal with matters like this, said: 'It was absolutely brutal, by far the most physical race I've ever experienced. I felt close to sort of fainting in that race; I've never experienced anything like it before. I asked my engineer to give me encouragement just to try and take my mind away from it. I do a lot of heat training in the sauna, so you push your body to the limit, and sometimes you just need to get out of that sauna. That's sort of how I felt from about lap 20. I opened my visor for the whole race, and it was hot air, but it was better than no air.'

Formula 1 drivers do carry a drink system on board the car, but the issue in Qatar was that the liquid inside the bottle was almost too hot to drink. 'You can drink but the drink is more of a tea than anything else because it's at [plus] 60 degrees Celsius,' said Charles Leclerc. Ocon described the experience as hell: 'I was feeling ill; lap 15 [and] 16 I was throwing up for two laps inside the cockpit, and then I was like, "Shit, that's going to be a long race." I tried to calm down, I tried to remember that the mental side in sport is the strongest part of your body, and I managed to get that under control and finish the race. But honestly, I was not expecting the race to be that hard. I can normally do two race distances, even in Singapore. Physically, muscle-wise and cardio-wise, I'm always fine. It was just like 80 degrees Celsius inside the cockpit this race. It was so hot that I wanted to open the visor on the straight line, because I had no air, and I was trying to also guide with my hand some air into the helmet. The more I was breathing to try and get everything lower, the more heat was coming inside the helmet. Honestly, it was hell in there.' Still, vomit and hellish conditions aside, Ocon said he never considered following Sargeant's lead and pulling out of the race. 'It's not an option, retiring,' said the Frenchman. 'I was never going to do that. You need to kill me to retire.'

One of the few voices that backed F1's decision to stage the race in the weather conditions was Lewis Hamilton, although it should be noted that he crashed out on the first lap and didn't endure the conditions like the other drivers. 'I'm going to be controversial as always,' he said in the aftermath. 'Obviously I didn't do the race, so didn't get to feel the pain that the drivers felt. But I have obviously been here a long time. Malaysia was much hotter than that race, and I know what it's like to lose four or more kilos in the race and barely being able to stand afterwards. My feeling towards it is . . . this is an extreme sport. You don't have marathon runners who are passing out after the marathon, saying you have got to make it shorter. This is an extreme sport, and we are paid very highly for what we do and from my perspective when I've not been feeling great at the end of the race, I've just got to train harder and that's how it's been for me.'

While it is likely a moot point, given Qatar was always going to be moved to later in the schedule, the issue raises some interesting points. Firstly, there were touring, GT and sportscar drivers around the world scoffing at the whining F1 drivers, given the extreme conditions faced by those in closed cars, who also often race over long distances. At least F1 drivers have moving air around them. And Formula 1 is yet to really flirt with cooling measures used in other motor-racing categories, such as helmet fans and cool suits, which are an undershirt covered in pipes that recycle cold water.

Obviously, these features add weight, so they are the enemy of engineering.

At the same time, similar to racing in the rain, at what point does calling an event off if the conditions aren't perfect go too far? Lewis copped some backlash for his comments, but he's right about at least one thing: Formula 1 is an extreme sport. That's part of its romance.

24

UNITED STATES

United States Grand Prix
Circuit of the Americas
20–22 October 2023

If people weren't already taking notice of Oscar Piastri, they certainly were after Qatar. Despite McLaren still sitting fifth in the constructors' standings behind Red Bull Racing, Mercedes, Ferrari and, at that point, Aston Martin, Red Bull's Max Verstappen named McLaren as the team that had his dominant outfit the most nervous heading into the final few races of the season. Not only that, the freshly crowned world champion also named Lando Norris and Piastri as the best line-up in the sport. 'I do think that as a team [McLaren is] probably the most consistent, compared to the others behind us,' Verstappen said. 'I do think they have the best driver line-up out of all of them, so they are operating really well. It's going to be interesting to the end of the year, but also I think the start of next year, to see where everyone is at.'

McLaren, meanwhile, was clearly dealing with some of the less comfortable elements of its incredible driver line-up. From the niggles between Norris and Piastri during the Japanese Grand Prix, to Norris pushing back at the team for being told to hold position behind his teammate in Qatar, there was undoubtedly a bit of tension. Earlier in the season, Andrea Stella had talked about how Piastri was pushing and elevating Norris. There were times, now, when the Australian wasn't just pushing Norris. He was beating him. 'Lando knows himself that Oscar is a unique talent – you don't see these kinds of talents in Formula 1 every day,' said Stella ahead of the United States Grand Prix. 'He's an absolute reference, even if he's a rookie, and at times Lando knows that he will set the bar very high. But if you are a champion like Lando is, you will have to take that from a positive point of view, because [Piastri] gives you so much information to keep improving. There's no champion in the world, in any sport, that wins everything, or as a driver is faster in every corner, faster every lap and faster every session. So, for me, Lando sees this as a bit of discomfort, but it's the discomfort you need to become the best. It's a curse and a blessing to be a champion.'

In Austin, for the United States Grand Prix, Norris fought back. Piastri struggled in the sole practice session of the sprint weekend. At one point, he had a huge moment on the way out of turn 9 when he ran slightly wide, straddled the exit kerb and was spat out towards the barriers. It took some quick hands to keep the McLaren pointing in the right direction as it bounced through the grass and dirt. Then, a scrappy soft-tyre run at the end left him way down in 19th place.

Given the ropey start to the day, Friday afternoon's qualifying session was much better for Piastri. He cruised through Q1 with the 10th fastest time. In Q2 he was eighth fastest. But in the final segment he couldn't nail his final run. In his official post-race comments, Stella described Piastri's issue as a 'large wheel-spin event at the exit of turn 11, which overheated his tyres and largely compromised the rest of his lap'. A 10th place start was locked in for Sunday's race, while Norris charged to the outside of the front row.

Saturday started out as a bit of a battle for Piastri too, as, much like was so often the case earlier in the season in the original-spec McLaren, he had to battle his way out of the first segment of the sprint shootout. From there, though, things looked more evenly matched between the McLaren drivers. They were fourth (Norris) and sixth (Piastri) in SQ2, then fourth and fifth, same order, in SQ3.

But Piastri's woes returned in the sprint race itself. The race started with light contact with Carlos Sainz, the only driver to gamble on the soft tyre, on the run to the first corner. That dropped Piastri to sixth, but he was very quickly under fire from seventh-placed Sergio Perez. Piastri defended for his life, which allowed Norris to skip away ahead, and George Russell to join the fight right behind Perez. On lap 3, Perez managed to get a nice, DRS-assisted run on Piastri down the back straight, forcing the rookie to the inside as they dived into turn 12, Red Bull and McLaren side-by-side. Perez nosed ahead on the way into the braking zone, but Piastri went deeper . . . a little too deep, it turned out. He ran slightly wide on the exit, allowing Perez to finally get through. That left Piastri under immediate fire from Russell, who charged around the outside at turn 15 to grab seventh place. Not legally, though. The Mercedes driver clearly had all four wheels outside the white line as he executed the pass. Pierre Gasly, who was following the pair, spotted it right away. 'Russell overtook off the track,' he reported on the radio. The stewards agreed and hit Russell with a five-second penalty. Not that it mattered to Piastri. His race pace was woeful as he sunk back to 10th by the end of the sprint, behind even Gasly at a time when McLaren had so clearly pulled away from Alpine in terms of car speed and points in the world championship. Norris finished fourth. Post-race, Piastri was at a loss to explain his lack of pace, except for knowing it didn't come from the first-lap contact with Sainz. 'Visually, like, there's a mark on the front wing, but I don't think it really made a difference. Certainly not anywhere near enough to explain the difference in performance. There's a few things to look at. I think battling with a lot of other cars at the start of the race really didn't help the state of the tyres . . .'

After some lessons learnt from Saturday, there were hopes of converting a 10th place start into points on Sunday. With Piastri being a little more conservative with the tyres in the early stages of the race and not pushing the rubber too hard, too early, it was a realistic aim. Unfortunately, those hopes were dashed on the very first lap. As usual, Piastri's race craft was impeccable at the first corner. As he watched the two Alpines chase each other from the inside of the road on the approach to the left-hander, he hit the brake a little early, turned in nice and shallow, and got brilliant drive out of the corner. It was great driving, except for the pure misfortune that it left him trapped in what was almost a four-car-wide situation, with Piastri on the inside, and George Russell on the outside, of a double Alpine sandwich. Piastri and Esteban Ocon managed to emerge ahead of the other two as they swept down to turn 1, but they then tripped over each other. It seemed like an innocuous contact and Piastri charged into sixth place. Ocon quickly slipped down the order, the team reporting to the Frenchman that he'd lost 40 points of downforce from the contact. On lap 6 he was told to retire the car. Piastri carried on in sixth place until lap 10 when he suddenly slowed. 'Oscar, recharge on and no full pedal. We need big lifts. I'm afraid we have to retire the car,' was the message over the radio. The engine was getting way too hot and, with limits imposed by the FIA on how many power units a driver can use per season, he just couldn't continue. Once back in the media pen, Piastri confirmed that the Ocon contact was the probable cause of the DNF, but he was happy to chalk it up to a racing incident. 'There's fluid all down the right sidepod, and that's where the contact was, so yeah, that was probably the cause of the end of the race,' he said. 'I didn't really think anything of [the contact], to be honest. I felt like I definitely had the right to be there. I don't think Esteban did anything untoward. We met and, unfortunately, it's caused damage for both of us. Just one of those incidents.'

Results Summary

Free Practice 1: 19th (1m 38.420s, +2.51s)
Qualifying: 10th (1m 35.467s, +0.74s)
Sprint Shootout: 5th (1m 34.894s, +0.36s)
Sprint: 10th
Race: DNF

United States Grand Prix: A brief history

It may have taken a Netflix docuseries for the popularity of Formula 1 to properly skyrocket in the US, but the sport has a long and storied history across the pond. The world championship has raced in the US since 1959, taking famous circuits like Sebring and Watkins Glen into the schedule over the years.

The most famous moment in United States Grand Prix history came at the most famous venue of them all. The Indianapolis Motor Speedway.

In the year 2000, the Brickyard became the home of the United States Grand Prix. It wasn't a return of the world championship era for the Indy 500, but rather a separate race on what is known as the Indianapolis Road Course, which snakes around the infield of the oval circuit before linking up with the heavily banked fourth corner of the speedway and onto the front straight. It's this banking that made headlines around the world, for all the wrong reasons, in 2005.

Back then, there was no control tyre supplier for Formula 1. Different manufacturers were free to develop tyres and pitch them to Formula 1 teams. In 2005, there were two tyre manufacturers in Formula 1 – Bridgestone and Michelin. Bridgestone had enjoyed a remarkable run of success with Ferrari between 2000 and 2004, but by 2005 it was Michelin with the upper hand. A move to new regulations, where drivers had to make one set of tyres last from the start of qualifying to the end of the race, favoured the French brand. It also had the lion's share of the teams: Bridgestone was supplying Ferrari, Jordan and Minardi, while Michelin was working with McLaren, Toyota, British American Racing (BAR), Renault, Williams, Sauber and Red Bull Racing (RBR).

On Friday 17 June, practice for the 2005 United States Grand Prix kicked off. In the first session, Toyota test driver Ricardo Zonta spun in the infield after his left-rear tyre lost pressure during Free Practice 1. Then, in Free Practice 2, Toyota race driver Ralf Schumacher had a monster crash in the banked corner. It was the second year running he'd destroyed a car there. A year earlier, he'd had a very similar crash while driving for Williams and broke his back, which sidelined him for six races. This time around, a furious Schumacher climbed from the wreckage and kicked it before storming off. But there were clear signs that it was more than driver error. Replays showed what looked to be a rapid deflation of his left-rear tyre before he slammed into the wall. When Toyota took a closer look at the tyres that came off Jarno Trulli's car, there were vertical cuts to the sidewall. Something wasn't right.

The matter was handed over to Michelin, and further analysis showed similar damage to that on Trulli's tyres elsewhere up and down the pit lane. Analysis continued throughout the night back in France, and the news wasn't good. There was a wave being sent through the tyre while cornering, and the frequency of the wave, combined with the load in the banking, was the perfect storm for the tyre to fail. It didn't look to be a batch issue, so it wasn't as easy as a recall and a fresh batch of rubber. Michelin advised its teams to take measures such as using higher pressures for the tyres, doing short runs, and running light fuel loads to limit the load on the tyres through the banking. In qualifying on Saturday afternoon, Trulli took pole position, thanks to running lighter fuel than most. But the concerns over the race continued. Turn 13 was the major worry for the seven teams using Michelin tyres, so a plan was hatched to build a makeshift chicane on the way into the banking, to slow down the cars. The head of F1 at the time, Bernie Ecclestone, was on board with the idea, as was speedway boss Tony George. As the teams left the track on Saturday evening, the general expectation was that, when they arrived the following day, a chicane would be built and ready to go for the race.

The chicane plan, however, fell down at one of the very first hurdles – getting it approved by the FIA. Then FIA race director Charlie Whiting immediately refused the proposal, on the basis that such a significant track upgrade couldn't be made without proper crash simulations and the like. The Brickyard circuit had been homologated without a chicane, and that couldn't change overnight.

So, the final Hail Mary was a trip to a Michelin R&D centre in Ohio. A random selection of 26 tyres were loaded into a cargo plane, while FIA technical delegate Jo Bauer and three Michelin engineers were given the use of McLaren's private jet. They put the tyres through various tests on Saturday night but couldn't learn anything useful. The tyres and the tired engineers arrived back in Indianapolis at around 6 a.m. on Sunday after an all-nighter.

When the teams arrived at a track with no chicane on Sunday morning, all hell broke loose. There were meetings between F1, the FIA, Michelin, the Michelin teams and the race organisers as they desperately tried to reach a solution. There was talk of letting the Michelin teams change tyres during the race, exempting them from the one-set rule. Or telling drivers to not use full throttle through the banking. Or making the Michelin cars come through the pit lane each lap. Or mandating a minimum lap time for the Michelin-shod cars, while those on Bridgestone tyres could go as fast as they liked. The teams didn't like any of the ideas except the chicane. And the FIA was adamant that a chicane was off the table. At one point, Ecclestone tried to pull rank and tractors started shifting tyre bundles around the track in the shape of a chicane, something that Whiting promptly put a stop to. Adding to the complexity of the situation, Ferrari saw the situation as a huge windfall, a chance to edge out McLaren in the constructors' title, and refused to give any ground. Jordan and Minardi showed willingness to stand with the Michelin teams and not race without a chicane. But Ferrari, led by the ruthless Jean Todt, had no interest in that. As the clock ticked down to the start of the race, things got desperate. The FIA harpooned the chicane idea altogether by stating that if the race organisers altered the circuit, the FIA officials would be withdrawn, and it wouldn't be an FIA race – and therefore not part of the world championship. Another factor to consider was that, due to the terms of the Concorde Agreement, the Michelin teams couldn't just refuse to race, either. They had to at least show up for the start of the grand prix.

And, when every other option had been exhausted, that's what they decided to do. Show up for the start. A plan was hatched for the 14 cars with Michelin tyres to go out on the grid, but then pull into the pit lane and withdraw from the end of the formation lap. The Concorde Agreement would be satisfied, and only six cars would be left out on the track for the start of the grand prix itself. Not all of the drivers were initially on board, given the plan meant they would all score zero world championship points, but eventually they came around and accepted there was no other option that ensured their safety. The world watched on in shock as 14 cars peeled into the pit lane rather than taking their place on the starting grid.

The remaining six cars battled it out for the United States Grand Prix. Michael Schumacher, who had won four titles for the Ferrari–Bridgestone alliance, led home teammate Rubens Barrichello in the farcical race. It was his and Ferrari's only win of what proved to be a tough season for anyone not on Michelin rubber. There were no dignitaries on the podium after the race, and Schumacher and Barrichello only made the briefest of appearances. The one person who stayed on the podium to celebrate was Jordan driver Tiago Montiero, who finished third. It was the Portuguese backmarker's sole podium finish in his two years in Formula 1. He did, however, go on to have an incredibly successful career in touring cars. Of course, having backmarker teams finish so high up in the standing skewed the points situation. Yes, Minardi had taken part in the race, but its haul of seven points, compared to 11 for Jordan, ruined any hope of avoiding the wooden spoon for the 2005 season. Minardi boss Paul Stoddart, who had been campaigning on Michelin's side despite his team running Bridgestones, was outraged. 'This is fucking crazy,' he said during a mid-race TV interview with the Dutch broadcaster SBS6. 'The FIA needs to get a grip with itself and sort this sport out before there's no fucking sport to sort out. The championship's over for Minardi. We were only fighting Jordan. This bullshit race has meant that the season finishes here. We can't ever overtake the points from today. It's over. This race, it's not just screwed the Michelin runners. It's screwed up the little fight between Minardi and Jordan that was getting quite good.'

Since Michelin was a supplier, not a competitor, the FIA couldn't issue a direct penalty. But the tyre manufacturer did agree to provide some compensation for ticketholders for Sunday's race, and it pre-purchased 20,000 tickets for the 2006 race that could be distributed among spectators who had been there in 2005. The seven Michelin teams, meanwhile, were ordered to face the World Motor Sport Council where they were found guilty of 'failing to ensure that they were in possession of suitable tyres for the 2005 US Grand Prix; but with strong mitigating circumstances', and 'of wrongfully refusing to allow their cars to start the race, having regard to their right to use the pit lane on each lap'. Three other charges were dropped. The teams faced legal pressure from angry spectators too; however, they found themselves protected, to a large extent, by local laws in Indiana. Put simply, if the teams had raced knowing there was a defect, and someone had got hurt, criminal negligence was on the table.

25

MEXICO

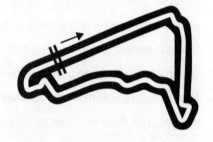

Mexico City Grand Prix
Autódromo Hermanos Rodríguez
27–29 October 2023

When Daniel Ricciardo got distracted by a spun Oscar Piastri in the Netherlands, crashed his car and broke his hand, it could have been a second end to his Formula 1 career in the space of a year. Particularly when Liam Lawson came along and did such a convincing job as his replacement at AlphaTauri. Lawson, young and clearly ready to step up to Formula 1, would have been a completely understandable choice to sign for AlphaTauri for 2024. In fact, it's the sort of signing that the Red Bull junior program exists to make. But Ricciardo must have done enough to convince Red Bull that he deserved another proper shot. Even while still on the sidelines with that broken hand, AlphaTauri announced that Ricciardo and Yuki Tsunoda would race its cars in 2024. Lawson, it seemed, would need to wait his turn.

In Austin, Ricciardo made his comeback. And, amid questions over whether Red Bull should have rolled the dice on Lawson and not played it safe with Ricciardo, it was an underwhelming comeback. His lack of race fitness was particularly obvious on the Sunday in the US as he crossed the line last on the road. He felt his hand had held up well, but after five races on the sidelines, racing a grand prix distance, in a car carrying damage after an early encounter with debris, was a tough ask. Despite having that 2024 contract in his back pocket, Ricciardo knew that the pressure was on. 'I still feel like I'm fighting,' he said as the F1 circus rolled into Mexico City a few days later. 'You are always fighting for something in this sport, always trying to prove a point or impress someone else. It's nice to be back, but I'm not just going to sail through the rest of this year and be like, "Oh, whatever."'

The pressure was on in the McLaren camp too. The upgraded MCL60 was significantly better than the car that had started the season, but it still had strengths and weaknesses. And with a series of slower-speed circuits coming up to round out the year, there were concerns that the team's best chances of a proper grand prix win were behind them. 'Do I think our best chances have gone? I would say yes,' said Norris. 'I think Qatar was our best chance of winning a race, and I missed out on that one. I don't want to say no, I don't say never, but there are no super high-speed Suzuka- or Qatar-style circuits left, which is where we're strong. And if you looked at the GPS and the overlays of how bad we are in the slow speed, I'm not looking forward to Brazil. I think we're going to be pretty shocking there.' But before Brazil, there was the high-altitude challenge of Mexico City, including the slow, tricky stadium section of the circuit that was unlikely to favour the McLaren. 'The stadium section is very, very slow and easy to make a mistake,' said a pessimistic Piastri ahead of the grand prix weekend. 'The whole track is difficult, and the altitude is very high here, so the grip is quite low. It just makes everything difficult.'

So, when Friday practice actually went well for the McLaren drivers, it was a pleasant surprise. In the first session, Piastri opted to use a prototype tyre compound, provided to all drivers by Pirelli, later in FP1 than the rest of the field. He ended up sixth fastest, while Norris was fourth. In the second session there were patches of rain as Piastri ended up ninth and Norris second. 'The car pace has looked reasonable,' said a relieved-sounding Piastri on Friday evening. 'The track is very low grip and takes a lot of getting used to, but it seems cool.'

Saturday started out equally promising. Piastri was a fine fifth in the final hour of practice, with him and Norris looking like easy Q3 contenders. That confidence led to some bullishness in the first qualifying segment as McLaren sent its drivers out on the medium-compound tyres, rather than the faster soft set. Then, there was confusion when Norris pitted at the end of a flying lap, rather than completing it. Piastri completed his run but wasn't overly quick. Both switched to the soft tyre for what became critical final runs. Once on the softs, Piastri jumped to the classy end of the timesheet and ensured his passage through to the next segment. But Norris didn't. He made a meal of his first run on the soft rubber with a scrappy effort, and the unlikely hope of his second lap on the softs being good enough was ruined by Fernando Alonso spinning in the first sector, prompting a yellow flag. Norris bailed out of his lap and resigned himself to the fact that he would be starting the race from the back of the grid. He emerged from the car perplexed about the early decision to run the mediums, but fully aware that he was the one who messed up the lap when it counted. 'That one opportunity, that one lap that I was given, I didn't put it together,' he told the broadcast. 'I went off and that was it. We will speak about it after, but I had one lap and I didn't do it. So it is on me.'

Once committed to the soft tyres, Piastri managed to stay clear of trouble. He cruised through Q2, and his Q3 lap was good enough for seventh on the grid, even if he felt the performance of the car was oddly fluctuating in the final segment. 'The car felt good through Q1 and Q2,' said Piastri. 'I saved a set of tyres for Q3 and, yeah, just didn't have the grip for whatever reason. We're still working out why; we had a bit of a similar thing in FP3. We're not 100 per cent sure why. We just didn't find the time when everyone else did.' That position was probably about par, based on practice pace. The real shock in qualifying was Ricciardo in the AlphaTauri. He charged to a remarkable fourth place on the grid. So much for that underwhelming comeback . . .

It didn't matter that Piastri was starting seventh. Or that Norris was at the back end of the grid. Nearly every set of eyes in the Autódromo Hermanos Rodríguez venue was trained on one thing at the start of the Mexico City Grand Prix: the Red Bull driven by hometown hero Sergio Perez. The accomplished Mexican driver was stuck in a form slump and coming under increasing pressure to retain his seat as the gulf between himself and his teammate, world champion Max Verstappen, widened. In Formula 1, it doesn't matter what you've done in your career, runs on the board will eventually count for nothing. Just ask Ricciardo.

The pressure for Perez to perform on home soil was intense, particularly as there was another Red Bull-backed driver in Ricciardo, in what should be a slower car, ahead of him on the grid. The thing about the Mexico City circuit is that the run to the first corner is very long, which means starting the race on the second or third row can be a real benefit. You can get a nice tow from the cars ahead and spring a surprise into turn 1. As Verstappen, third on the grid, split the Ferraris that started on the front row and then pulled to the inside line, Perez found himself right at the front of the pack, but on the outside. For a split second, he had a nose ahead of everyone as he, Verstappen and Charles Leclerc went three-wide into the braking area for turn 1. And then, as so often happens when you're on the outside line, the space disappeared. The crowd went wild as Leclerc and Perez clashed, sending the Red Bull flying through the air. Perez's hopes of a miracle at home were dashed . . . on a weekend when Ricciardo was reminding the Formula 1 world just how good he can be. A reminder in itself of the brutality of motor racing at the ultra-elite level.

Amid that turn 1 chaos, Piastri worked his way up to sixth on the first lap. But that was as good as it got. It was by no means a poor race for the rookie, but on a track that wasn't predicted to suit the McLaren, he never looked overly comfortable. He held his own, but couldn't maximise the package like Norris, who put in a hell of a drive from way down in the field. When Kevin Magnussen went off track at turn 9 at a little under half of the race distance, destroying his Haas, Piastri was still in sixth, while Norris had worked his way up to eighth. Between the barrier damage and the flames licking out from the bottom of the broken Haas, a safety car was inevitable. Even a red flag wasn't out of the question. McLaren responded by pitting Norris and dropping him back to 10th once the yellow came out. If the team had waited a few more seconds, he would have got a free set of tyres when the red flag appeared.

After a brief pause, the race got underway with a standing restart. Piastri dropped a spot to seventh. Norris went all the way back to 15th. From there, however, the momentum changed. Piastri found himself under fire from Yuki Tsunoda, while Norris sliced his way back through the field for a second time. On lap 48, the Piastri–Tsunoda battle hit new heights as the AlphaTauri, well suited to the track and on the more durable tyre, came good. Piastri was forced into ultra-defensive mode as Tsunoda made a big play heading into the turns 1/2/3 complex. There was a little bit of contact, but they carried on in position. Tsunoda tried again on the following lap, with an ambitious move around the outside of Piastri into turn 1. Just like Perez earlier in the race, Tsunoda was a long way up. But the outside is a low-percentage place to be, and once again the lane disappeared as he and Piastri raced into the braking zone. They made heavier contact than the previous lap and Tsunoda was sent into a spin. That helped Norris up to eighth, a spot behind Piastri who was now sporting damage from the AlphaTauri crash. Norris ran down his teammate quickly, and eventually the inevitable radio message arrived. 'Oscar, if this is our pace, we would let Lando past to go and attack Ricciardo. We would need to find half a second,' was the message from the pit wall. The order was clear as day: pick up your pace by half a second per lap or let Norris through. Piastri almost immediately pulled over and let Norris go past him. It was a smart call. Norris ran down Ricciardo and George Russell and ultimately finished fifth, after starting at seventeenth. Andrea Stella would later describe the drive as a 'masterpiece'. Piastri cruised around to finish eighth.

After the race, Piastri was asked about his calm, complying reaction to the team's message about Norris in the closing stages of the race. A fair question, given he'd shown reluctance to let his teammate pass him in other races earlier in the season. 'I mean, I had some damage at that point,' he said. 'Lando was very quick compared to everyone; I think it didn't make any sense to try and battle each other. And in the end, it meant Lando got another two spots. So, it worked out well for the team.'

Results Summary

Free Practice 1: 6th (1m 20.463s, +0.74s)
Free Practice 2: 9th (1m 19.163s, +0.48s)
Free Practice 3: 5th (1m 18.392s, +0.50s)
Qualifying: 7th (1m 17.623s, +0.46s)
Race: 8th

Mexico City Grand Prix: A brief history

The name Rodríguez is synonymous with Formula 1 and Mexico.

Pedro and Ricardo Rodríguez were Mexico's first racing super-stars. Backed by their wealthy father, the pair took on the wider motorsport world in the 1960s. It was the younger brother, Ricardo, who led the way. He appeared on the radar by winning an international sportscar race at Riverside in the US in 1957 – aged just 15. The following year he tried to enter the 24 Hours of Le Mans but was turned away for being too young. A year later he made his debut at the famous endurance race, and another year later he finished second alongside André Pilette. At 18 he was the youngest podium finisher in the history of the event. And his star was on the rise. Having caught Ferrari's attention, Ricardo was invited to drive for the team at the Italian Grand Prix in 1961. He qualified second, solidifying his superstar status even if his fuel pump failed 13 laps into the race. Ferrari snapped him up for the 1962 F1 season, but it was a bit of a disaster for the team and he didn't get his chance to shine in what was an often uncompetitive car. Even worse, the lack of form from Ferrari led to the team deciding against the late-season trip to the US, South Africa and Mexico. Ricardo was desperate to race on home soil at the new Magdalena Mixhuca circuit for what would be a non-championship Mexican Grand Prix, so he did a one-off deal to drive a Lotus entered by Rob Walker. If only he hadn't. Tragically, in practice, Ricardo was killed in a crash. It's not clear if it was driver error or a mechanical failure. Either way, the world was robbed of one of its brightest racing talents, aged just 20 years old.

Pedro wasn't quite as prodigious a talent as his younger brother, but a heck of a driver all the same. He was meant to take part in that 1962 race in Mexico City, which would have been his Formula 1 debut. But after his brother's death, he pulled out. He even considered retiring altogether but ultimately decided to press on. Pedro didn't make his grand prix debut until the end of the 1963 season, and it wasn't until 1967 that he finally made a full-time commitment to motor racing. He signed with Cooper that year and, in just his ninth grand prix start, won the season-opening race in South Africa. A first for a Mexican driver. That cemented his spot in Formula 1, and he won the Belgian Grand Prix in 1970 and the non-championship Spring Trophy at Oulton Park in 1971. That same year, he too tragically lost his life, driving a Ferrari sportscar in an Interserie race at the Norisring street circuit in Germany. The Magdalena Mixhuca circuit was renamed Autódromo Hermanos Rodríguez in honour of the brothers.

The circuit came and went from the Formula 1 calendar over the years before Hermann Tilke had a crack at it, and the track returned in 2015 for its modern era in the sport. There are some peculiarities to Autódromo Hermanos Rodríguez. For example, between the time it last hosted a grand prix in 1992 and the next time it hosted a grand prix in 2015, there was a baseball stadium in the middle of the circuit. Foro Sol, as it was known, was initially built as a concert venue before becoming the home of the Diablos Rojos del México and Tigres de México baseball teams. Its origins, now known as the stadium section of the modern circuit, are very clear.

Another unique feature is the altitude. At 2285 metres above sea level, it's the highest stop on the F1 schedule by 800 metres (the next highest being Brazil). Given that air pressure drops with altitude, and air pressure is super important in Formula 1, it's quite the challenge for teams to deal with. For one, the turbos have a lot more work to do. Power doesn't dip in high altitudes like it used to in the naturally aspirated days, but that turbo has to spin a whole lot harder to feed the motor the air. Cooling is another issue, given there is literally less air available. Ambient temperatures aren't crazy, but the low density makes it difficult to keep the engine and brakes cool enough – hence bodywork adjustments, with additional cooling louvres, are the norm for racing in Mexico City. Less air also means less downforce, which means, regardless of the layout, teams run the highest downforce levels possible. And drivers still complain about there being no grip. The straight-line speeds are not dissimilar to Monza, despite the downforce levels being at the very opposite end of the spectrum.

26

BRAZIL

São Paulo Grand Prix
Autódromo José Carlos Pace
3–5 November 2023

Expectations were certainly held in check inside the McLaren garage heading to the famous Interlagos circuit. Lando Norris had already flagged the event as a tough outing given the MCL60's low-speed deficiencies, although the pace in Mexico had, at least, been slightly better than expected. For the second weekend running, Oscar Piastri found himself facing a brand-new circuit that he'd never seen in the flesh – which left him relying on simulator work he'd done weeks earlier, before the Austin/Mexico/Brazil triple-header kicked off. And with São Paulo being a sprint weekend, he only got one practice session, instead of three. He finished that sole hour of practice 20th and last – although it wasn't entirely representative of his pace. Given the tyre constraints of the sprint format, McLaren decided to keep a set of soft tyres up its sleeve for both drivers.

That meant Piastri had familiar company at the bottom of the practice times, with Norris just ahead of him in 19th.

From there, it was straight into qualifying on Friday afternoon – and suddenly the McLaren came alive in the muggy, overcast conditions. Piastri cruised through Q1 with then fifth fastest time while Norris was eleventh. In the second segment, Norris beat everybody, while Piastri was ninth. But by the time Q3 rolled around, the weather had become a factor. The heavy clouds were starting to spit, and, unlike a dry session, the rush was getting out and getting a lap down before the heavens opened and track conditions deteriorated. Piastri was one of the last out of the lane and it cost him when he got to Junção and slid off the road. In the moments that followed, the conditions continued to deteriorate. Before anyone could improve on their first laps, the sky darkened, as if it instantly became midnight. The wind charged across the track and lightning lit up the sky. Out came the red flag as the thunderstorm brought qualifying to an end. Norris was left stranded in seventh, and Piastri was tenth without a Q3 time to his name. 'I just lost a lot of grip,' said Piastri. 'I don't know if it was already raining or whatever, but I was struggling a lot already on the lap – I think everyone was. I just went in [to the corner] how I thought I did the last lap and slid straight off. Shame. The pace of the car was looking good.'

On Saturday conditions started out more consistent in terms of weather. Norris fired to the top in SQ1, while Piastri was a little lucky to be 14th fastest when the segment was cut short by Esteban Ocon and Fernando Alonso making contact, which sparked a premature end. In the second sprint qualifying session, Norris was quickest, a replication of Friday evening's success, while Piastri was ninth. For the critical final segment, Piastri decided to go first. There was method to the madness as the pit exit became a logjam of drivers trying to get the best of the conditions at the end of the session. But despite the method, it proved to be madness all the same, Piastri fighting an unhappy McLaren as he slumped to 10th on the sprint grid. Norris timed his run much better and took pole for the sprint.

The sprint didn't quite go to plan for either McLaren driver. Norris made a poor getaway from pole position and was beaten to the first corner by Max Verstappen in what proved to be a race-defining moment. Norris, once again, had to settle for second. Piastri spent most of the race in a three-way fight for eighth, and the last world championship point on offer in the sprint, with Daniel Ricciardo and Carlos Sainz. Around the mid-race distance, it became quite a heated battle as Ricciardo, who was faster than Sainz, tried and failed to get through several times. His failure to execute the pass opened the door for Piastri to dive under Ricciardo with 10 laps to go and grab ninth place. All of the battling took its toll on Piastri's tyres, though, and Ricciardo was able to work his way back into ninth in the closing stages of the race, while Piastri found himself working overtime to keep the wily old fox Fernando Alonso at bay on the final lap, which he was narrowly able to do. While he missed out on points, the upside, said Piastri, was some important learnings on his journey of tyre-management discovery. 'I learnt a lot from a tyre-management point of view and from a racing point of view, where to position the car,' he said. 'Still some things to try and improve for tomorrow, definitely, but a lot in the bank.'

Everyone on the grid, except pole-sitter Max Verstappen, scored a free position before Sunday's race even officially started. Charles Leclerc had qualified second for the race, only for TV cameras to cut to his Ferrari buried in the tyre wall at Ferradura. There are few things more humiliating for a driver than a warm-up-lap spin, but it does happen. Speeds may be low, but the aggressive measures taken to warm tyres and brakes, such as weaving and bursts of throttle to spin the rear wheels, are not without risk. In this case, however, it wasn't a driver error. Instead, his car had suffered a hydraulic failure, which had tipped it into a spin and put him out of the race before the lights had gone out. 'No!' the exasperated driver screamed over the radio. 'I lost the hydraulics! Why the fuck am I so unlucky?'

The drama didn't stop there. No sooner had the race got underway than there was contact in the pack, Williams driver Alex Albon clipping Nico Hülkenberg before clattering into Hülkenberg's Haas teammate, Kevin Magnussen, destroying both cars. Piastri was collateral damage, an out-of-control Magnussen hitting and damaging the McLaren's rear wing as he slid past facing the wrong way. The race was immediately neutralised by the safety car and Piastri trundled around and into the pits. The crew fitted new tyres and a mechanic inspected the rear wing. 'Oscar, kill the engine,' he was told over the radio. 'The car is not safe to continue.' His race was over . . . at least until the safety car turned into a red flag. The stoppage opened a window for McLaren to fix Piastri's car, and the team immediately went to work. The stoppage lasted for the best part of 40 minutes, enough time for the team to patch up the car. It wouldn't be brilliant, and Piastri would have to take the restart from the pit exit, as stipulated by the rules if you work on a car in the garage during a red flag. But at least he had some familiar company as he watched the rest of the field charge by; Daniel Ricciardo was another to get caught up in the crossfire, after a tyre from one of the crashed cars went flying towards his head. Fortunately, he wasn't hurt, but the same couldn't be said of his car, which, like Piastri's, had needed repairs during the stoppage.

Starting from the pit exit put the two Aussies way behind the pack. Even if Piastri had been able to restart the race in position, though, it wouldn't have made much difference. His car was still carrying way too much damage to be remotely competitive, and last on the road, two laps down, was all the afternoon was going to yield.

It all looked terribly unlucky, but Piastri didn't play the luck card on Sunday evening after the race. Instead, he rued not doing a better job in qualifying and starting further up the grid, closer to Norris, who had started sixth. 'I hit the brakes for turn 1 and then looked in the mirror,' he explained. 'I saw someone's tyre flying through the air and thought that didn't look very good. And then yeah, sure enough, got the impact after that. There was nothing I could have done, but when you qualify in those kinds of positions, you leave yourself at much more risk. Friday, we didn't execute as well as we should have. If I was starting even where Lando started or further up the front, I wouldn't have been in that crash. You've got to try and put yourself in the best position possible. There's no point blaming bad luck and not reflecting on things you can improve . . .'

Piastri also noted an important silver lining that reflected how precious laps in current Formula 1 cars really are, given modern testing restrictions. 'Thanks to the amazing effort of everyone to get the car back together in 20 minutes, which was no easy feat, I got an extra 70 laps that I otherwise wouldn't have,' he said. 'After yesterday I had some clear things I wanted to try and improve on. And I experimented with that a lot, some things successfully, some not. But it's very rare to get an opportunity to try things like that. Of course, I would prefer the opportunity didn't come up in the first place. But when it's there, you've got to try and capitalise on it with the lack of testing we have.'

An even brighter silver lining was that, despite his own predictions on how bad Brazil would be for McLaren, Norris finished second. And not just second, he'd at times pushed the race leader Verstappen incredibly hard. Paired with his second place in Saturday's sprint, it had been a mighty impressive weekend for the Briton. And another sign that McLaren was making genuine progress with the weaknesses in its car.

Results Summary

Free Practice 1: 20th (1m 13.838s, +2.10s)
Qualifying: 10th (No Q3 time)
Sprint Shootout: 10th (1m 11.189s, +0.56s)
Sprint: 10th
Race: 14th

São Paulo Grand Prix: A brief history

Brazil has produced some incredible Formula 1 drivers. Three of them are world champions, and all three won multiple titles. First there was Emerson Fittipaldi, the first Brazilian to win a title, in 1972. He then backed it up with another in 1974. Next up was Nelson Piquet, who was world champion in 1981, 1983 and 1987. Then there was the man who many consider to be the greatest of all time, even if he *only* won three world championships: Ayrton Senna.

Senna was a megastar around the world. He dated supermodels, such as Elle McPherson. He was, and still is, really, a household name. And in Brazil, that was all taken to another level. He transcended Formula 1 in a country obsessed with football. Racing at home was always something special for Senna, even if it took eight seasons for him to win there. And what a win it was. For much of Senna's career, the Brazilian race was held in Rio, until it moved to the Autódromo José Carlos Pace, better known as Interlagos, in 1990. For Senna, a native of São Paulo, that was a big deal. The first race at Interlagos was won by Senna's bitter rival Alain Prost. But in 1991, Senna pulled off a miracle. The hometown hero qualified fastest in his McLaren but found himself under relentless pressure from Williams driver Nigel Mansell throughout the race. At least until Mansell picked up a puncture, spun, and then his gearbox failed. That left Senna cruising towards victory . . . until his gearbox started to fail as well. The car repeatedly jumped out of gear, Senna eventually deciding that his safest bet was to leave the transmission in sixth gear. That turned the closing laps into an incredible test of physical endurance as Senna manhandled the McLaren around the slow corners in a high gear, desperately trying to keep the momentum up to stop the engine from bogging down. At the same time, Riccardo Patrese was reeling him in at a rate of knots. As if by some divine intervention, the heavens opened a couple of laps from home, putting a dampener on Patrese's charge and helping Senna take a memorable first home win. He was both emotionally and physically drained as he crossed the line, screaming with joy down the radio back to the McLaren pit wall. When he stopped on the cool-down lap, his arms immediately spasmed. The on-track medical team had to help him take off his gloves and pull him out of the car. Senna was then helped onto the podium, where he found one last bit of strength to hold the trophy and the Brazilian flag above his head, sending the crowd into raptures.

It was a dramatic finish, but no match for the 2008 Brazilian Grand Prix – one of the most dramatic Formula 1 races of all time. A rookie Lewis Hamilton had joined McLaren in 2007 at a time when the team was a title contender – and very nearly snagged a title in his debut year, despite having the highly rated, two-time world champion Fernando Alonso as his teammate. Ultimately, he couldn't get the job done at the season finale in Brazil, with Ferrari's Kimi Räikkönen emerging ahead of both McLarens in the final points. But Hamilton returned a year later with a huge shot at redemption. In 2008 he went into the season-decider with a five-point lead, at a time when points were only awarded to the top eight. The situation was that fifth place or better was all Hamilton needed, even if Brazilian hero and title contender Felipe Massa won the race. Both drivers did what they needed to in qualifying. Massa took pole; Hamilton was fourth fastest. Advantage Hamilton – until the heavens opened shortly before the start of the race. It was a wildcard the points leader didn't need. The rain didn't hang around for long, though, and the field ended up on slick tyres. Massa continued to lead, while Hamilton filtered up to fourth ... until the rain returned, eight laps from home. Most of the field pitted for intermediate tyres, including the two title contenders. But Timo Glock was one of two drivers to gamble on the slick. Staying out elevated him to fourth, ahead of Hamilton. A mistake from Hamilton as the laps counted down helped Sebastian Vettel into fifth, putting Massa at a mathematical advantage. Hamilton did his best to recover that vital position, but Vettel's defence was robust. When Massa crossed the line to win the Brazilian Grand Prix, he was world champion. He was world champion for a whole 39 seconds. The Ferrari garage went crazy, as did Massa's family ... and the Interlagos grandstands.

Amid the celebrations, it was lost on nearly everyone that Hamilton had run down a struggling Glock on that very last lap. Massa hadn't won the championship after all. As he pulled into parc fermé as the race winner, Massa sat in his car, opened his visor and wiped tears from his eyes. He defied the heartbreak of losing the title by celebrating winning his home grand prix with a passionate, and hugely admirable, outburst on the podium, thumping his chest and shouting at the top of his lungs, while his eyes glistened with tears. 'I was proud,' he would later say. 'Winning the Brazilian race is the most important thing a Brazilian driver can achieve. I was looking at the people, my people, the Brazilian people, under the podium and just wanted to show them that I was proud to be there and that we always fight until the end. This was my feeling ...'

27

LAS VEGAS

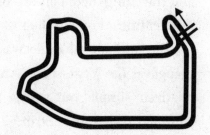

Las Vegas Grand Prix
Las Vegas Strip Circuit
16–18 November 2023

No event on the 2023 schedule was as highly anticipated as Las Vegas. The expansion of the schedule to include three races on US soil was all about riding the Netflix wave of popularity, with Vegas positioned as the absolute pinnacle of that push. The idea was to set a new standard for glamour and spectacle at a Formula 1 race, with cars screaming down the Strip, past the most famous casinos in the world, at night. And to really harness the party-round-the-clock Vegas vibe, the decision was made to have Formula 1 on track at all sorts of weird hours, with the double benefit of the more critical sessions (i.e. qualifying and the race) falling in favourable windows in Europe and Asia as well. Everything was basically shifted forwards a day, with track action still starting on Thursday, but not until 8.30 p.m. local time. Qualifying then technically started on

Saturday morning . . . at the stroke of midnight. The race then started 22 hours later, at 10 p.m. local time on Saturday night.

It was an ambitious concept, and ultimately a tough one for teams to deal with. It lacked the straightforward nature of the Singapore Grand Prix, where the schedule is as simple as the Europeans staying on a European time zone. For example, there were rumblings about Las Vegas hotels not being as well prepared to have team and category personnel, and travelling media and so on trying to live on a completely different time zone to the rest of the local population.

The oddball schedule was just one of the quirks of the inaugural Las Vegas race. Another was the unique layout – relatively simple, but with a monster 1.9-kilometre straight running down the Strip. Then, there was the ambient temperature. When you think of Vegas, you think of the sun and the hot Nevada desert. At least, that's what Formula 1 bosses did when, back in 2022, they were deciding where to slot the Las Vegas Grand Prix into the schedule. Ross Brawn, who was the Formula 1 CEO at the time, admitted as much to *Talksport* in the UK in the lead-up to the race. 'The one thing we hadn't considered initially . . . is it gets very, very cold at night,' he said. 'So when the race is happening, which is Saturday night, it has been known to drop down to three or four degrees [Celsius]. So, it can be really quite cold, and of course getting the cars to work in those temperatures can be a challenge. We're definitely facing some new challenges which we've never had before, but I think it'll be spectacular.'

The biggest issue from a climate perspective would be tyre temperature, followed closely by brake temperature.

And having that whopping long full-throttle blast between turns 12 and 14 would only make the issue worse, with tyre and brake temperature plummeting as the cars rocket along in a straight line.

In true Vegas style, Formula 1 was taking a gamble with this race. Traditionally, the Formula 1 financial model is to have a local promoter pay big money for the series to come and race in their city. You want a race? Here's what it will cost you. But with Vegas, F1 took the incredibly rare step of promoting its own race. Working on projected figures of US$1.2 billion in economic impact to the region, and, likely, also willing to run the event as a loss leader to showcase the sport, Formula 1 invested an estimated US$500 million of its own money to get the Las Vegas Grand Prix up and running.

So, plenty was at stake. But it wasn't a PR home run from the word 'go'. First, there were the insane ticket prices (general admission started at around US$500 for three days – compared to AUD$280 for a four-day GA at Albert Park). Then, there was the failure to deliver the fans, who had all spent so much money to be there, what they expected on the Thursday evening.

The event had barely got going when the weird schedule bit Formula 1 on the backside. At 8.30 p.m. on the Thursday evening, the cars hit the track for the first time. It was a spectacle, no doubt about it, particularly as the cars danced past the Sphere through turns 7, 8 and 9. But the first practice session only lasted eight minutes. It was at that point that Ferrari driver Carlos Sainz ran over a water-valve cover, which had worked its way loose after being sucked up by the ground effect of the cars. The debris did a remarkable amount of damage to Sainz's car, so much so that he had to switch to a spare chassis for the remainder of the weekend. It also meant Free Practice 1 had to be abandoned entirely so track crews could inspect the estimated 30 valve covers located around the track. Eventually they decided to pull them all up and fill the holes with asphalt . . . which would need to be dug out again after the event, given the valves are used by firefighting crews.

By the time the track was deemed safe to be used, it was 2.30 a.m. local time. Still, F1 persisted with a lengthened 90-minute Free Practice 2 session. Unfortunately, nobody was there to see it. Given the late hour, F1 was unable to properly staff the venue for the gates to be opened. Fans were gathered up by police and security guards and promptly kicked out, off the circuit precinct, and like an odd throwback to the COVID-19 pandemic, the session took place behind closed doors. Not that there was much to see at McLaren, anyway, with both Lando Norris and Oscar Piastri struggling to get their heads around the brand-new surface and the cold temperatures as they finished 11th and 14th fastest, respectively.

In a broader sense, it was an embarrassing start to Formula 1's showcase event. The fans who had paid a fortune for a Thursday-only ticket, and who ended up seeing a grand total of eight minutes of running, were offered compensation . . . in the laughable form of a US$200 voucher that could be spent at the online merchandise store. A statement from Las Vegas Grand Prix CEO Renee Wilm didn't go down all that well with the wider audience, either. In lieu of any sort of apology to fans, Wilm's statement outlined the reasons that attendees had to be booted (concerns for public safety of the security officials, transportation workers, as well as corporate areas needing to be cleaned and restocked) and then read: 'We know this was disappointing. We hope our fans will understand based on this explanation that we had to balance many interests, including the safety and security of all participants and the fan experience over the whole race weekend. We have all been to events, like concerts, games and even other Formula 1 races, that have been cancelled because of factors like weather or technical issues. It happens, and we hope people will understand.'

The final pillar of the PR disaster was that Sainz was slapped with a 10-place grid penalty because the energy store on his car had been too damaged to be carried over to the spare chassis. He had already been through three units for the season, with the use of a fourth at Las Vegas drawing the penalty – even though its failure was purely down to damage from the valve cover. Ferrari applied to the FIA for dispensation, but it was knocked back. There was one little bit of good luck, though. According to Formula 1 rules, a driver can't drive two separate chassis on the same day. If you destroy a chassis in FP1, you'll be sidelined for FP2. But, given the clock struck midnight well before FP2 got underway, it was a new day – and Sainz was free to take part in the second session.

The last hour of practice on Friday night was significantly more promising for McLaren. With 10 minutes to go, Piastri had a crack at a qualifying sim lap on soft tyres, going fastest of everyone with a time of 1m 34.491s. Norris did likewise a minute later, slotting into ninth. With just under seven minutes to go, George Russell used a combination of track evolution, plus a very handy tow from Norris, to pull nearly four-tenths clear of Piastri. It was a well-timed lap, too, the session ending abruptly moments later when Alex Albon rolled to a stop with a wheel missing from his Williams. The decision from race control not to restart the session robbed a lot of the field of their final runs, leaving Piastri in second and Norris in ninth.

There were enough signs to suggest that McLaren was in the fight for Q3 when qualifying rolled around at midnight. Between the brand-new surface (laid specifically for the race) and the cold conditions, getting the tyre to 'switch on' (i.e. start making peak grip) without sucking the life out of it was a real challenge. Conservation was key. The fewer sets each team could use in each segment of qualifying, the better. The early runs in Q1 weren't perfect for the McLaren drivers, with Piastri brushing the wall and Norris copping a nasty block from Sergio Perez, but, heading into the final runs, both were well clear of the bottom 16th. With around four minutes to go, the segment reached its critical point, where drivers had to decide if they wanted to roll the dice on their current set of tyres, or pit for a new set. McLaren decided to roll the dice on the current set . . . and the gamble failed. Both Norris and Piastri were pushed into the drop zone as the clock ticked down and couldn't climb their way out. Norris ended up 16th and Piastri 19th. 'In hindsight, maybe using the one set of tyres wasn't the right decision,' rued Piastri after the session. 'But from practice, and even during the session, there was nothing to really indicate that putting a second set on was going to be the best way forward, so that was one element. I think we were damaging the tyres quite a lot, which we didn't really see in practice earlier, either. The tyres are just the name of the game this weekend. We've seen that across a lot of teams. Some are making it work, some aren't. It's just not really worked for us that much this weekend.

'Honestly, the pace in the car was not bad. If we had got through [into Q2] then we had the potential to be in Q3 and perform decently. So I don't think the car is a complete disaster. It's just [that] the circumstances didn't really work out for us, and maybe there is a feeling we could have done better.'

It may have felt like things could only get better for the McLaren drivers, but Vegas had one last twist for Norris. When the grand prix got underway late Saturday evening, the track resembled an ice rink as the field tried to snake through the first few corners on cold tyres and with cold brakes. Not everyone made it through, Fernando Alonso spinning his Aston Martin and making contact with Valtteri Bottas. Through the madness Piastri made a blinder, getting all the way up to 12th place, a spot ahead of Norris. That was at least until lap 4, when Norris had a snap of oversteer through the fast turn 11, which spat him straight into the wall. His McLaren was engulfed in sparks as it slid down the wall and came to a rest in the barriers on the run-off for turn 12. A winded Norris climbed out of the wreckage to end a tough weekend.

The race went green again on lap 7 with Piastri sitting 11th in the queue on the hard tyres. That quickly became 10th as he mugged Yuki Tsunoda into turn 1 on that restart lap.

A lap later, he passed Nico Hülkenberg for ninth, before he dispatched Kevin Magnussen for eighth on lap 10. Four laps later, Piastri closed up on the back of Logan Sargeant along the Strip before launching a spectacular move under brakes into turn 14. Passing was possible in Las Vegas after all, and Piastri was the one proving it. At the same time, he had pressure from behind. Lewis Hamilton, also on the hard tyres, had been following him through the pack, and, on lap 16, the seven-time world champion decided to pull a move on Piastri at turn 14. There was what looked to be light wheel-to-wheel contact between the pair, but it was heavy enough to leave them both with punctures. Piastri was able to dive straight into the lane for a new tyre, so the isolated loss of time was minimal. But he was left in strategic no man's land. It was too early in the race to get a set of mediums to last to the end, so he had to take on another set of hards. And given the requirement to use two different compounds per race, he was suddenly committed to the non-preferred two-stop strategy.

A double whammy in terms of strategy arrived on lap 25 when Max Verstappen and George Russell made contact, the debris from which prompted another safety car. That gave the drivers who had started on the medium tyre a cheap stop for hards, while also bunching up the field. Piastri had made good progress since his stop, and he filtered up to fourth as the medium-tyre starters all headed to the lane. But the timing of the safety car had really worked against him. The next restart came on lap 29, Piastri pulling another incredible passing move to barge past Pierre Gasly's Alpine at turn 5 to move into third place. An out-of-sync Verstappen would demote

Piastri back to fourth on lap 33, before Piastri took that painful second stop on lap 43, seven laps from home. The McLaren team did limit the pain by completing a rapid 1.9-second stop as they fitted the car with lightly used medium tyres. Piastri resumed in 12th place, clearing Albon and then Gasly again to earn a solitary world championship point for 10th (and a bonus point for the fastest lap). It was a solid recovery, but a case of what could have been given the car speed.

'That's disappointing,' said Andrea Stella after the race. 'It's just a massive shame because Oscar was absolutely brilliant. I think I said that certainly [being] eliminated in Q1 wasn't our position because we knew we had improved the car from practice. But somehow, today was a bit of a surprise as to how quick we were. So it's a shame that, because we had started the race on hard tyres, then we needed to pit before the due time because of the contact with Hamilton.'

As usual, there was no explosion of emotion from Piastri as he calmly explained the clash with Hamilton. 'It was kind of just an awkward one,' he said. 'Neither of us had really committed to the corner that much. And then we both committed at the last minute. Then I was trying to back out of it, but we just ended up meeting in the middle. I was really wishing the rule of using two compounds didn't exist, because I would have just gone to the end on the hards. And I think we had the pace to hang on to people [in front of us]. So that was a shame.'

At the very least, the Las Vegas experiment paid off for Formula 1. After the issues earlier in the weekend, the race itself delivered in spades between the likes of Piastri charging through the field, and a thrilling battle at the front between Verstappen and Charles Leclerc (decided in the Dutchman's favour). Good racing can recover a lot of lost PR ground.

Results Summary

Free Practice 1: 17th (No time)
Free Practice 2: 14th (1m 36.987s, +1.72s)
Free Practice 3: 2nd (1m 34.491s, +0.40s)
Qualifying: 19th (1m 34.850s, +2.12s)
Race: 10th

Las Vegas Grand Prix: A brief history

Ever heard the one about a Formula 1 race in a car park?

The 2023 Las Vegas Grand Prix broke a lot of new ground for Formula 1, such as it being a self-promoted race, and that spectacular chute down the glittering Strip.

But it wasn't the first time Formula 1 had raced in Sin City.

The idea of Formula 1 heading to Las Vegas was first bandied about in the 1970s. The casinos had long clocked on to the idea of bringing things like high-profile music acts and boxing matches to town to increase their entertainment offering for gamblers. Formula 1, a sport associated with luxury and money, and with a history linked to another famous gambling city in Monaco, seemed like a perfect fit. At least as far as the Ceasars Palace casino was concerned.

At the time, there were two F1 grands prix in the US – one on the west coast (Long Beach) and one on the east (Watkins Glen).

As early as 1980 there were genuine plans in place to add a third race in Las Vegas, but local resistance over closing the public roads preferred for the circuit meant it didn't happen. A year later, getting the Las Vegas race off the ground became a matter of necessity. The Watkins Glen venue was in dire financial straits and its race, initially scheduled for October, was cancelled. If F1 wanted to retain its two US races, it needed to make Las Vegas happen. The task fell to Bill Weinberger, a former president of Caesars Palace. A 22,000-square-metre plot using the Caesars Palace car park and an adjacent vacant block owned by the Summa Corporation was earmarked for the race. Weinberger did try to incorporate around 400 metres of the Strip, but there were issues with approvals and delays with construction. Eventually, it was decided that the entire circuit would have to be crammed into those 22,000 square metres. Weinberger reportedly traced his hand on a placemat to see if it could be done. Three of his fingers fit. And the infamous 3.6-kilometre-long circuit was born.

The venue was built in a matter of months and when the Formula 1 circus arrived for the season finale in 1981, it was an underwhelming experience. It was hot and dusty, and most drivers hated the tight, slow, boring layout. Aussie Alan Jones was the reigning world champion and had announced plans to retire from Formula 1 at the end of the season. He was among those who were, initially at least, unimpressed with the Ceasars track. 'It's like a goat track, dragged down from the mountains and flattened out,' he told journalists at the time. 'What a bloody place to be ending your career . . .'

Frenchman Jacques Laffite, meanwhile, arrived in Nevada as an outside shot at the world championship. He immediately labelled the track as unfit to host anything resembling a grand prix. His comments were run by the *Gazzetta dello Sport* newspaper in Italy, which was promptly sued by Ceasars Palace. It wasn't just the pokey nature of the track that annoyed the drivers; it was also highly physical due to its anticlockwise nature, the opposite of most European circuits, making it a stern test for the drivers' neck muscles.

The race itself was anything but a classic. Jones, always bull-like in his strength and resilience, dominated what was (at the time at least) his final race, wearing a golden wreath on his head when he took to the podium. An exhausted Nelson Piquet battled his way to fifth and the world title – and could barely stand after the race.

Heading into the 2023 Las Vegas race, Jones spoke to Fox Sports about his memories of 1981. Understandably, his stance had softened given both time and his success there. 'They did a fairly good job with the space that they had available, and as it turned out, it didn't make a bad little circuit, to be honest,' he said. 'It was all right – I mean, I had a very good time there! And the circuit went in an anticlockwise [direction], a different way than what we were normally doing. A lot of the drivers were suffering very badly on their neck fatigue because of the g-forces. I did [struggle], actually. With about 10 laps to go, I'd go through a left-hander and my head would fall over to the right, and I had to wait to get to a right-hander for it to come back up again. There were a lot of drivers suffering from neck problems because it was quite hot. It was fairly flat; there were no trees or shade or anything. It really was a bit of a test of stamina.'

The circuit being something of a disaster wasn't the real issue with the Ceasars Palace race. The problem was that, commercially, it bombed. Given it was entirely housed within one casino, there was no collective marketing effort from others in the area. And unlike other major events in Vegas, it just didn't draw a crowd. An estimated 35,000 people showed up for the race (compared to the 315,000 people who, according to F1, attended the Vegas race in 2023). Much worse than that, it didn't bring in even a handful of high rollers. 'We thought there was an untapped market in Europe, Asia and the Middle East with Formula 1 fans,' Weinberger told local news outlet KTNV Las Vegas before the 2023 race. 'We said, "Look at what's going on in Monaco. All these fancy people are walking up and down the street spending money like it's water." We figured they'd probably like to come gamble at Caesars Palace. They didn't. If a dozen great gamblers showed up, it would have been a huge success. That was the problem with the race, from our point of view.'

The event lasted one more year before Ceasars Palace was dropped from the schedule and Las Vegas was sent into a four-decade F1 hiatus.

28

ABU DHABI

Abu Dhabi Grand Prix
Yas Marina Circuit
24–26 November 2023

Just a few days after Las Vegas, the Formula 1 paddock descended on the more familiar surroundings of the Yas Marina Circuit in Abu Dhabi to bring the longest season in the category's history to a close. With both the drivers' and the constructors' world championship long since decided, and a frantic end to the season with five races in six weeks, there was a sense of weariness from almost everyone involved in the sport, from fans, to broadcasters, to drivers, to teams. Still, McLaren did its best to inject a bit of excitement into the season finale by announcing a new engine deal mere moments before Free Practice 1 on the Friday evening of the Abu Dhabi Grand Prix. It was fundamentally an extension of the existing customer deal with Mercedes-Benz, but one that would run until 2030.

The deal was interesting in two ways. One, it extended beyond the existing power-unit rules (set to expire in 2026) – and you never know how each PU supplier will handle a change in regulations. Two, it was effectively a seven-year commitment to being a customer, instead of remaining open to a factory engine deal. Despite the raised eyebrows around the paddock, Andrea Stella was adamant that it was an easy decision. 'It was quite straightforward because we are very happy with the ongoing collaboration,' he explained. 'They were absolutely instrumental, even, in the progress of the team this year, I have to say. But above all, the kind of reassurance we got from a technical point of view, the operational standards, just how solid [what we saw was] . . . when we checked what was at stake for 2026, [it] made this decision quite simple for us. So, we are just delighted that we have this level of continuity and stability as we look forward.'

It was an odd field for the final Free Practice 1 of the year. The vast majority of teams opted to send a young driver out in one car for some valuable grand prix weekend miles, at a time where there was less than usual on the line. Red Bull Racing went as far as benching both its primary drivers for the hour-long session, with Jake Dennis and Isack Hadjar replacing Max Verstappen and Sergio Perez. McLaren left Piastri in his car, while IndyCar star Pato O'Ward took over Lando Norris's car. As expected, the primary drivers filtered to the front, Piastri finishing up sixth behind the likes of Lance Stroll, Valtteri Bottas, Daniel Ricciardo and pacesetter George Russell. The only 'blow-in' near the front was Aston Martin reserve Felipe Drugovich, who was second fastest.

Perhaps the most curious moment of the session came just five minutes in when Dennis – a world champion in the all-electric Formula E – came over the radio to report that he had to pit because his helmet was 'nowhere near tight enough'. It doesn't matter how accomplished and experienced you are in other categories, the forces that a Formula 1 car puts your body through are always surprising.

For Free Practice 2, it was back to a full field of primary drivers, the session getting underway shortly before sunset. The sun hadn't yet set when the session was stopped, though, after Carlos Sainz buried his Ferrari in the barriers at turn 3 at speed. The Spaniard was fine, but the damage to the barriers was significant. It took more than 25 minutes for the session to get going again. And even then, it only continued for four minutes before Nico Hülkenberg dropped his Haas at turn 1 and hit the wall, resulting in a second red flag. After another seven minutes, the session got going for a third time. Through all the interruptions Norris ended up second fastest and Piastri tenth.

Not for the first time during the season, things started to come to Piastri on the Saturday. In the final hour of practice of 2023, he finally showed his hand as a contender, sitting third after his early run, and locking down the same position on his final run, albeit a spot behind Norris.

An incredibly strong finish to the season was now within McLaren's grasp. And true to that form, the pair cruised through Q1 with Norris in P5 and Piastri P11. There wasn't quite as much breathing room in Q2, Piastri only sneaking through to the final qualifying segment in 10th as Norris harried Max

Verstappen with the second-fastest time. But when it counted in qualifying, Piastri, nearing a year as a Formula 1 driver, stepped up to the plate. He had been slightly outpaced by Norris on their first runs in Q3, but on the critical runs, Norris was the one who blinked. As he came into the hotel complex in the final sector, he lost the rear end, recovering it with the car facing the right way, but dumping a heap of time in the process. Piastri nailed his lap, sealing third place on the grid as Norris dropped back to fifth. 'I don't know what happened to Lando on the last lap,' said Piastri. 'I was struggling a little bit in the first two parts of quali. Before qualifying, I hadn't done a lap without a major mistake this weekend; I was struggling to get everything together. I think I did a much better job of that in qualifying.'

Piastri held position as the final race of the 2023 season got underway, but it wasn't long before he came under fire from a familiar foe ... his teammate. Norris made a rapid start to move into fourth and, as much as Piastri was able to put early pressure on second-placed Charles Leclerc, he had his fellow McLaren driver right behind him. There was a bit at stake for Piastri and Norris. McLaren was fourth in the manufacturers' standings, but only by 11 points over Aston Martin. There was no scope at all for the teammates to take each other out. By lap 5 Norris had worked his way into third and that was the order the two McLaren drivers stayed until the finish. Unfortunately for them, they were both jumped by George Russell and Sergio Perez, and rounded out the season fifth and sixth. Nothing Hollywood about it, but it did seal a comfortable fourth in the constructors' for McLaren, behind powerhouse squads Red Bull, Mercedes and Ferrari.

'It feels like it's been a while since I've had a race without contact or something crazy going on,' said Piastri on closing out the 2023 season. 'The race was maybe not as strong as we would have liked as a team. I think my first and second stints weren't my best of the year, but I think the final stint looked quite strong, so it was nice to end on a decent note. We had hoped for a bit more pace, but we know our car is still weak in a few areas, and this track definitely exposed that in places.'

With that, Oscar Piastri's rookie season in Formula 1 came to an end. A fitting end, in a way, between his workmanlike approach to practice, his rapid qualifying speed, and the ongoing learning about tyre management during the race. It really summed up his 2023.

Results Summary

Free Practice 1: 6th (1m 26.665s, +0.59s)
Free Practice 2: 10th (1m 25.361s, +0.55s)
Free Practice 3: 3rd (1m 24.810s, +0.39s)
Qualifying: 3rd (1m 23.782s, +0.34s)
Race: 6th

Abu Dhabi Grand Prix: A brief history

In its relatively short time as the season finale, there have been two memorable title showdowns in Abu Dhabi – both concerning Lewis Hamilton.

The most famous, or infamous, depending on which side of the Verstappen/Hamilton debate you sit, is of course 2021.

That year, there was little to split the Mercedes and Red Bull packages and, after several run-ins between the pair during the season to really heighten the tension, it came down to a winner-takes-all scenario at Yas Marina.

For the most part, Hamilton did what he needed to do to win an eighth title. He had controlled the race and was leading when Williams driver Nicolas Latifi crashed with five laps to go, bringing out the safety car. As the leader, Hamilton couldn't afford to gamble on new tyres and cede track position. But Verstappen could. He pitted for brand-new rubber and resumed in second place ... except with five lapped cars in between. Given there was never going to be more than a couple of green laps at the end, that should have easily been the breathing room that Hamilton needed to win the race and the title. Until Red Bull Racing successfully lobbied the race director, Aussie Michael Masi, to let those five cars un-lap themselves. It was a perfectly legal decision under the race director's power, but also somewhat unprecedented – and highly controversial given it left Hamilton as a sitting duck and effectively handed the title to Verstappen. After the race, Hamilton was so disillusioned that he contemplated walking away from the sport. Masi was made a scapegoat by the FIA, lost his job and was subject to horrible abuse from the Hamilton faithful. The FIA did at least clamp down on the direct line of in-race communication between race teams and the race director, which had clearly influenced Masi's decision at the 2021 Abu Dhabi Grand Prix. It was a mess in a lot of ways. But what a blockbuster for Formula 1 at a time when its popularity was booming. Sometimes sport has to be the loser for entertainment to be the winner.

It wasn't the first time Hamilton had tasted bitter defeat at Yas Marina. Back in 2016, it was also where he lost the Silver War.

There was a time when Hamilton and Nico Rosberg were good pals. They came from remarkably different backgrounds, Rosberg growing up in Monaco as the son of another Formula 1 world champion, Keke Rosberg, while Hamilton grew up in working-class Stevenage, north of London. But despite their differences, the two quickly became close friends once paired up in karting in the early 2000s, a friendship that continued as they climbed the junior open-wheel ladder and broke through into Formula 1 (Rosberg in 2006 with Williams, Hamilton in 2007 with McLaren). In 2013, they became teammates once again when Hamilton was lured over to Mercedes, which Rosberg had joined in 2010. Initially, that partnership too was fine ... until the hybrid era kicked off in 2014. Mercedes nailed the new regulations and suddenly had the fastest car in the field. As the two ambitious, talented and ruthless drivers became title contenders, the rivalry between them grew fierce – to the point that it eroded their friendship entirely.

Signs of the teammate tension were clear as early as 2014 at places like the Hungaroring, where Hamilton refused to let Rosberg, on an entirely different strategy, past. And at Spa, where the pair crashed into each other. Both were still in contention for the title heading to Abu Dhabi that year, a race won by Hamilton to become a two-time world champion.

The following season very much went Hamilton's way, and he had a third title sealed before the finale in Abu Dhabi. Rosberg, however, finished the year in remarkable form with three wins on the bounce, including the final race. In the cool-down room before the podium, Hamilton picked up one of the Pirelli caps, mandatory for drivers to wear while collecting their silverware, and flicked it across the room to Rosberg. An unimpressed Rosberg threw it straight back at him. In the press conference, the antics continued. 'I'm feeling very happy,' said Rosberg when asked for his reaction to the race victory. 'Being world champion sounds a lot better than winning the race,' was Hamilton's reply.

Rosberg carried that late-2015 form into the 2016 season and managed to pull a handy little points lead on Hamilton. In Barcelona, at the race won by future world champion Max Verstappen, Hamilton and Rosberg took each other out of the race. They then did the same thing in Austria. By the time they got to Abu Dhabi, the situation was simple – if Rosberg finished on the podium, he would be world champion. If he was outside the top three, and Hamilton won the race, Hamilton would be champion. Hamilton led the race from start to finish with his teammate behind him. Right behind him, in fact. Because Hamilton spent the whole race only going as fast as he needed, clearly trying to back Rosberg into the rest of the pack. The Mercedes pit wall repeatedly asked Hamilton to speed up as third-placed Sebastian Vettel got closer. 'I'm actually in the lead right now. I'm quite comfortable where I am,' was his response over the radio.

Hamilton's plan didn't work, and Rosberg finally joined his father on the list of world champions. In one final power move, he immediately announced his retirement from Formula 1, ensuring that he would always have the last laugh over Hamilton.

'[The friendship broke down] immediately when we were fighting for the world championship, not before,' Rosberg told

Eurosport in 2022. 'But that's always the case. When you're fighting for success in every race and for titles, it doesn't work anymore. It was a build-up from one race to the next. If you want to decide the world championship for yourself, you can't play "love, peace and harmony". You have to test limits and go into grey areas to win, especially when two drivers are at such a high level. I don't regret anything from the battle with Lewis. That was a sensational time and a mega fight. I'm very proud of that. In the meantime, we've returned to neutral, which is okay.'

CONCLUSION

When Alpine went through its management reshuffle in the middle of 2023, it wasn't only Otmar Szafnauer and Alan Permane who left the building. They were joined by chief technical officer and Formula 1 veteran Pat Fry.

Unlike the other two, whose exits were described in the press release as the outcome of a 'mutual agreement', Fry had made the decision to leave Alpine all on his own, opting to move to Williams instead. His resignation wasn't as high profile as Szafnauer losing his job, but it was significant in another way. Fry had started his career at Benetton, the forerunner to Alpine, back in the late 1980s and had been a part of the team's transformation into contenders in the early 1990s. In 1993, he left and worked at McLaren and Ferrari before returning to Alpine in 2020.

It was meant to be a bit of a full-circle move, Fry returning home to Enstone, where his career had started. A second chance to take the team from the midfield to the front. And initially, he felt like he was making the right sort of progress.

And then it stopped.

'I look back at the first three years I was [back] there, and we improved Enstone, dramatically,' Fry said at the end of the 2023 season. 'Year on year, we built a better car. If you put the three cars (2020, 2021 and 2022) next to each other, each one was a massive step [forward]. It's a credit for everyone there; the various teams were collaborating a huge amount better. I think everyone there should be proud of what we achieved for those three years. I guess I'd gone back there to go back to the place you started your career and try and rebuild it. And I think we did really well. From a distant fifth [in 2021], we were a solid fourth [in 2022]. But I didn't feel there was the enthusiasm or the drive to move forward beyond fourth . . .

'I decided at the start of March [2023] that I want to be pushing things forward; I don't just want to sit there and not be able to do things. So, for me, that was time to stop and move on, really. It's one of those things; I think as a company, they weren't almost set up to push hard enough. You can say you want to be first. But the difference between saying it and achieving it is monumental, as we all know.'

Based on Fry's thoughts, the attitudes between Alpine and McLaren couldn't be more different. From where McLaren had started the season, it would have been so easy to write the year off. But, in a way very rarely seen in Formula 1, the team persisted with its aggressive updates program and found it paid very real dividends. Like Alpine had been a year earlier, McLaren was a solid fourth in the 2023 standings – comfortably ahead of the fast-starting Aston Martin squad, and a whopping 182 points clear of Alpine. And McLaren had finished the season so strongly, with pace that would give Mercedes and Ferrari, and perhaps even Red Bull, something to really think about over the off-season.

'It's definitely been a bigger rollercoaster than I expected,' said Piastri after the Abu Dhabi Grand Prix. 'I knew there would be ups and downs . . . maybe not as down at the start or as up at the end! But I've really learnt a lot. I feel like I've had basically every situation you could have [in Formula 1], apart from a championship fight.

'As a team, we're learning how to compete at the front, which is exciting. It's not a position we've been in for 10 years. It's so nice to be having these conversations, going through these scenarios. And for me, it's really a privilege to be fighting at the front so early in my career. There are people that go their whole F1 career that don't have the opportunity that I've had in 22 races. I'm very, very grateful for that.'

When later asked if he was proud of what he had achieved in 2023, Piastri said, 'It's definitely been a great season. A lot of highlights that I wouldn't have been able to achieve without the team improving the car. But also, I guess to pat myself on the back, I had to deliver in those moments, too. That's probably my proudest moment – Silverstone, where we rocked up with a car that was competitive [and] I was able to get the most out of it. Japan, not my finest race, but I did enough to score my first podium. And Qatar, we had one opportunity, really, in the whole year to actually win something, and we managed to take it. For me, I can be very proud of that.'

But it wouldn't be Piastri without he himself adding a bit of balance to the discussion. '[There were] definitely some trickier weekends,' he continued. 'And things to work on as a whole season. You don't win championships by one or two weekends. I know that from my junior career. So I just need to make that happen more often.'

After all those peaks and troughs, Piastri ended up ninth in the drivers' world championship standings. The same place Ayrton Senna finished in his maiden season. It was the highest finish for a rookie since Alex Albon in 2019, although Albon did have the advantage of spending half that rookie season in a Red Bull Racing car. Other than that, you have to go back to 2007 to find better rookie performances, when Heikki Kovalainen finished seventh and Lewis Hamilton second (albeit in a super-competitive McLaren).

Following the Qatar Grand Prix weekend, undoubtedly the highlight of Piastri's season, with a win in the sprint and second in the grand prix, Jonathan Noble penned a telling piece for Motorsport.com. The premise of the story was that there was a little trick on offer for more clever drivers in the field on sprint weekends. Given they qualify for Sunday's race on Friday afternoon, they go through the whole Saturday – a sprint shootout and a sprint race – knowing where they will start the actual grand prix. At some point, Fernando Alonso clocked on to the fact that if you're going to start the Sunday race from an even grid position, which means the dirty side of the track, you can spend Saturday 'cleaning' your grid slot.

Whenever applicable, Alonso can be seen darting off the racing line down the straight and using his hot tyres to pick up dust and dirt and rubber marbles from where he'll start the grand prix. It's genius. And in Qatar, Noble spotted one other driver doing the same thing. Oscar Piastri.

At the end of each segment of the sprint shootout, Piastri would wait for permission from his engineer to drive off the racing line, and then sweep to the inside of the track and straight through grid position six. 'The grid-cleaning opportunity seems such an obvious thing to do, especially for someone so experienced as Alonso,' wrote Noble. 'But for a rookie driver like Piastri, who has not even had a full season under his belt, unleashing these tactics already says an awful lot about the qualities he has brought with him to F1. Piastri is the epitome of calculated coolness. There have been plenty of times – especially when Lando Norris had got hold of upgrades first – that he could have thrown his toys out of the pram and got himself wound up over things. But no, he has been completely measured. With his mentality, his driving and his tactics on track in leaving no stone unturned, Piastri is showing he has all the potential needed to be at the very top of F1.'

It was a little over a month after Qatar, right as Piastri was closing in on the end of his rookie season in Formula 1, that I interviewed René Rosin for this book. The Prema boss spoke so passionately about Oscar's junior career, but the enthusiasm didn't stop as our conversation moved on from the Piastri–Prema era and into Piastri's rookie F1 season.

'Honestly, Formula 1 is a big step,' Rosin told me. 'Oscar had the downside of the gap season in 2022, when all of the mess happened. But he turned it in his favour. I knew that he could put Lando under pressure. Lando is an extraordinary driver, he's very fast. But Oscar is relaxed. He takes his time to learn. But then he's there. His results in Formula 1 make me so happy. You can see those Oscar traits in Formula 1. He builds up to things. But when it counts, he's right there on pace. Even in moments when it's a sprint race, with one Free Practice session, you can see how he learns from it, and then he's there in qualifying. If he keeps on this path, he has an incredible future ahead of him.'

Once the recorder was off, Rosin continued to talk about the Piastri family. He told me how close he'd grown to Oscar's father Chris. How he had travelled from Italy to Melbourne for no other reason than to be at Chris's 50th birthday party. How Chris was so proud of his son's achievements that he had bought the title-winning Formula 2 and Formula 3 cars from Prema as a keepsake. Esteban Ocon, Lance Stroll, Logan Sargeant, Zhou Guanyu and Charles Leclerc all came through the Prema system, so Rosin isn't just romanced by Piastri's success in Formula 1. He's seen all of that before. Instead, this is a clear admiration of both the driver and the young man.

And that's a common theme. When those closest to Piastri speak about his ability, both how good he is and how good he could be, it always comes back to his focus and demeanour. After the season-ending Abu Dhabi Grand Prix, Andrea Stella addressed the media one last time. When the McLaren team principal was asked what had impressed him the most about Piastri, he said, 'It's the rapidity with which he learns that I think makes him exceptional. And this has been true in whatever scale you take: within the timeframe of a race, within the timeframe of an event, within the timeframe of the season. His gradient is so impressive, which obviously creates expectation for next season. And expectations require work to be [realised]. But the good thing with Oscar is that he's such a grounded person, he's so committed. And if anything, working with him will be more about what we need to do to confirm this gradient, work that effectively has already started in terms of planning ahead on to the winter.

'Maybe one of the key enablers [as to] why he can grow so rapidly is just the man beyond the driver. He's so calm, he's so good at keeping himself in a [mindset] in which he can use the best of this talent. I don't have that quality. I have to think about my psychology to actively keep myself in the most productive state. For Oscar, this seems to come quite naturally. Maybe he worked throughout his young career on that. I don't know, but it is remarkable. And even when I've seen great drivers, currently or in the past, all of them sort of sometimes underperform because they don't stay in the [mindset] in which they give their best.' When Stella mentions 'great drivers', he knows what he's talking about, having worked with the likes of world champions Michael Schumacher and Fernando Alonso during his time at Ferrari.

There is no way Oscar Piastri and Mark Webber could have predicted how McLaren's 2023 season would play out. Or how Alpine would implode. But, back in 2022, they saw something in McLaren. And the decision to go to McLaren, based on Piastri being wanted in a race seat immediately, without being farmed out to another team for two years, proved to be a stroke of genius. At least in the short term, of course. There are no guarantees in Formula 1. But even if Alpine does one day make good on its factory status and becomes a powerhouse team, and McLaren gets mired back in the midfield with its long-term customer-engine deal, there's a good chance it won't matter for Piastri. McLaren gave him the exact platform he needed for that critical rookie season. He was able to showcase that he belonged in Formula 1. He was able to showcase that he has the drive, focus, mentality and – most importantly – the X factor that a driver needs if they want to be world champion.

ACKNOWLEDGEMENTS

My first thanks go to Jonathon Noble, who I firmly believe is the best F1 journalist in the entire business. Knowing I could reference his work with absolute trust made a big difference to this book. Not only that, his support, friendship and mentorship over the past decade has helped my career immensely. I wouldn't be in a position to write books like this without him.

Thanks to Karun Chandhok for being so generous with his time and so earnest with his insight. Thanks to René Rosin for speaking so passionately about Oscar. And thanks to James Sera for the remarkable insight into the karting days.

Thanks to Brandon VanOver, first for bringing the idea for this book to me in the first place, and then for being an incredibly supportive publisher throughout the process. I am still new to the book world and his gentle guidance and enthusiastic support has built my confidence and allowed me to take creative risks. I look forward to working on many more projects in the future.

Thanks to Shané Oosthuizen for her editing work – and for embracing the importance of calling corners by their traditional names, not their numbers.

Thanks to Oscar Piastri for delivering on the promise that we saw in him when we decided to bring this book project together.

And thanks to McLaren for creating the perfect rags-to-riches story arc with the development of the MCL60.